Economics, Bureaucracy, and Race

POWER, CONFLICT, AND DEMOCRACY

AMERICAN POLITICS INTO THE TWENTY-FIRST CENTURY

POWER, CONFLICT, AND DEMOCRACY:

AMERICAN POLITICS INTO THE TWENTY-FIRST CENTURY

Robert Y. Shapiro, Editor

This series focuses on how the will of the people and the public interest are promoted, encouraged, or thwarted. It aims to question not only the direction American politics will take as it enters the twenty-first century but also the direction American politics has already taken.

The series addresses the role of interest groups and social and political movements; openness in American politics; important developments in institutions such as the executive, legislative, and judicial branches at all levels of government as well as the bureaucracies thus created; the changing behavior of politicians and political parties; the role of public opinion; and the functioning of mass media. Because problems drive politics, the series also examines important policy issues in both domestic and foreign affairs.

The series welcomes all theoretical perspectives, methodologies, and types of evidence that answer important questions about trends in American politics.

Economics, Bureaucracy, and Race

How Keynesians Misguided the War on Poverty

JUDITH RUSSELL

COLUMBIA UNIVERSITY PRESS

NEW YORK

Cau

COLUMBIA UNIVERSITY PRESS
Publishers Since 1893
NEW YORK, CHICHESTER, WEST SUSSEX

Library of Congress Cataloging-in-Publication Data

Russell, Judith, 1946–
    Economics, bureaucracy, and race : how Keynesians misguided the war
on poverty / Judith Russell.
        p. cm. — (Power, conflict, and democracy)
    Includes bibliographical references and index.
    ISBN 0-231-11252-1 (cloth : alk. paper)—ISBN 0-231-11253-x (pbk :
alk. paper)
    1. Poverty—Government policy—United States—History—20th century.
2. United States—Economic policy—1961–1971.   3. Economic assistance,
Domestic—United States—History—20th century.   4. Manpower policy—
United States—History—20th century.   5. Racism—Economic aspects—
United States—History—20th century.   6. United States—Politics and
government—1945–1989.   I. Title: Keynesians misguided the war on
poverty.   II. Title.   III. Series.
HC110.P6R896 2003
362.5'56'0973—dc21   2003051652

∞

Columbia University Press books are printed on permanent and durable
acid-free paper.
Printed in the United States of America

c 10 9 8 7 6 5 4 3 2 1
p 10 9 8 7 6 5 4 3 2 1

Contents

Preface

This book had its beginnings in my fascination with the notion of ideas having effects on outcomes and how that might happen. I anticipated a very theoretical book. I thought it would be a book about political consciousness. Given my interests, I thought it would be about ideology and working-class politics. In fact, this book barely touches on those themes or the Marxist theory and analysis that I expected would be at its heart. For a book about ideas, it is light on theory, almost anti-theory.

Indeed, this book on economics, bureaucracy, and race deliberately shies away from big-picture ideas, preferring to tell a reasonably focused story about how the swirl of politics and personalities shaped the struggle of a secretary of labor and a Council of Economic Advisors chairman in the Kennedy and Johnson administrations. Outcomes in this story are affected also by ideas, particularly economic ideas and ideas about race, but not in ways that lead to sweeping policy statements about how these phenomena happen.

Wrestling with ideas about poverty that would in fact remain at the center of this book, I was struck early on by a simple contradiction. Why is it so hard for poor people to earn a living in a nation where virtually every feature of contemporary life is business driven? Many others have asked and answered that question, or similar ones, and I learned from them about how business interests, employment policies, economic theories, and racism work to drive down job availability, ironically for the very people who need jobs the most. Still, I felt it was inevitable that essential information about how ideas actually worked to produce these outcomes slipped through the cracks in big-picture explanations.

Finally, and perhaps most important, as I worked on this book I discovered that the role of racism grew in importance. I knew race would be a factor but did not know how key a role it would play. I also felt that the operation of racism in the early sixties in the United States and how it worked against efforts to obtain employment definitely needed proper explanations. Interestingly, although this started out as a book about poverty and jobs, nothing gives me greater pleasure than the small contribution I hope it makes to the story of African American efforts to obtain jobs and the nature of the opposition they faced.

Acknowledgments

Many people, none of whom are responsible for the result, have given me counsel, advice, and encouragement. I wrote my earliest draft of this book as a dissertation while I was a doctoral student at Columbia University. There I was most fortunate to encounter a range of talented and interested individuals who furthered my education and shaped the way I thought about problems. Among them, Charles V. Hamilton, Robert Y. Shapiro, and Allan Silver were leading influences. In addition, at Columbia and later as a political science faculty member at Barnard College, I had the benefit of sharp and incisive comments and advice from faculty, colleagues, students, and friends. Among them was Richard M. Pious, who never gave me advice that I did not follow. The first time I handed Dick a draft he said he liked it, but handed me ten single-spaced pages on what he did not like. I knew I was almost home two years later when I handed it to him again and he only gave me a single page. Other valuable advice and support came from Robert Amdur, Alan Barton, Jim Caraley, Dennis Dalton, Herb Gans, Ira Katznelson, Mark Kesselman, Fritz Kratochwil, Kenneth T. Jackson, Peter Juviler, Xiaobo Lu, Alan Matusow, the late William McNeil, Sumner Rosen, Rosalind Rosenberg, Herb Sloan, the late William Vickery, and former New York Federal Reserve Bank secretary Arthur Hunt Willis.

I wish to thank my fellow colleagues in the Willen Interdisciplinary Faculty Seminar at Barnard College in 1995–1996, including Lynn Chancer, David Farber, Bob McCaughey, Kelly Moore, and Lesley Sharp, with whom I discussed the ideas in chapter 5. The American Society and

Politics Seminar of the Center for the Social Sciences at Columbia University gave valuable responses to a talk I gave in April 1993.

Research assistance was absolutely key to the early stages this work. The contributions of Pamela Alexander, Amelia Burgess, Sofia Quintero, Kohanya Ranch, and Pauline Yoo were indispensable. Nell Dillon's professionalism, resources, and friendship were always in great supply and great demand. My graduate and undergraduate students at Columbia and Barnard never failed to amaze me with their insights and enthusiasm for the book. I also drew strength and inspiration from the politics, activism, and long-term up-close scrutiny of my two Rhodes Scholars, Eric Garcetti and Benjamin Jealous. John Kastellec closed the last few critical gaps at the end.

Secretary of Labor W. Willard Wirtz was giving of his time and patient with my questions. Although I did not turn to him until I was deep into the research for this project, his enthusiasm for and acceptance of my arguments were enormously consequential in moving it forward, as was my own conviction of his early recognition of the relationship between poverty and unemployment. I thought his recognition deserved greater acknowledgment. Even before my archival research began, Nicholas Lemann was generous with advice resulting from his own trips to the Johnson and Kennedy Presidential Libraries. Financial support for research and travel came from both institutions. In particular, I received support from a John F. Kennedy Library Foundation Research Grant. Anyone who has ever done research at those libraries knows that their exceptional archival staffs are national treasures.

Finally I would like to thank John L. Michel, my editor at Columbia University Press, for his support, advice, and patience. Thanks are due also to his assistant Jeannie Lu and Managing Editor Anne McCoy who was in charge of editorial production. My copyeditor, Sarah St. Onge, was masterful at pulling together the manuscript. Publishing the book in Bob Shapiro's series, Power, Conflict, and Democracy: American Politics Into the Twenty-first Century, could not have given me more pleasure.

Last, and not least, thank you Suzanne McMillan, and you know why.

My children, Matthew and Hillary, have always been extraordinary sources of strength. At times just staying a step ahead of them has been a genuine catalyst. Hillary's husband, Peter, and now Hawthorne complete a treasured family circle.

No influence has been greater on my life than that of my beloved father, Robert Wood Russell, to whom this book is dedicated.

Economics, Bureaucracy, and Race

1. Introduction: The Other War on Poverty—the Battle for Jobs

Nearly 125,000 jobs in New York City were lost or displaced, virtually overnight, after the terrorist attack on the World Trade Center's Twin Towers on September 11, 2001.[1] While job loss because of depression, recession, and cyclical and structural causes has long been a recurrent and, in fact, regular feature of the American economy—indeed, by September 11, the city and national economies had been experiencing persistent economic slowdown for many months and had actually entered a recession—this instantaneous and catastrophic job loss has no parallel in American history. Hardest hit were the financial services sector, travel and tourism, the retail sector, and small business and manufacturing.[2] To make matters worse, New York City's capacity to mobilize for a quick response to both recession-related and attack-related layoffs was effectively nonexistent, New York being the only major city in the nation without a coordinated, business-driven job-training system.[3] Mayors had neglected workforce training programs for decades, consequently the city had no comprehensive, well-oiled employment and training machinery to fall back on to establish emergency networks of job centers after September 11 or to spend the federal funds earmarked for workers dislocated by the attack.[4] By spring 2002 the recession was considered over, but the weakness and joblessness of the national recovery meant that by June 2002, with unemployment at 5.9 percent, employers remained cautiously focused on efficiency rather than rehiring laid-off workers, a jobless recovery similar to that of the early 1990s. New York's ability to rebound from recession has repeatedly lagged behind the nation's as a whole, and the city's experience of the slow recovery—already exacerbated by the consequences of the terrorist attacks—was even more pronounced.

While there is much we do not know about the extent of job losses stemming from the recession or how the recession will be affected by the terrorist attack and the consequent shocks to the city's already faltering economy, we can ask how—or if—these economies will reabsorb the lost jobs.

In 1932 President Franklin Roosevelt responded to the nation's biggest employment crisis, the Great Depression, with an unprecedented range of federal jobs programs intended for the most part to provide temporary income to laid-off workers. Roosevelt's New Deal had been largely constructed in New York City when the president was still the governor of New York state. As president, Roosevelt went to the Capitol with a platoon of New Yorkers armed with programs that had been worked out in New York City. Henry Hopkins was at FDR's right hand, as was First Lady Eleanor Roosevelt, with her settlement house and labor reform connections, and his secretary of labor, Frances Perkins, whose career in pursuit of industrial reform had been galvanized by the tragedy of the Triangle Factory fire. In the end, the New Deal completely transformed the nature of the relationship between citizens and government, in particular, how people viewed their government and its responsibility to intervene in economic crises.

While it may have been novel at the time, the scenario of federal economic intervention in the New Deal meant that billions of dollars flowed into things that were socially useful, creating public works like parks, roads, electrification projects, dams, bridges, hospitals, schools, federal and state buildings, and countless other public works programs with the object of rebuilding and renewing civic life while at the same time giving gainful employment to workers desperate to stave off poverty. But the Roosevelt administration's response to joblessness would be the last time the federal government successfully intervened on a grand scale to enable workers to maintain their relationship to the regular workforce. Not until the Kennedy and Johnson administrations in the 1960s would important national programs be proposed that aimed to redress inequalities in labor market absorption of unemployment, and these programs—the subject of this book—would aim to leverage the poor into the regular labor market. This was the last time presidential efforts to redress employment inequalities and bring everyone into the workforce increased an administration's political capital.

Sixty years later, on August 22, 1996, only a few months away from the end of both his first term and his reelection campaign for president, President Bill Clinton signed into law the Personal Responsibility and Work Opportunity Reconciliation Act of 1996. The bill was a historic piece of legislation for a twentieth-century Democratic president, eliminating federal responsibility for welfare after sixty years, transferring it to the states with the charge that recipients must work to receive benefits and that assistance be limited to five years in a lifetime. Clinton claimed after he signed the act that "welfare will no longer be a political issue."[5] Clinton's decision to jettison the AFDC program at the national level demonstrated two things. It reflected his—correct—recognition of the continued vitality of the idea of work in the American ethos, and it showed that he had finally, as his first term was closing, developed the political nerve and skills to "end welfare as we know it."

Yet early in his administration, in spring 1993, Americans observed a new Democratic president falter and lose his first battle on Capitol Hill because he could not change four votes in the Senate. The Clinton administration had responded to unemployment by proposing a modest amount for job training in its economic stimulus program. That was not the administration's major tool, as it was hoping that improvement in the general economy would be the principal factor in cutting down unemployment. The jobs component was in effect a buried antipoverty measure intended to bring some portion of relief to the unemployed in a jobless economic recovery. A quarter of the money would have gone to unemployment insurance and another $1 billion was targeted for short-lived summer jobs. Its problems were twofold. The package added $19.4 billion to the deficit Clinton was trying to cut, and this weakened support for it even within his own party. And he did not then have the political savvy to understand the first rule of domestic politics: persuasion.

This was a far cry from January 8, 1964, when newly inaugurated president Lyndon Johnson boldly announced to the nation that his administration would eliminate poverty across the land. We would be the first nation ever to attempt such a feat; there was no doubt that we would succeed. Johnson recognized that the national economy and mood would permit such a large-scale governmental effort to fight poverty, and he knew he had the political capital and skills to lead the fight. He viewed the poverty program as a showpiece of domestic legislation that would capture and define the spirit of his administration. The paradox is that Johnson saw a public program benefiting the poor as increasing his political popularity, while thirty years later Clinton had to submerge relief in an economic program promoting the general economy.

Such radical renovations in our approach to antipoverty policy have been characteristic of the United States. Goals in this area have consistently been ambiguous and failed to devise effective public policy to assist the poor.[6] We cannot come to agreement on what the national government can do, or should do, to alleviate poverty and how it can best do this. And, as both Clinton's 1996 transfer of welfare responsibility to the states and Johnson's 1964 War on Poverty illustrate, we have often lurched between contradictory and untested programs without a clear idea of how they will affect the poor. These concerns have long been at the center of American public policy debates, yet we have never had systematic overall planning to fight poverty, and, most important, we have never had serious jobs programs on a national scale to address its chief cause: unemployment. Why has our approach to poverty and its victims—most of whom are children today—been so halfhearted, so inconsistent, and so misguided?

A range of views regarding American's antipoverty policy has been offered by experts and observers, including some with firsthand experience in crafting American public policy. According to former senator and poverty expert Daniel Patrick Moynihan, the first comprehensive attempt to address poverty in the United States directly—the War on Poverty— was a political expediency that came from a select circle at work on a campaign agenda for President Kennedy's second term. Antipoverty policy arose as a byproduct of that work. "The plain fact," he says, ". . . is that the attempt to address the issue of poverty in the whole of the United States came in the first instance from an informal committee of a half dozen persons thinking up themes for President Kennedy's 1964 reelection campaign."[7] Political scientist Charles V. Hamilton suggests that Americans have never really tried to erase poverty because "this country has only recently—very recently, the last 20 to 25 years—seen poverty as a condition that public policy ought to try to *eradicate*. . . . There has always been the assumption that in a market economy there would be rich people and poor people, with a reasonably stable group in between."[8] As

Hamilton says, in the public mind the business of government is not to eliminate poverty through public policy but only to buffer its most pernicious effects. Public policy specialist Hugh Heclo believes it is useful to see the past as a collection of heterogeneous moments containing many emergent policy probabilities and tendencies, only some of which were ever realized. In the history of antipoverty policy, a clear, unambiguous political commitment has never had its moment. Heclo, then, conceives of antipoverty policy as an accident of political moments when only some ideas are realized out of the universe of possible political answers.[9]

These are diverse views, and they provide context—not explanations—for poverty policy in America and the role of government in addressing it. More systematic political analysis has reexamined established views of economic and social policies in the United States to uncover linkages between ideas, politics, institutions, and society in American political life, and such work has furthered understanding of poverty policy, and the War on Poverty in particular, by examining the course of employment policy generally in the United States.[10] Yet to consider the War on Poverty in the broader category of failed or truncated efforts to achieve full employment obscures the importance of immediate political and economic factors that were directly relevant to its outcome as an antipoverty policy. While the failure of the War on Poverty to take a jobs-centered turn can be told as a chapter in the larger story of the long-term quest to achieve full employment, it is also a tale of the short-term enthusiasm for policy ideas that is characteristic of, not anomalous to, antipoverty policy making in the United States. The aim of this book is to explore particular ideas about poverty in the political setting that critically affected government antipoverty policy making. Specifically, this book examines ideas about jobs policies in the War on Poverty to understand why jobs programs, which might have become the centerpiece of the first large-scale antipoverty initiative undertaken in the United States, did not.

Prevailing attitudes in post—World War II America viewed poverty and unemployment as anachronistic economic malfunctions that could be confronted through concerted national efforts, and the elimination of poverty became a national goal for the first time anywhere in the world with the enactment of the Economic Opportunity Act of 1964.[11] The War on Poverty was formulated in a policy atmosphere of extreme lability; the absence of any clear consensus among the program's creators as to the causes of poverty and the optimal policy to eradicate it meant that this was a period of opportunity for ideas that otherwise might never have reached the policy agenda. The greatest failure of the War on Poverty, consequently, was in missing the mark on the most optimal solution to poverty at a singular time when, in fact, more conventional work-oriented solutions on a large scale might have had a remarkable impact on the poor. Furthermore, jobs policies were the solution sought by critical constituencies that would have most benefited from concerted programs to address unemployment: the black poor. The War on Poverty could have been an inclusive program of government-sponsored jobs and job-training programs in conjunction with the private sector. This book examines and explains why it was not.

Why examine employment policies and antipoverty policy in the War on Poverty nearly forty years later? First, because work is a central human activity, public policy concerning work illuminates important ideological or philosophical underpinnings of society, and these have continuing relevance for public policy today. In the United States, public policy concerning work is shaped by the American ethos and its deeply embedded values and preferences concerning the market, capitalism, individualism, and limited government. This ethos forms a strong undercurrent in American politics that is expressed in public policy. Moreover, the larger context of employment policy involves structural postindustrial economic changes and their effects and reflects the ability of American business to incorporate the demands of advanced capitalism.[12] Twentieth-century governments have a role in easing the adjustment during this transition. In particular, the status of the United States Department of Labor (DOL) in 1960 exemplified the dynamics of this transition. The DOL's situation perfectly illustrates how changes in the nature of unemployment were the outcome of difficult contractions in capitalism and the emergence of a new stage, in which higher unemployment was to be the rule not the exception. The DOL's struggles demonstrate how the existing capacities of government, located in the Labor Department, were inadequate to the transition at the time.

Particularly relevant here are Ira Katznelson's arguments on the inhibited range of American social and economic policy.[13] Katznelson describes as "silences" the noninitiation of policy ideas, in which certain ideas and options in American public policy are not presented, let alone proposed and rejected. Instead of encompassing the full range of welfare state options, the debate here about the scope and role of government is limited to positions of the positive or social security state that offer various forms of market assistance or social security for all citizens. The social welfare state is never considered because it is too far to the left of accepted ideological discourse. Such limits to government activity are distinctive to the United States. The consequences of this for antipoverty policy are captured by Hugh Heclo when he says that "any attempt to ground American anti-poverty policy in a highly egalitarian, social democratic vision of society is trying to recreate a possibility that has passed, if such a chance ever existed at all."[14]

The idea of silences is significant not only with regard to left-leaning public policy in the United States but also for deeply embedded elements of racism in American life and its effects on American government. And this provides another reason for concentrating on the range of ideas and policy options characterizing the War on Poverty. A range of public policy options has not been presented—or responded to—because the governmental will to redress injustice and inequalities that have differentially affected black Americans has been profoundly limited. In particular, as demonstrated in this book, black Americans' concerted parallel pressure on government to respond to their struggle for full economic inclusion with substantive employment programs failed to affect definitively the antipoverty agenda in the War on Poverty. The astonishingly broad exclusion of important black voices presents a paradox. Many scholars writing since the 1980s have regarded the War on Poverty as a "black" program. Political scientists have argued that the War on Poverty programs of the 1960s disproportionately benefited African Americans, or so it was perceived at the time. This fact or perception in turn contributed to the white backlash that led to the beginning of the end of high liberal public policy from 1932 to 1981, which we now know as the American Welfare State. In their retrospective assessments of American politics in the sixties and seventies, influential analyses like those of Thomas Edsall and Mary Edsall and Kevin Phillips and Margaret Weir, among others, argue that public resentment of perceived black advantage in controversial public programs fueled an electoral turnaround in 1980 as black-favoring, budget-busting liberal majorities at every level of government were turned out of office, ushering in, if not a genuine electoral realignment, a new era of conservative policy and politics.[15] It is argued that racial preference was demonstrated in a range of public policies from antipoverty programs that originated in the sixties to affirmative action in hiring and education, housing preferences, and income distribution. Yet any discussion of the racial character of the antipoverty policies of Lyndon Johnson's Great Society has not only to distinguish between the intentions and goals of policy makers and policy outcomes but also to separate these dimensions from perceptions of policy outcomes. These distinctions are often missing from critical analyses of policy making in the period, and so too is close examination of the racial attitudes and assumptions of the specialists who created, in particular, the much-maligned War on Poverty.

A third reason for concentrating on ideas about jobs policies is that jobs are necessary to eliminate poverty in the United States, if poverty is described as the inability to earn a living income. Except for the very old and the very young, the "essential characteristic of the poor is unemployment or underemployment."[16] This is true today and was true during the early 1960s when planning for the War on Poverty commenced. Jobs policies could have been the most successful antipoverty strategy in the early 1960s when persistent and hardcore joblessness was relatively new. Many of the structural unemployment problems we talk about today—and that appear to have spread widely throughout the workforce, transforming the meaning of work even for Americans at higher ends of the income spectrum—already existed when the War on Poverty was in its planning stages. It was in the 1960s and 1970s that factories, plants, and steel mills began to disappear from the cities and relocate in the suburbs to benefit from the better tax, transportation, and workforce advantages growing there. These were the source of jobs for unskilled and low-skilled workers, white and black. In the two decades from 1967 to 1987, New York City and Chicago alone lost more than 825,000 manufacturing jobs, and this pattern was repeated over the industrial Northeast and Midwest.[17] Moreover, the idea that unemployment, low levels of employment, and employment in low-paying, low-skilled, so-called dead-end sectors of the economy have hit black Americans disproportionately has been around a long time. In one way or another, these work-oriented causes continue to be seen as major contributors to wide-scale poverty among black Americans, and they have been connected causally to the mushrooming of ghetto poverty in cities. Today there is no lack of material telling us how structural changes in the economy, locational decisions of firms, macroeconomic factors, and persistent, or evolving, discrimination have hit black Americans hard. William Julius Wilson revalidated academic interest in poverty in the black community in the 1980s, but he did not discover the problems of structural unemployment and its impact on black unemployment—nor does he claim he did.[18] These problems originated back in the early and midsixties. In fact, they dogged the planners of the War on Poverty, who could have addressed them through a substantial employment strategies program.

Jobs programs concentrated on adult unemployment and underemployment were believed to be the right strategy to combat poverty by key participants at the moment in the spring and fall of 1963 and early in 1964 when planning for the Economic Opportunity Act of 1964 was under way. The fact that they were not the central strategy had important consequences for antipoverty policy. Had it had a stronger jobs component, the War on Poverty would have been more politically viable in the long term in Congress than it was with amorphous experimental programs such as Community Action Programs (CAPS) at its center. Jobs programs, such as the popular Manpower Development Training Act 1962, were unambiguously related to the central domestic issues of the early sixties—unemployment and civil rights—and popular support of a government guarantee of work was high.[19] Further, jobs programs—including job training, job creation by government, and jobs in the private sector for which the poor were prepared—were what the poor wanted and were perceived to need by important interests in the society at the time; in particular, a major jobs initiative would have been more responsive to the "Negro job crisis," and it was called for by the civil rights leadership and other black spokespeople.[20] Finally, if jobs programs on a large scale had been the centerpiece of the War on Poverty, the second-, third-, and fourth-generation effects the United States has experienced—the swelling of the ranks of the ghetto poor—might have been greatly attenuated.

The United States continues to experience the consequences of this unemployment and underemployment, and the economic, social, and private costs of such joblessness have been enormous.[21] Even as the U.S. economy enjoyed low unemployment and high growth from the mid-1990s through the turn of the century, the long view—even before September 11, 2001—suggested that the prospect of a definitive end to recession and unemployment was unlikely. The recession, which started in March 2001, had already begun to broaden the range of unemployment as the nation was attacked in New York City, to the extent that corporate layoffs had reached the tens of thousands by fall of that year. In the ten-year period from 1977 to 1986 the average yearly cost (in constant 1986 dollars) was nearly $90 billion. This cost the average American household more than $1,000 per year. Moreover, the social costs are twofold. Not only are income maintenance benefits paid out of the national wealth, but society also pays again in the costs of lost production of goods and services that would be produced if everyone who wanted to work were employed. The ten-year cost of such lost production between 1977 and 1986 was nearly $1.2 trillion, or about $14.2 billion annually, a forfeiture of about $1,600 in goods and services per household per year.[22] This does not include the cost of the private pain and hardship associated with unemployment: broken homes, marital strife and abuse, child abuse, mental illness, poor health, crime, and homelessness. While unemployment may not be the direct cause of such suffering, there is no doubt that the two are linked and that joblessness increases their effects.

Unemployment levels for the very poor have not improved much over the past century, and economic expertise and institutions have not diminished the problem of entrenched joblessness for this category since World War II.[23] A large-scale government effort at job training, job creation, and job placement during the early 1960s might have altered the dynamics of hardcore unemployment as it has developed since. Large-scale jobs programs were an essential complement to aggregate economic measures to bring down persistent unemployment in the early 1960s and would have been more successful as an antipoverty strategy to eliminate hardcore unemployment. These ideas were part of the policy discourse at the time, and they could have led to another War on Poverty—a war fought with jobs. We had, and missed, the opportunity at that time to put in place significant measures to ensure economic participation by everyone in the society.

Planning for the War on Poverty began in the Kennedy administration early in 1963, when a series of articles and books on poverty prompted the president's interest and he directed Walter Heller, chairman of the Council of Economic Advisers, to undertake a study of potential antipoverty initiatives.[24] In May 1963 Heller brought in income distribution expert Robert Lampman, who produced guidelines that would be the factual basis for the potential poverty program, as well as Kermit Gordon and William Cannon of the Budget Bureau. By the end of the summer, Heller had been directed by Kennedy's special assistant, Theodore Sorensen, to pull together measures that might constitute an attack on poverty as part of the president's 1964 legislative program. Heller did so by directing one of his assistants, William Capron, to create an informal interagency task force of officials from various government agencies that might be involved in social welfare issues: Health, Education, and Welfare (HEW), Labor, Commerce, the Economic Development Administration, the Appalachia Program, and the Justice Department, among others.[25] What emerged were outdated, stale program ideas that had never gone very far, "often for rather good reasons."[26] Dissatisfied with the conventional proposals that emerged and seeking a more striking concept for the poverty program, Heller, Gordon, and Capron seized on the idea of Community Action Programs (CAPS), which had been evolving at the President's Committee on Juvenile Delinquency (PCJD), as the organizing mechanism for antipoverty policy. While Kennedy continued to express interest in the potential program over the fall, he failed to give Heller an unequivocal commitment to the poverty program until three days before his death, when, on November 19, he gave Heller a guarded go ahead. After Kennedy's death, Heller presented the proposed poverty agenda to President Johnson, who immediately took to the idea and directed the groundwork to continue. Johnson formally declared war on poverty in his January 8, 1964, State of the Union address, well before the program had developed clear outlines. On February 1 he appointed Peace Corps director Sargent Shriver to head up the Task Force on Poverty, which would direct the planning of the War on Poverty. Its work ended in the Economic Opportunity Act, which became law on August 20, 1964. The Economic Opportunity Act contained seven titles offering youth programs, rural grants, employment and investment incentives, work training and study, social services, health, education, and income assistance, and community action programs. Its total funding for the first year came to $962.5 million, only $500 million of which was newly appropriated; the rest would come out of existing funds and budgetary legerdemain. The most important and controversial idea to come out in the act was the inchoate coordination mechanism, CAPS, an idea that would serve more as a lightning rod for congressional attacks against the War on Poverty than as a benefit to poor communities.

It is now time to revisit the War on Poverty, using the full archival evidence available. While we know a great deal about the War on Poverty generally, most of the policy and historical literature is not focused on what happened to proposals for jobs strategies during that period. Until Margaret Weir's and Gary Mucciaroni's books on unemployment, not one major study substantially tracked what happened to ideas about jobs strategies in the War on Poverty.[27] Additionally, either because of its inherent difficulty or its controversial nature, no sustained attention has ever been given to close exploration of the racial motivations of the architects of the EOA.[28]

Almost forty years have passed since the Task Force on Poverty under newly inaugurated president Lyndon B. Johnson began to plan the nation's only large-scale government antipoverty program. Most of the existing accounts and analyses were written in the 1960s and 1970s, some without access to the pertinent Kennedy and Johnson Presidential Library archival material. Important questions remain unanswered, including those pertaining to the connection between ideas and jobs policies. Today, increasingly few people even know what the War on Poverty was, much less imagine a world in which the national government, without prompting, would initiate a large-scale effort to address the problems of poor people. As a generational event, the War on Poverty is as remote to the college graduating class of 2003 as 1928, the eve of the great market crash of the Depression, was to the baby boomer generation. Yet an important distinction is that as boomers studied the Depression from the vantage point of 1963, they discovered the origins of an American welfare state that continued to have relevance for them. Today, as twenty-year-olds study the Kennedy/Johnson years, they discern the origins of the demise of the American welfare state, and they recognize as well that the relationship between government and the polity has changed hugely since that time. Even so, students are invariably fascinated by the goals, politics, agenda, and very existence of the War on Poverty. Most students I have taught are dissatisfied with the pervasiveness today of narrow self-interest as an organizing principle for life and look back longingly to this last period of aggressively unselfish public policy.

This book, then, has the perspective of time and the advantage of historical documents. It attempts to bring a new perspective to the oft-told tale of the origins of the War on Poverty by reexamining the historical record and uncovering the hidden story, based on new evidence, of the fate of jobs policies.

This book examines important ways in which ideas affect government policy making. Specifically, it consolidates processes through which distinct economic ideas came to dominate in one social welfare initiative at a particular point in time. In other words, it illustrates that ideas have consequences, but only in specific ways at specific times. Bowing to E. P. Thompson's great work *The Making of the English Working Class*, it does not posit a law governing how ideas have consequences but suggests a logic to how this occurs; to paraphrase Thompson, while ideas may have consequences in the same way in different times and places, it is never in *just* the same way.[29] It is hoped that the approach to policy analysis demonstrated here can be applied more broadly to other policy areas as well, since the ways ideas influenced, or failed to influence, the development of the War on Poverty may offer insights into policy formation in other cases.

This book draws on a variety of evidence. To investigate the ideas that actually were in debate in Congress, I examined legislative histories for the Economic Opportunity Act of 1964, the Manpower Development and Training Act of 1962, the Emergency Employment Act of 1971, the Trade Adjustment Act of 1961, the Area Redevelopment Act of 1961, the Accelerated Public Works Act of 1962, the Public Works and Economic Development Act of 1965, the Appalachian Regional Development Act of 1965, the Civil Rights Act of 1964, the Wagner-Peyser Act of 1933, the Manpower Services Act of 1966, and the subsequent extensions and amendments to these acts throughout the Johnson years.

To trace how ideas affected antipoverty policy in this period, I examined leading journals of opinion and publicly available records of the antipoverty agenda such as congressional committee hearings and reports, presidential addresses, party platforms, press reportage, and public opinion surveys for evidence of the flow among elites of ideas related to jobs policy. Content analyses of the *New York Times* revealed what the dominant ideas on the agenda were and helped to establish the public debate. Frequency or emphasis (headlines) illustrated salience or lack of it.

I also interviewed at length former secretary of labor W. Willard Wirtz in Washington, D.C., as well as corresponded and spoke frequently with him between July 1991 and November 2001 to obtain more direct information than is publicly available on his critical role in promoting jobs policies in the War on Poverty.

Most revealing and useful was a thorough examination of archival materials and oral histories in the John Fitzgerald Kennedy and Lyndon Baines Johnson Presidential Libraries. The primary sources here were principally oral histories and other archival documents from individuals who were instrumental in the development of antipoverty policy, economic policy, and jobs policy in the Kennedy and Johnson administrations. Specific ideas associated with the War on Poverty emerged from close analysis of the archival materials of the period, spring 1963 to August 1964, that led to the Economic Opportunity Act of 1964.

Could jobs strategies have been the central idea in the War on Poverty? In the chapters that follow, this book answers yes, the idea of jobs strategies could have prevailed, and illustrates why it did not.

Chapter 2, "Economic Ideas and the War on Poverty," demonstrates how particular attributes of economic decision making in the administration of President John F. Kennedy affected the War on Poverty. These economic influences were the role of President Kennedy's Council of Economic Advisers (CEA) in shaping presidential decision making, the competition of particular economic ideas in the Kennedy administration, and the prevailing understanding of unemployment by key policy makers in the administration. A critical factor in the demise of the idea of jobs policies in the War on Poverty was the lack of consensus among experts as to the technical causes of unemployment and how unemployment was related to poverty.

The next chapter, "Change and Incapacity in the Department of Labor," analyzes, as it was perceived, the stark incapacity of the Labor Department to administer the kinds of large-scale jobs programs it was proposing in the War on Poverty. Secretary Willard Wirtz's goal was a massive government-sponsored jobs program to be administered by the Labor Department, but the Department of Labor was considered too set in its ways and administratively chaotic to make the transition to a new kind of policy initiative. In the end, Wirtz failed to promote successfully the idea of jobs programs as the central antipoverty strategy, and the War on Poverty took a broader course.

Chapter 4, "Social Forces, Civil Rights, and the Struggle for Jobs," describes the black community's struggle to raise the issue of black employment in the sixties as a catalyst to a War on Poverty centered on jobs programs. The role of black leadership in and outside the civil rights coalition exemplifies the longstanding history of economic analysis and political pressure by the black community, which raised employment issues as being central to its well-being. This chapter documents the shift in the civil rights movement in 1963 to a more pronounced emphasis on jobs and employment issues.

Chapter 5, "Governmental Will: The Limits of Noblesse Oblige," demonstrates the Kennedy administration's ambivalence about committing government resources to meet the call for jobs from the black community. It also considers Lyndon Johnson's potential to reverse the historical pattern of governmental institutional racism in the United States. Pressure from the black community for jobs and employment programs brought to bear on the Kennedy and Johnson administrations was ignored because of relative powerlessness to affect the national agenda. This chapter raises the issue of the racial attitudes of the white liberal architects of the Economic Opportunity Act of 1964 and concludes that, in part, institutional racism accounted for their failure to incorporate the black job agenda into the War on Poverty.

Chapter 6, "Ideas and Government Policy Making," emphasizes the context of ideas in which public policy making was situated in the period under study. This chapter examines three decisive arenas in which the idea of jobs policy competed for dominance. It posits the centrality of the prevailing economic ideas in the early 1960s in undermining the appeal of the idea of jobs policies as the preferred government antipoverty strategy and shows how these economic ideas were consequential to the War on Poverty. The lack of consensus on technical economic ideas about unemployment was decisive to the fate of the idea of jobs policies in the War on Poverty. If government had provided an emphatic sense of sponsorship and social agency, then poverty and jobs would have been linked. We had a national mood and an economy that permitted large-scale intervention. The decisive reason for the failure of the idea of jobs policies was the lack of a clear consensus among experts, early on, about the nature of unemployment and its relation to economic performance and how these two factors relate to poverty. A second reason was the incapacity of the Labor Department—the chief sponsor of the idea through the advocacy of Willard Wirtz—to administer such a program effectively. A third reason for the failure of jobs policies was the halting and partial nature of the government's commitment to the civil rights leadership and the black community's struggle for full economic participation in the society, an issue of governmental will.

Finally, the book contains an appendix, "Joblessness, Poverty, and Public Policy in the United States," that provides a brief compendium of the general governmental response to joblessness and poverty since the Depression.

This book gives prominence to ideas and their role in the formation of the War on Poverty. It has involved close study of the social, political, and technological thought and assumptions of an era and its institutional environment and introduces the role of ideas in a new way by making them variables in the policy-making process, bringing them into the foreground.

2. Economic Ideas and the War on Poverty

This country thinks it has got full employment. As far as the economics of employment is concerned, that is probably right. As far as the humanities of unemployment are concerned, it is dead wrong.
— WILLARD WIRTZ

The country was not ready at that point to accept 4 percent unemployment.
— WILLARD WIRTZ

Economic ideas are part of the history of antipoverty policy, particularly the economic ideas during the Kennedy and Johnson years. The debates that began among economic experts in the earliest days of the Kennedy administration over the causes and consequences of unemployment had repercussions beyond macroeconomic management. These debates also shaped the strategies chosen two years later in Walter Heller's poverty committee under Kennedy, which evolved, many recompositions later, into the Shriver Task Force that formulated the War on Poverty under President Johnson.

During the early 1960s, Heller and his Council of Economic Advisers argued that the economy would respond to aggregate stimulation by returning to full employment and maintaining long-term secular growth and thereby reducing poverty. The cost of economic slack, Heller maintained, was a drastic slowdown in the rate at which the economy reduced poverty.[1] Heller's thinking was that reducing economic slack would increase the rate at which the economy took people out of poverty, presumably bringing this rate up to the levels of the immediate postwar years when, between 1947 and 1957, the percentage of families with less than $3,000 total money income declined ten points, from 33 percent to 23 percent. Heller was distressed that the rate of decline from the years 1956 to 1961 was only 2 percent, from 23 percent to 21 percent. With a successful tax cut, full employment, and faster growth, the 1957–1967 rate would fall from 19 percent to 14 percent, a rate similar to that of 1947 to 1957.

In contrast, structuralists argued that the nation was experiencing structural problems in the labor market that fiscal measures alone would not solve; what was needed were interventionist jobs policies on a large scale. This lack of consensus in economic thinking on the nature of unemployment was present at the onset of Kennedy's administration, with the CEA and the Treasury Department, on one side of the issue, favoring aggregate stimulation through fiscal measures such as the tax cut, and, on the other side, Department of Labor officials, labor specialists such as Charles Killingworth, and Chairman William McChesney Martin of the Federal Reserve Board favoring large-scale jobs measures to address structural unemployment.[2] Had there been clear resolution among experts over the nature of unemployment in this period and the way it was related to hard-core joblessness, and, in particular, had the structuralist arguments prevailed, the idea of jobs policies as the solution to poverty would have been considerably strengthened. Based on hindsight, the structuralists were right, because unemployment did not respond to aggregate demand policies by taking deeply entrenched poor people out of poverty. The notion that the rising tide of economic growth would lift all boats was wrong, because the residue of hard-core joblessness among the poor remained, even in the face of increased growth.[3]

Grasping the meaning of this critical period and this critical lack of consensus requires understanding particular attributes of economic decision making in the Kennedy administration. This chapter focuses on three important economic influences in the Kennedy administration: the role of Kennedy's Council of Economic Advisers in shaping his economic thinking and decisions, the competition of particular economic ideas in his administration, and the prevailing understanding of unemployment in these years when key decisions were made that would go on to affect the War on Poverty. This chapter will show how commitments made established the prominence of decisive economic ideas that would later limit the possibilities for antipoverty policy.

ECONOMIC ADVICE IN THE KENNEDY ADMINISTRATION

The Employment Act of 1946 assigned an economic advisory role to the Council of Economic Advisers: to bring the best available economic knowledge to bear on presidential decision making.[4] In its advisory role to President Kennedy, the council, under Walter Heller, was extraordinary in its influence—perhaps more influential than any other council has been. Particular characteristics of the Heller council and its relationship with the president explain the council's striking influence.

John F. Kennedy entered the presidency with virtually no commitments on economic matters except "to get the country moving again"—a commitment to growth.[5] Although as a candidate Kennedy had promised economic growth and vowed to stimulate investment, economic issues had not been a hard-hitting theme in the 1960 presidential campaign. Unemployment in February 1961 totaled 8.1 million workers unadjusted for seasonality. For the first half of 1961, seasonally adjusted unemployment averaged close to 5 million, nearly 7 percent of the labor force. In 1962 seasonally adjusted unemployment fell to 4 million, 5.6 percent of the labor force, and in 1963 it was slightly higher than in the previous year.[6] Kennedy faced two major financial problems when he came into office: how to promote recovery from the economic slowdown of the previous summer and fall and how to maintain the strength of the dollar. The nation was in the middle of its fourth recession of the postwar period; gross national product had fallen 1 percent between the second and fourth quarters of 1960, and nearly 20 percent of the nation's manufacturing capacity was idle.[7] Kennedy's economic policy making has been hailed as evidence of the triumph of Keynesianism, or the "New Economics," the consolidation of the economic doctrine that government should actively pursue policies that ensure long-term stable growth.[8] Examination of documentary evidence from the Kennedy administration, however, reveals how ambivalent the economic thinking of the president was. The main story in economic policy making in the administration was the triumph of Kennedy's Council of Economic Advisers in achieving intellectual preeminence in the president's sphere of economic advisers. As in no other administration, Kennedy's council played a central role in shaping the president's economic thinking. This had direct consequences for the centrality of the idea of jobs policies in antipoverty policy, particularly because of the council's understanding of the relationship between poverty and unemployment and the way it would respond to macroeconomic manipulation but also for the effects of particular Keynesian measures they chose to stimulate the slack economy, using fiscal Keynesianism measures such as the tax cut instead of targeted Keynesian measures such as large-scale public spending.[9]

To understand better the dilemma Kennedy faced as he tried to forge new economic policy for a new decade, it is necessary to consider certain influences that impinged on his economic policy making. These influences were his economic advisers, the competition of particular economic and political ideas, and the opinion of what Richard Neustadt would call "the Washington community of influentials."[10] In addition, an important consideration that dogged Kennedy's thought process in making economic choices was political feasibility: would he be able to get the votes in Congress to pass innovative economic measures such as the tax cut?

The Council of Economic Advisers

In the early 1960s macroeconomic policy-making responsibility in the executive branch was distributed among the Council of Economic Advisers, the Treasury Department, the Bureau of the Budget, and the Federal Reserve Board.[11] President Kennedy—who preferred less structured arrangements than his predecessor had—was principally advised on fiscal policy by the CEA's Walter Heller, the BOB's secretary, David Bell, followed later by Kermit Gordon, and Treasury Secretary Douglas Dillon. This group was called the Troika when the chairmen met together. The independent Federal Reserve Board set monetary policy, as it does today. When the Troika was joined by the chairman of the Federal Reserve, William McChesney Martin, the group was called the Quadriad.[12]

The primary job of the CEA was to provide expert economic analysis to the president, although it also functioned as coordinator for his views at times.[13] In its role as counselor to the president, it forecast economic trends, analyzed economic issues, and prepared an annual economic report to Congress.[14] The council met on an ad hoc basis at Heller's request, after consultation with the president, and convened only when it met with the president. During the Kennedy administration, it reported to the president every two or three months, more often if necessary. Functional specialization developed to a degree among the parts of the Troika and the Quadriad, and this too was formalized during Heller's tenure.[15] What is striking about these arrangements is the extent of decentralization of economic advice and counsel they illustrate. The Troika issued quarterly projections on GNP, unemployment, revenue, and the budget as a more or less mediated report of its three members. These were the economic facts the administration had to go on in making up the budget and in economic policy making.16 While differences among the members were generally negotiable, there were "a few occasions quite early when the differences were fairly sharp" and remained unmediated.17 Specialization evolved according to the expertise of each agency. The CEA was chiefly responsible for economic projections, the BOB for budget expenditure projections and expenditures on national income accounts (which the council would use in its economic forecasts), and Treasury for revenue estimates. Contention would arise over the issue of revenue forecasting, when, for example, the council and Treasury could not agree on the accuracy of each other's revenue equations and would use their own so that "on both sides there was coverage of the whole forecast and the original division of labor couldn't be carried out."18 In spite of such variance, the remarkable thing about the relationships among the members of the Troika and the Quadriad was compatibility and the frequency with which they reached consensus.19

At every level President Kennedy, and later President Johnson, had access to particularly distinguished economic advice from the CEA and its consultants.20 There were also other economic advisers to President Kennedy, such as Kenneth Galbraith and Seymour Harris of Harvard, who were personally closer to the president than was his council, and Carl Kaysen, who was concerned with certain issues of foreign economic policy. Harris had been advising the president on economic matters off and on since his work on Kennedy's first senatorial campaign in 1952. Galbraith had been friendly with Kennedy at Harvard and "among the economists, there [was] no question that Galbraith was closer to the president"; this friendship gave him access to the president and "meant that the president was fully exposed to his ideas all the way through. [Yet] it did not mean that he accepted the ideas."21 (It has also been suggested that, in spite of the president's great affection for him, he also viewed Harris with less than full confidence.)22 The most direct evidence that Kennedy did not accept Galbraith's views over those of his council is that he eschewed the joining of economic and public goals in interventionist public spending on the scale proposed by Galbraith. Kennedy respected expertise and had an independence of mind—there was a "cold, matter of fact quality of his mind," according to Paul Samuelson—that enabled him to make pragmatic judgments.23 He had no dogma and was willing to change his mind depending on the nature of the evidence. He was not easily led in his economic thinking and had to be convinced of the rational and logical correctness of the decisions he would make, which, in the end, would also be tempered by their political feasibility.

That the Heller council was able to be so influential with Kennedy is attributable in part to the tutorial function it played in his economic education. This is well illustrated by James Tobin's account of one of his sessions with the president.

> He wanted to talk about economics, economic theory indeed. He wanted to ask me some questions, but it turned out he wanted to give his own answers to them too and see if I agreed, almost as if he were showing how well he had learned his lessons. So he did most of the talking, and my own interventions were largely to confirm that his own answers to his questions were right. There were two subjects; the budget deficit and gold. On the first he said, "Is there any economic limit to the deficit? I know of course about the political limits. People say you can't increase the national debt too fast or too much. We're always answering that the debt isn't growing relative to national income. But is there any economic limit to size of the debt in relation to national income? There isn't, is there? Well, what is the limit?" I said the only limit is really inflation. He grabbed at that. "That's right, isn't it? The deficit can be any size, the debt can be any size, provided they don't cause inflation. Everything else is just talk." We had a similar conversation about gold and the balance of payments. . . . This was the gist of the conversation. He spent more than half an hour from a busy day on this conversation, and he was obviously having a good time. Obviously too, he and I both recognized that the talk was an academic one, divorced from the day to day policy decisions where he realized so keenly that the political and ideological myths from which he was showing his intellectual liberation were so constraining and compelling. I was extremely gratified, of course because these were points he had certainly not understood in 1961 and points I had tried persistently to make orally and in writing for almost two years. Maybe he was just showing that he understood my points, without indicating that he agreed with them. But that was definitely not the tone of the conversation. Rather it was that he understood them and accepted them but that he was, as I well know, hemmed in.[24]

Paul Samuelson also felt that while somebody like Galbraith "could have been a Harry Hopkins to [Adlai] Stevenson, or Svengali, and really had a tremendous control over his mind in economic affairs . . . I never had the impression that any one person would ever be able to do that with Senator Kennedy, candidate Kennedy, President-elect Kennedy, or President Kennedy."[25] But Kennedy's preference for analytical expertise and pragmatism in his advisers made him particularly open to the Heller council of experts and pragmatists. He gave them great access—spending virtually hours at a time with the council, individually or as a group—especially before the Bay of Pigs, when his schedule was more flexible. Heller successfully convinced the president early on not to bring other economists into the White House, which meant that the council had a monopoly on economic expertise, thus enhancing its influence with him.

The council's chairman, members, and staff were Keynesian in their economic philosophy, activists in promoting an aggressive public posture for the council, and pragmatists in not joining economic goals to collective public goals through the use of targeted large-scale spending. As economic advisers to the president, council members influenced his economic policy in important ways. They helped to diffuse the New Economics among noneconomists in the administration—and publicly—so that Keynesian economic ideas came to be more a part of the general philosophy of the administration and more widely accepted by the public. Their thinking departed from the Keynesian thinking of the 1930s in not espousing public spending, relying instead on fiscal stimulation measures like the tax cut to stimulate the slack economy.[26] For some economists, such as Leon Keyserling and Kenneth Galbraith, this departure was an important misapplication of Keynesian principles.[27] The council's economic philosophy was consistent with mainstream textbook economics of the time; by 1960 the ideas they espoused were not radical but orthodox in academic economics. Full employment and economic growth were the central problems in their view, both addressable by fiscal and monetary measures. Economic stability was measured in terms of full employment, and both were the goals of fiscal policy. These ideas "not only justified the big tax cut but made it the centerpiece of Kennedy's entire economic policy."[28] As economic policy, the tax cut was Keynesian, with modifications from the 1930s, and was ushered in by general agreement that total spending and the level of total money income were affected by both monetary and fiscal policy, thus bringing monetary policy into a Keynesian orbit.

The council diffused economic ideas through a process of education on three levels: it educated the president on the New Economics, and it—and he—educated the public. "There was a combination, simultaneously almost, of getting to the President on the one hand and simultaneously having the President get to the nation with some basic principals and precepts."[29] Kennedy's Yale speech in 1962, a "fundamental economic speech written in the myth-shattering tradition," was an example of this.[30] The council also educated Congress through its testimony to the Joint Economic Committee (JEC) in a way that set it apart from some earlier councils, especially the divided Nourse council under Truman, which was severely split on whether to testify before Congress. This was a role the president explicitly encouraged the Heller council to adopt.

In this process, the council also influenced the president's economic philosophy and came to change many assumptions to which he was predisposed before assuming the presidency. Council members engaged Kennedy hour after hour in educational discussions on specific policy matters and in tutorial sessions on theoretical economics.[31] Furthermore, they peppered him with educational memoranda of outstanding clarity and precision, and these were tremendously influential.[32]

President Kennedy was unusually open to education by economists; his capacity for abstract thought was great, and he was open to new ideas. Herb Stein said that before becoming the president Kennedy's ideas on fiscal policy were "lightly held. He did not consider himself as knowing economics."[33] Among the economists who worked closest to Kennedy, there is agreement that Kennedy waged an inner battle on matters of economic policy, torn between what he knew logically and doubts he had that "still hung in his mind from earlier training or conditioning" that caused him to cling to more moderate economics than those of his Heller council tutors.[34] Paul Samuelson suggested that at the beginning Kennedy was predisposed to reject New Deal Keynesianism with its focus on spending out of hand; in fact, Samuelson said that his own influence with the president stemmed in part from Kennedy's perception of him as a "sober and respectable and even a conservative New Deal type, and that this was a quality that was very much valued."[35] James Tobin believed that New Deal liberal economics and fiscal policy were perceived as politically unviable during Kennedy's campaign and afterward by the Kennedy entourage, and this feeling influenced the choice of economic advisers in the Heller council.

The council had a role in consolidating the idea that maximum full employment and balanced economic growth were proper measures of the health of the economy, replacing the previous orthodoxy of a balanced budget and price stability.[36] The success of the economy in moving out of a recession came to be gauged by where it was in relation to a full-employment growth target rather than by whether it was moving up or down. Contrary to the council's belief, as Walter Salant correctly notes, this growth emphasis was not initiated by the Heller council; rather, Leon Keyserling had emphasized this growth while he was a member of the Nourse council.[37] The Heller council reintroduced this idea, however, and was successful in implementing the emphasis on economic growth as a policy idea in the form of the 1964 tax cut. The correct trajectory, then, of the idea of maximum employment was that it was first introduced in the Truman administration with the Nourse council, disregarded in the Eisenhower administrations, and reintroduced with the Heller council under Kennedy.[38]

The analysis that follows examines the interplay of particular economic ideas in the Kennedy administration and how they affected policy choices available to antipoverty planners in the period.

THE COMPETITION OF ECONOMIC AND POLITICAL IDEAS

Kennedy was genuinely torn by a personal inner battle in accepting Keynesian economic policies.[39] This struggle made for a highly ambivalent commitment on his part to activist fiscal measures such as the tax cut. As noted, the Heller Council of Economic Advisers played a key role in the development of his economic thought and the particular pattern of Keynesian economic ideas he came to espouse—especially seasonally adjusted unemployment—but above all it was pivotal in winning Kennedy over to the cause of the tax cut, a victory that would go on to affect future policy choices.[40] This further examination of the documentary and other evidence illustrates how economic decisions and assumptions would go on to limit the options available to antipoverty planners as they deliberated on what would become the War on Poverty. Especially important were economic ideas about unemployment and the measures to address it, the understanding of how unemployment related to poverty, and the consequences of going for a tax cut to stimulate the economy instead of large-scale public spending.[41] All these ideas would have relevance for the fate of jobs programs in the War on Poverty.

The actual economic practices of the Kennedy administration were perceived at the time to be eclectic and more oriented to problem solving than to doctrinal principles. Because there is no center of economic policy making in the United States, and because Keynesian policy had never gained a secure foothold here, Keynesian economic measures had to contend with other approaches, commitments, and goals in interpreting economic issues.[42] Economic issues were muted in Kennedy's presidential campaign; outside of increasing the rate of growth up and getting the country moving again, they were not a prominent theme.[43] Although Kennedy made no economic commitments, his occasional emphasis on the "public sector need for keeping up with the expanding population" could have "built up, on the part of liberals, a very great hope that he would come in with a big spending program."[44] Yet he had already made decisions about the kind of economic advice he would have in his choice of economic advisers that eschewed serious consideration of the New Deal variant of Keynesian economics—targeted Keynesianism—that focused on public spending. Kennedy's choice of Walter Heller to head up his Council of Economic Advisers meant that fiscal Keynesianism would be the leading economic technique to manage the economy.[45] Kennedy may have started out "with a desire to disbelieve" in New Deal Keynesianism; his rejection could have stemmed from a number of sources, including his conviction that it was politically unviable—that "an unmitigated or old-style Democratic liberalism in regard to economics and fiscal policy wasn't going to pay off politically both during the campaign and afterwards"—and from the influence of his economically conservative father and upbringing.[46] In addition, a detailed critique by James Tobin of Leon Keyserling's memorandum on economic growth policy, which was submitted to the Democratic Advisory Committee (DAC) policy meeting on economic policy in the campaign, was used by the Kennedy forces within the DAC to contribute to the rejection of large-scale public spending as a statement of Democratic policy.[47] According to Tobin, the memorandum contained only one growth policy, even though it went on for a hundred pages, and that was "more spending, more spending, more spending."[48]

Within the context of spurring national economic growth, Kennedy entered the presidency with the idea of sacrifice in mind, based on his reading of the mood of the country. At the same time, he wanted to maintain a degree of fiscal responsibility. His commitment to these two goals would eliminate Heller's and the council's chances of winning the president over to a tax cut strategy in the first stage of Kennedy's economic program.[49]

Shortly after the Democratic convention, in a daylong session with his economic advisers at the Kennedy compound in Hyannis Port, Kennedy said that he sensed "that the mood of the country is that it's politically favorable to ask for sacrifices, not promise good things."[50] This was a theme he began to stress: that it was "the time to ask the people for sacrifices" and to place emphasis on people's doing things for their country.[51] While it was not especially prominent in the campaign, this became one of the dominant—and most rousing—themes in Kennedy's inaugural address. His receptivity to Heller's introduction of the idea of a tax cut as an economic technique to spur the economy would be limited by the sense that "he was boxed in by two things. One was the sacrifice theme and the other was fiscal responsibility."[52] According to Paul Samuelson, in this period every time he mentioned the tax cut to Kennedy, the president would wince as it was "incompatible with his whole posture of sacrifice. How could the first act be to give a handout?"[53] At the same time, fearing that it would jeopardize every program he was contemplating and because of his close election, "the last thing . . . the president want[ed] to have [was] the reputation of a reckless spender."[54]

Kennedy's political advisers were also wary of Keynesian economic expansion techniques, more so than Kennedy himself. In the early days, Ted Sorensen viewed Keynesian fiscal measures as a "bit of traditional liberal dogma with which his man may have been saddled as a candidate but which was a definite political handicap to him as he tried to be a middle-of-the-road president."[55] Neither president-elect Kennedy nor his staff had thoroughly studied, or been unequivocally confronted with, the politically unappealing side of fiscal economic techniques to stimulate the economy: deficits. Apparently, they had not thought through the economics of what a commitment to growth meant, particularly in regard to the deficit, as the Samuelson preinaugural task force (on economic policy) findings "produced great surprise and consternation on the part of one and all in the Kennedy camp as to what it was going to take to get the country moving again." Paul Samuelson felt that the candidate's "education should have been carried further on the need for deficits" in the campaign and that Kennedy's economic advisers never "really shot home the unpleasant point" that more fiscal stimulation involved "an extenuation of the deficit."[56] Kennedy's political advisers—Ted Sorenson, Myer Feldman, and Richard Goodwin, for example—"were horrified" at the concept of fiscal stimulation leading to deficits; not realizing the mechanics of the economic situation, "they just hoped they could get away with an antirecession program which did not involve deficits."[57] Heller thought that Kennedy's political advisers, "the lawyers," did not understand economics at the beginning of the administration but developed a more sophisticated grasp of economic theory over time.

One early effect of these constraints was that in his task force report to the president-elect, Samuelson, having been cautioned in advance by Kennedy's advisers not to ask for a tax cut because it would embarrass Kennedy and would not happen, made no such request, and, in fact, the report suggested various ways of increasing expenditures as an antirecession economic program.[58] The report vacillated on "the subject of fiscal stimulus, just saying that we might consider a temporary tax cut and not actually recommending it."[59] Kennedy's reception of the report was very positive. In fact, he seemed "to be quite open-minded on the question of the deficit," stressing that the council use the White House "as a pulpit for public education" to "promote better understanding of the fiscal and monetary policy effects on the economy" and to educate "the American people in order to set the record straight" about how the Republicans got the nation "into the recession and into the deficit."[60] Paul Samuelson felt that the president's concern with public opinion was as great a political constraint as his concern with congressional opinion. One way Kennedy chose to resolve the tension between the need to use more aggressive economic techniques and the political constraints he faced was to use the White House "as a pulpit for public education." Public education would change public opinion and foster receptivity to the greater deficits and activism he was ready to go along with.[61]

What were the political constraints that troubled Kennedy? In the transition period before the new president took office, the Kennedy team seemed reluctant to take decisive policy positions in economic matters. It appeared that "the whole team around the new administration was still acting as if they were campaigning, as if there was still an election. They were very much concerned about relations with the press and about comparisons with the Eisenhower administrations and the tactics of competing with the outgoing administration for a good press during the transition. It was a great preoccupation and remained so for quite a while."[62] Kennedy was concerned with his position with the leaders of the Democratic Party and both houses of Congress, and out of this concern, shortly after his inauguration, he explicitly agreed with leaders in Congress on what the council termed "the bombshell" that he would balance the budget.[63]

As members of Paul Samuelson's preinaugural task force, the council had assumed that the new Democratic administration would want to offer active measures to fight the recession that the Eisenhower Administration had been loath to recognize.[64] They were deeply disappointed when they received the word "that no strong fiscal medicine could be used—the new administration must be very sound on the budget."[65] When the council introduced the idea of the tax cut to Kennedy, who was already constrained by the need to maintain consistency with the ideas of sacrifice and fiscal responsibility, it was checked with "one of the earliest and hardest blows we at CEA received . . . the news that the congressional leaders had exacted from the president the promise that the 1962 budget would be balanced."[66] Yet Kennedy was not a budget balancer by nature and considered deficit spending "perfectly acceptable as part and parcel of expansionary policy."[67]

In Kennedy's first year, the budget had moved into deficit after a variety of programs were enacted to address the domestic economic problems of recession and unemployment.[68] The president retreated on his domestic economic program when, "after a violent argument within the Administration," he agreed to balance the 1962 budget.[69] His initial antirecession program to revive and accelerate the economy was received as "cautious and tentative."[70] Such interpretations of Kennedy's initial economic policy as not going much beyond Eisenhower's on fiscal measures, the council believed, did not take into account "that he felt he couldn't go much further at that time" with Congress and his concern for the administration's standing with the financial community.[71]

"Shortly after the transmission of the budget in January of 1962, the atmosphere [seemed to change] from the balanced budget philosophy to tax reduction as a method of stimulating growth."[72] In the late spring of 1961 events related to the Berlin Crisis had acted to consolidate the role of the council and its reputation for expertise with the president. (The CEA had argued strongly and nearly alone against a tax increase to pay for the $3 or $4 billion of additional government expenditures to cover the Berlin commitment, stating that the economy could handle a program under $5 billion without inflationary effects.) The council considered its role in dissuading Kennedy from the tax increase a clear turning point, showing the president's faith in his economic advisers.[73] It prevailed on Kennedy to present a bolder second-stage program. By the end of March 1962, recognizing that its economic forecast had been too high and that the economy was not going to make it to full employment (4 percent to the CEA), the council renewed its efforts with the president and pushed resolutely for a large net tax cut in the range of $7 to $10 billion for fiscal stimulus purposes, to remove fiscal drag. During the spring, the president had been saying publicly that the administration would take a look at the economic picture, but he made no commitment to act, hoping for an upturn.[74] Widespread recession fears, fueled by the steel episode and the stock market crash, led Kennedy to commit himself to tax reform and the tax cut. His June 7, 1962, news conference led off with an unequivocal statement of these goals. The president declared that the existing tax structure exerted too heavy a pull on the economy and that an $8 billion surplus would result were the U.S. economy operating at full employment and full capacity; this constituted "full acceptance of the full employment surplus analysis by the president."[75] The council had won the tax cut commitment it sought from the president. Near the end of 1962, Kennedy submitted to Congress the largest, up to that time, intentional peacetime budget deficit in history: nearly $12,000,000.

The council's victory on the tax cut moved fiscal measures to the forefront of the president's economic strategy. Kennedy discovered over time—as "his full understanding of the modern fiscal policy and economics won out"—that the "unbalanced budget didn't cause as much furor as he had feared. He resolved the struggle between his "fiscal responsibility . . . narrow margin of victory kind of thinking, which made him very, very cautious quite apart from what he could or could not get through Congress" and his understanding "of the fact that deficits weren't evil."[76] The council's role in promoting the aggregate demand perspective on unemployment would be similarly instrumental. Were it not for the council's powerful influence on the president's economic thinking on unemployment, the structuralist argument, with its allies in Congress, might have had a better chance at prevailing.

President Kennedy saw unemployment as a political embarrassment for a Democratic president but considered his capacity to address it limited. At least in the beginning, Kennedy "felt that an unbalanced budget was more of a political and public opinion threat to him than unemployment was, because the political impact of unemployment on Congress, on the country, was surprisingly little in 1960, 1961; even 1962."[77] In hearings before the Joint Economic Committee (JEC) on March 6, 1961, the council pressed for expansionist fiscal and monetary policy to defeat unemployment and get it down to 4 percent, unequivocally stating that structural unemployment had not worsened as a percentage of total unemployment.[78] The next day Federal Reserve chairman William McChesney Martin contradicted the council, dismissed their analysis of cyclical unemployment, "and played up the structural account in his testimony."[79] This divergence of views on unemployment was challenged by the JEC, and the council and the Federal Reserve were sent back to reconcile their differences. A subsequent meeting, on March 8, "brought the president into the picture," with Douglas Dillon, Robert Roosa, William Martin, David Bell, Walter Heller, Kermit Gordon, and James Tobin coming to an agreement on the structural versus aggregate demand interpretation of unemployment that was so conciliatory it was bland.[80] The issue was never actually thrashed out; it was merely announced that the problem stemmed from a difference in emphasis and definition, not a basic disagreement. This conclusion disappointed many of the principals, in particular the council, which felt it had definitive economic evidence that belied the structural argument.[81] The outcome did not amount to a preference for the analytical merits of one position or the other but a resolution to set aside the differences of opinion. This lack of resolution would have important consequences for antipoverty policy.

In February 1962 Kennedy had thought the unemployment issue could be somewhat neutralized by pulling together respectable opinions in a blue ribbon commission that would moderate conclusions on what needed to be done. The council was firmly opposed to such a commission because "It was a threat to the CEA, certainly. We knew the reason for unemployment, low total demand, and we also knew that no blue ribbon commission would say so, especially with structural employment ideas so prevalent."[82]

Kennedy's dilemma—how to incorporate the conflicting goals and commitments he felt he had to meet—demonstrates the importance of the economic advice and instruction of his Council of Economic Advisers.

Without confidence in the economics of his advisers, "the likelihood is that non-economic reasons could overwhelm [presidents] in any given instance."[83] It has been said that, perhaps more than any other postwar president except Ronald Reagan, Kennedy's economic policy making using the New Economics was guided by a clearly articulated ideology that was firmly rooted in Keynesianism and gave consistent and practical direction to his economic decisions going "beyond mere public rhetoric to serve as a continuous guide for his actions and policies."[84] While this may to some degree describe Kennedy's Council of Economic Advisers, it does not reflect the state of President Kennedy's economic thinking at the start of his administration or the way he dealt with the constraints of competing commitments, goals, and political considerations on his decision making.

Kennedy was torn by ambivalence about the applicability of the Keynesian policies advocated by his council, ambivalence that was rooted initially in his superficial understanding of Keynesian economic principles. The council played a key educative role in resolving his uncertainty by instructing him on the principles of the New Economics. But Kennedy was also torn by doubts about the political feasibility of the economic measures he was advised to take, and he encouraged his council to play a similar educative role with Congress and the relevant public: the Washington community of influentials. According to James Tobin, the closeness of the 1960 election left Kennedy without the mandate he needed to push through his economic policies. "The president felt trapped . . . by his political inability to get through Congress."[85] This was on his mind throughout his presidency. He was eagerly looking forward to a second term when, he felt, the political strictures on him would not be so binding.

The competition between certain, at times incompatible, economic and political ideas should be considered in the context of political feasibility. For Kennedy, the political feasibility of the economic ideas he wanted to promote rested in part on being able to influence the opinions of the relevant public. He saw the council as instrumental—as a positive political force—in molding this opinion and enhancing the political feasibility of Keynesian economic ideas, particularly with the leaders of the Democratic Party, both houses of Congress, and the financial community. Kennedy saw a need for public education, meaning in both Congress and the nation, to pave the way for Keynesian measures, and one role of the CEA was to coordinate such public education to change or prepare opinion for the new economic policy. His concern with political feasibility rested, in part, on the absence of a mandate from the close presidential election in 1960. He was also concerned with the standing of his administration's economic record in comparison with that of the Eisenhower administration. But political feasibility was also relevant for the issue of unemployment in the Kennedy administration, as the next section will show.

UNEMPLOYMENT IN THE KENNEDY ADMINISTRATION

> We encountered in Washington—at least I did, and it was a new and shocking experience for me—the theory, very widespread, that we had shifted to a new stage of the economy in which it was necessary to operate at higher levels of unemployment, considerably higher than we'd operated in the past, and there wasn't anything abnormal or disturbing about unemployment rates between 5 and 6 percent, and this was because of structural changes in the economy.
> —JAMES TOBIN

Another reason political feasibility was important for Kennedy was the lack of consensus in his administration on unemployment, which came to an impasse in March 1961 before the Joint Economic Committee, as discussed above, and how to address it. As mentioned earlier, Kennedy thought that one way to strengthen his political ability to get controversial fiscal measures like the tax cut through an economically conservative Congress would be through public education. Such education could serve two goals: it could rationalize budget deficits as a legitimate economic measure through the diffusion of Keynesianism, and it could create consensus on the nature of unemployment. To this end, he proposed in February 1962 a blue ribbon committee on unemployment, a proposal the CEA was able to defeat. According to Tobin, the "true purpose of the committee . . . would be to explain how difficult the unemployment problem is and therefore would have a kind of nonpartisan, higher, respectable excuse for any failure of the administration to solve it. . . . One job of the committee would be to consider the extent to which unemployment is due to inadequate demand and the extent to which it is structural, and in particular, to what extent does the latent federal surplus prevent us from getting to full employment."[86] As reported above, the council was convinced that its explanation of unemployment as being a matter of inadequate total demand would not be the consensus of such a commission because of the prevalence of ideas about structural unemployment, and it argued against it. Indeed, some of the council's reluctance to acknowledge the persuasiveness of the structural interpretation stemmed from its belief that such a focus on specific factors in the labor market appeared to give support to conservative forces in Congress that had consistently opposed Keynesian economic measures.

Paul Samuelson remembered that Kennedy had a recurring wish for blue ribbon committees to bring in "respectable people who would bring pressure to bear on Congress and middle of the road people to do what his experts told him really ought to be done, but which the country didn't seem ready to do."[87] Kennedy felt that if he could create consensus on the nature of unemployment by bringing together the disparate views of the demand proponents, such as his council, and the structural proponents, such as Chairman Martin of the Federal Reserve and the Labor Department, he could get expansionary fiscal measures like the tax cut through Congress.

Was unemployment, then, a result of insufficient demand, and could it therefore be affected by economic growth policies like the tax cut to increase aggregate demand; or was unemployment a result of structural problems that required active labor market policies such as large-scale job creation and job training? As described in the preceding section, there had been sharp disagreement of a technical nature on these questions early in the administration among the president's top economic advisers, with important consequences for the idea of jobs policies. In the hearings before the Joint Economic Committee on March 6 and 7, 1961, Chairman Martin of the Federal Reserve and James Tobin of the CEA had flatly contradicted one another on this basic issue, with Martin dismissing the cyclical thesis and calling for noninflationary structural measures and Tobin calling for fiscal and monetary measures to increase aggregate demand.[88] This disagreement was thinly papered over after a meeting with the president, but it had the effect of focusing attention on the problem of structural employment. Moreover, it could be argued that Kennedy himself had tried to synthesize these disparate viewpoints by creating the blue ribbon committee to study the causes of unemployment. Yet in this contest the CEA won, and President Kennedy was ultimately drawn over to the idea of the tax cut. Nevertheless, what the disagreement evidenced was the deep lack of technical consensus among experts on the causes of unemployment.

Similar differences over the causes of unemployment and how it related to poverty were replayed in the planning of President Kennedy's antipoverty initiative in spring and fall of 1963. In planning that led up to the War on Poverty, Walter Heller and Secretary of Labor Wirtz repeatedly had sharp differences of opinion over the structural explanation of unemployment and consequently over the role and scale that jobs programs should play in the poverty program.[89] Wirtz attached "unqualified priority importance to the enactment of the tax bill as the most important step toward the reduction of unemployment" and spoke out regularly on its behalf. Yet the facts of the strong "concentration of unemployment among the uneducated, the unskilled, and the untrained" convinced Wirtz of the inescapable need for considerable additional measures to address structural unemployment.[90] Wirtz pointed out that 34 percent of the unemployed were unskilled or semiskilled, two-thirds of them had less than high school education, and 23 percent of the unemployed were minorities. At the same time, long-term, or hard-core, unemployment had risen from 12 percent of total unemployment in 1952, to 18 percent in 1957, to 27 percent in 1963.[91] These facts demonstrated a "strong, strong, dangerous, bitter concentration of unemployment today in the uneducated, in the unskilled, in the untrained."[92] Wirtz's position was that, while economic growth was a key first step, and the first approach to reaching that goal would be the tax cut, something needed to be done in terms of moving in on hard-core unemployment, the kind of unemployment that was central to poverty and would not respond to the tax cut alone, as the tax cut would not eliminate persistent poverty by bringing down the general rate of unemployment. What was important, he maintained, was to bring regular employment to the male heads of households. While acknowledging repeatedly the importance of aggregate demand measures like the tax cut, Wirtz pressed for job-creation policies and a public works strategy if needed.[93] He wanted to make adult employment the central strategy of the War on Poverty.

Wirtz's outlook on the respective roles of economic and interventionist labor measures was a reflection of his experience, not his economic philosophy. He was a labor lawyer and had been a law professor, but although he understood the economic debates he waged with Heller and the council, he had not studied economics and consequently had not come to his role as the head of the Labor Department with a firmly held economic philosophy. Although Wirtz steadfastly refused to be categorized as a member of an economic school or philosophy, his views on the economy and the state would be most consistent with those of John Kenneth Galbraith. Wirtz did not deny the logic of Keynesian economics, but he did question its adequacy to meet the particular situation before him and the council and maintained that it would inevitably not meet the needs of the hard-core unemployed: "There is some validity to macroeconomic approaches, but they are not sufficient. I could be described as recognizing the validity of Keynesian economic theory but recognizing also that it was not adequate to meet the situation that confronted us at that time. It was essential to move away from a total reliance on macroeconomics."[94]

The CEA position that increasing economic growth was the first step in reducing poverty made the tax cut the central unemployment strategy of the War on Poverty. Their assumption that unemployment would respond to fiscal stimulation and take people out of poverty meant that a welter of additional social programs would address other specific needs of the poor, including job training for the young. While Heller at times acknowledged the applicability of structuralist measures, he had comparatively little commitment to such approaches and did not appear to espouse them from a sense of conviction.[95]

Two issues are central to understanding the significance of this dispute over unemployment for antipoverty policy in the United States. First, what is the definition of full employment, and, second, can full employment be achieved in the United States chiefly through macroeconomic measures, as the council claimed in 1961, or are interventionist measures necessary, as structuralists like Wirtz claimed, to provide jobs and training for those unable to find jobs in the regular labor market?

There is no quantitative definition to the term "full employment," and terms such as "full employment," "maximum employment," and "high employment" have been used interchangeably without precision.[96] Full employment has often meant what economists and politicians have wanted it to mean in relation to some other economic goal such as curbing inflation or stabilizing prices. In the 1940s, in *Full Employment in a Free Society*, Sir William Beveridge defined full employment as always having more jobs available than unemployed men. He meant jobs at fair wages, in reasonable locations, and that the lag between losing a job and finding a new one would be very short.[97] This idea of full employment underlay the failed Full Employment Act of 1945 and President Roosevelt's 1944 State of the Union Message to Congress, when he called on Congress to create a new economic bill of rights including the "right to a useful and remunerative job" and the right "to earn enough to provide adequate food and clothing and recreation."[98]

But what did unemployment mean to the Heller council? To realize genuine full employment as an economic goal in the United States, according to James Tobin, would have required that "Congress and the president and the whole administration" embrace the targets and goals mandated by the Employment Act as the single most important objective of economic policy.[99] The unemployment goal publicly set by the Heller council in its first testimony before the Joint Economic Committee on March 6, 1961, was 4 percent.[100] It had adopted this rate as "a reasonable target for full utilization of resources consistent with price stability."[101] One reason the Heller council adopted the 4 percent rate was that it was compatible with other important economic goals such as price stability (in the Eisenhower administration, 4 percent had been widely regarded by economists as the lowest rate of unemployment that was compatible with price stability), the U.S. competitive position abroad, and the balance of payments.[102] Another reason, one that the Tobin quotation at the beginning of this section illustrates, was that structural changes in the economy had caused higher levels of unemployment than the economy had operated with in the past to become accepted. Evidence for this was "the fact that at the peak of the previous boom, unemployment had been 5 percent, so that showed that even in 'good times' you didn't get unemployment very far down."[103] In the absence of a governmental consensus on the priority of genuine full employment as a goal of government policy, the full employment target of 4 percent set by the council had to be consistent with the total economic goals of the Kennedy administration. What this target did not do was to bring the poor into the economic mainstream, as was intended in the War on Poverty. Even if full employment could be achieved through aggregate policy, unemployment rates like 4 percent leave a residue of unemployed—millions of potentially employable people. It was to this residue of hard-core unemployment that antipoverty policy in the form of jobs policies was crucial. In a labor force of about 100 million, which was the size of the U.S. labor force at the time, 4 percent unemployment meant about 4 million people out of work at a given time, and that meant that in the course of a year, about eight or ten million people would go through unemployment. The specter of four million unemployed did not sit well with the Joint Economic Committee, which understood and accepted structuralist measures. When Wirtz appeared before the JEC, it did not express satisfaction with projected unemployment levels that were compatible with the council's other goals: "In terms of their reaction to these unemployment percentage figures that we took up there, they didn't like 5 percent. They didn't like 4.5 percent. They didn't like it when we got to 4, and of course we did. . . . They said 'that's four million unemployed people. Why are we settling on that?' " Wirtz's experience with the JEC points out another reason for the viability of jobs programs to address poverty related to structural unemployment. "The country at that point was not ready to accept 4 percent unemployment."[104]

As to whether aggregate economic policies could ever create full employment in the United States, economic history says no. Aggregate stimulation policies would not operate in the United States to create full employment. The only point in economic history in which the United States achieved full employment was in 1944, at the height of wartime production during World War II.[105] The Heller council was wrong, and the consequences for antipoverty policy were that, because of the weight of Heller and the CEA in influencing the president to adopt the tax cut and in deemphasizing the importance of structural unemployment, and because of Heller's central role subsequently in orienting the initial policy-planning stage of the War on Poverty, the war was premised on important misunderstandings of poverty's causes. The structuralists had a good argument. While certain kinds of unemployment were reduced through increased growth, hard-core joblessness was not. Poverty—which, as Wirtz and other structuralists maintained, was principally caused by the absence of a decent, steady income—could not be reduced without additional measures to create jobs and train people who did not have the skills for the jobs that were available.

Evidence abounds that the U.S. economy is incapable of creating enough jobs in normal times for everyone who needs a job. As Philip Harvey has shown, between 1890 and 1988, nearly a century, the United States reached 2 percent or less unemployment only seven times (1906, 1918–19, 1926, and 1943–45); it reached 3 percent or less only nine times; and a rate of 4 percent or less was reached only twenty-four times, one year in four. The average (mean) unemployment rate was 7.1 percent, which, corrected for the effect of the 1890 and 1930 depression years, produces a median annual unemployment rate of 5.5 percent. This historical record suggests that neither the normal workings of the economy through free market forces nor macroeconomic policy alone will produce full employment.[106] In its normal state, the United State's economy operates with high levels of involuntary unemployment.

The War on Poverty was thus directed away from jobs. The idea of jobs policies failed because consensus was not formed among experts on the priority of unemployment as a cause of poverty. In this case, the dominance of the aggregate demand perspective of the CEA was largely attributable to their enhanced role and influence with the president. Wirtz and the Labor Department did not have the same reputation for economic expertise, even though they were in the process of developing it. Moreover, Labor's position was viewed as the result of a jurisdictional interest that did not help their claim to impartiality. The idea of jobs policies may have been the right idea at the right time; jobs policies may have been able to take the poor out of poverty by giving them the training and work they needed. Yet economic ideas in the Kennedy administration, particularly the critical lack of consensus among experts on unemployment and how it was related to poverty, weakened the persuasiveness of the structuralists' ideas and directed the War on Poverty away from the jobs programs sought by the Department of Labor. This was a key factor in the demise of the idea of jobs policies as the centerpiece of the War on Poverty. There were, however, two other important considerations. These were the extent to which the Labor Department was capable of administering the kind of jobs programs it was advocating and the lack of governmental commitment to respond to the demonstrated call for jobs from the black community.

3. Change and Incapacity in the Department of Labor

The United States Department of Labor (DOL) was at the brink of a critical period of transition and innovation when Kennedy became president. The sixties was a decade in which the boundaries of government policy would be transformed as the responsibilities and goals of the department came to include antipoverty policy making.* The ambition of Secretary of Labor Willard Wirtz in this period was to bring government manpower policies together under the control of a fully modernized Labor Department. As part of this goal, Wirtz advocated the idea of large-scale government job policies as the heart of the War on Poverty. He was only partially successful: jobs policies played an important role but did not dominate the War on Poverty, and the Department of Labor at the end of the decade was only incompletely consolidated. The DOL never achieved the administrative coherence it needed to launch successfully the idea of jobs programs as the centerpiece of the War on Poverty.

At the beginning of the decade, when concerted manpower policy began to emerge for the first time, the term "manpower" was intended to embrace a set of concerns beyond the traditional employment and labor market functions of the Labor Department. At the same time, in the beginning of its evolution the department was narrowly focused on emerging structural employment problems—technological, industrial, occupa-

---

*See the appendix "Joblessness, Poverty, and Public Policy in the United States" for a brief overview of the governmental policy response to joblessness from the Depression through the 1960s.

tional, regional, and demographic changes—and policies such as those propounded in the Area Redevelopment Act of 1961 were designed to retrain workers who had either been displaced as a result of foreign competition or lost their jobs because of automation. The United States Employment Service (USES) was the agency through which the Labor Department had historically provided basic manpower services, originally aimed at reducing unemployment through job matching. Entirely financed by the federal government, the system was locally oriented, administered at the state level and run by a member-state employment service bureaucracy of 35,000. The USES was the oldest and largest employment service structure in the United States and the only nationwide one.[1]

In the early 1960s the Labor Department began to shift its emphasis from labor programs and labor-management relations to the field of manpower, although it continued generating labor statistics and handling labor disputes. Over the course of the decade the responsibilities of manpower came to include such antipoverty measures as expanding job opportunities for the disadvantaged in the public and private sectors, facilitating regional economic development, reducing the welfare rolls, reducing job discrimination by promoting equal employment opportunity, raising worker incomes, easing the transition from school to work, improving the procedures of searching and matching jobs and applicants, and reemploying returning veterans, in addition to its more traditional role of raising worker productivity and participation in selected occupations to combat unemployment and inflation.[2]

William Willard Wirtz headed the Department of Labor during the administration of President Lyndon Johnson, from 1963 to 1969. Wirtz had been appointed by President Kennedy on August 30, 1962, after having served as undersecretary of labor to Arthur Goldberg for the first twenty months of the Kennedy administration. He was sworn in as secretary of labor on September 25. The Labor Department, during his vigorous tenure, sought to expand and consolidate its hold over federal manpower policy. In the spring of 1963 Wirtz was a key figure in the initial Kennedy poverty committee that evolved into an interagency task force to explore policy options for a possible presidential initiative on poverty the following year; he was also at the center of the Shriver task force, which formulated the Economic Opportunity Act of 1964. Wirtz believed that a large-scale government program of public works, public employment, and job training would be most effective in attacking poverty.[3] And this was his goal for the War on Poverty. He sought a five-billion-dollar-a-year jobs program to be administered by the Labor Department.[4] A massive jobs program, he thought, would be the most effective means to attack employment-related hard-core poverty. It would also give the Labor Department effective control of the War on Poverty.

In the end, however, Wirtz and his idea of jobs programs for combating poverty were left standing at the post, largely because of the effects of three key factors. The first of these, described in the previous chapter, was the lack of consensus among experts as to the causes of unemployment and the way it related to poverty. Another factor, to be examined later, was the failure of government policy makers to incorporate demands from the black community for jobs and training. These were compounded by a third: the incapacity of the Labor Department to administer the kind of large-scale jobs program it was advocating. Instead, the idea of community action was promoted by the Budget Bureau as a cheaper, more coherent program to serve as the centerpiece of the War on Poverty.[5] Rather than being central in the War on Poverty, job creation was one policy alternative among many.

This chapter begins with an examination of the Department of Labor, its organization, administration, and operating methods. This analysis reveals the formal limitations in governmental arrangements existing at the time of the War on Poverty. Evidence is then presented to show that concerns about the administrative problems in the Labor Department were widely shared. Finally, the last part of the chapter presents an analysis of the thinking of Secretary of Labor Willard Wirtz in the 1960s. This last section concludes that if there had been technical consensus among experts on the causes of unemployment and how unemployment related to poverty, and if the administrative capacity of the Labor Department had been adequate, then the stage would have been set for government to provide the emphatic sponsorship and social agency required for linking jobs to the eradication of poverty. But this did not happen.

THE DEPARTMENT OF LABOR, 1961–1968

Scholarly explanations and arguments descending from sociologist Max Weber's work on bureaucratic structure and behavior began to emerge in the social sciences in the 1980s. Theda Skocpol and Margaret Weir, among others, began to emphasize in much of their work the effects of institutional histories and the structures of administration on the outcome of policies.[6] According to their analyses, the histories and administrative arrangements of bureaucracies have shaped the way in which policy ideas have taken form. In this view, a proper explanation of how ideas emerge and become influential must address the structures in and around the state that pattern the interactions of experts and politicians.

> If a given state structure provides no existing, or readily foreseeable, "policy instruments" for implementing a given line of action, government officials are not likely to pursue it and politicians aspiring to office are not likely to propose it. Conversely, government officials (or aspiring politicians) are quite likely to take new initiatives, conceivably well ahead of social demands, if existing state capacities can be readily adapted or reworked to do things that will bring advantages to them in their struggles with competitive political forces.[7]

In 1960 the Department of Labor was at the edge of transition. The status of the department illustrates, in a compelling way, how state capacities can influence the success or failure of policy ideas to take hold. At the helm of the Labor Department was a dynamic administrator, Willard Wirtz, who sought over the decade to nationalize a department virtually handicapped by competition among its own nearly autonomous agencies. In planning for the War on Poverty, Wirtz had promoted a poverty program with "an immediate, priority emphasis on employment" at its center.[8] He sought a large-scale, integrated program of job training, public employment, and public works, believing that job training alone was insufficient to address the extent of employment-related poverty. His idea of jobs policies—as the centerpiece of government antipoverty measures in the War on Poverty—did not, however, take hold, in part because of the belief among policy makers that the Labor Department was too set in its ways to administer the innovative policy ideas being contemplated for dealing with the poor. At the heart of the problem was the inertial drag of the United States Employment Service (USES) and questions about its willingness and ability to provide services to a new constituency: the poor. Recognition that the Employment Service was a hidebound agency in need of renovation was widespread among policy makers, in Congress, and among top-echelon administrators in the Labor Department itself, which sought to reorganize and redirect the agency to make it responsive to new jobs policy initiatives for the poor. By the end of the decade, the Employment Service had made an imperfect transition—under great pressure from the Labor Department—from its historical role as an agency that provided employers with the kind of workers they wanted, screening out applicants who did not meet the requirements and specifications set forth by employers, to a new role reoriented toward the problems of the poor. In the end, the transition was incomplete, and it occurred too late to be instrumental for the War on Poverty.

Concerns about the levels, patterns, and persistence of unemployment in the 1950s contributed to recognition in the Labor Department of the need for the comprehensive manpower policy that began to be implemented in 1961.[9] Over the decade, change was sought through three means: legislation, administrative reorganizations of the department, and modifications in its operating methods.

One of the early organizational changes highlighting the emphasis on manpower was the creation on April 20, 1961, of the Office of Manpower and Automation, one of the first acts of Secretary Arthur Goldberg.[10] Emanating from this office were concepts that served as the basis of new manpower legislation such as the Area Redevelopment Act of 1961, the first program of the New Frontier and principally concerned with capital investment but also containing a small training component. The Office of Manpower and Automation also initiated the popular Manpower Development and Training Act of 1962 (MDTA), which was of "historic importance in recognizing the responsibility of government for training individuals who might otherwise be stranded by the changed requirements of industry."[11] Sparked by the concern for automation-related joblessness, the MDTA provided for occupational retraining for those unemployed who had an attachment to the workforce. As the second program of the New Frontier, and the first to survive the economic and political trials that confronted the Kennedy administration, it was redirected toward unemployed youth and the disadvantaged when no automation-related displacement had been found after six months of looking. The act was passed in mid-1962, funded late in 1962, and got under way in 1963. By 1964, however, it was clear that automation and technology were not the real problems; the real problems were "the hardcore, disadvantaged individuals, the individuals with low levels of education and training and individuals with less than eighth grade education, individuals who were over forty-five years of age or minority individuals. Individuals who were on welfare or drawing unemployment compensation—these were the kind of people that it became evident that we had to shift to."[12] In this way, the act became the first of the manpower policies to serve as an antipoverty policy, and, as such, it set the pattern for subsequent manpower and antipoverty programs.[13]

In the hierarchy of economic policy making, the annual manpower report by the president to Congress mandated by the act had "raised manpower policy to a visibility and status second only to fiscal and monetary policy."[14] The act was highly popular in Congress, passing both houses with overwhelming bipartisan majorities, and it experienced an extraordinary absence of congressional pressure for results, allowing its administrators freedom to adapt the program to changing problems. State and local governments, the public, and the academic community all evaluated the program positively. Garth Mangum has attributed the legislative honeymoon experienced by the MDTA to the fact that it appealed to factions on both sides of the economic debates between the structuralists and proponents of aggregate demand that occurred in Congress in 1961 (see chapter 2). While the lack of consensus on the causes of unemployment could not be authoritatively settled, the MDTA's retraining approach was something with which all involved could live. Retraining offered politicians direct benefits for constituents back home; it permitted direct attacks on the structural problems identified by the structuralists centered around the Labor Department; and it satisfied the CEA's aggregate demand advocates by providing for government spending, which would increase demand and training to address the mismatch the council recognized between jobs and available skills.

Responsibility for implementation and appropriations for the MDTA lay principally with the Labor Department. HEW, which also had legal obligations mandated by the act, backed off because of lack of interest. From the outset, three operating agencies within the Labor Department vied for control of the new MDTA: the Office of Manpower, Automation, and Training (OMAT), which replaced the Office of Manpower and Automation with the passage of the MDTA; the Bureau of Apprenticeship and Training (BAT), which promoted and registered labor-management sponsored apprenticeships; and USES, which, with the Unemployment Insurance Service (UI), was a unit of the Bureau of Employment Security (BES).

The Office of Manpower, Automation, and Training initially dominated departmental decisions for the program by assuming broad powers, having the advantage of the secretary's support and sole responsibility for administering the MDTA appropriation. Specifically, the office prepared manpower reports for the president, directed research and training activities, used its budgetary authority to fund experimental and demonstration projects aimed at the disadvantaged, planned programs and evaluated results, and—in an attempt to remedy its greatest weakness, lack of state and local bases of power—built a field staff with eleven regional directors.[15] This field organization was eventually stripped away, however, through the influence of its departmental competitors, and certain operating functions were given to other bureaus. OMAT remained a staff arm for the Manpower Administration (created in 1963) with the new name Office of Manpower Policy, Evaluation, and Research (OMPER).

The Bureau of Apprenticeship and Training was given the responsibility for handling the on-the-job-training (OJT) component of MDTA and contracted this out directly to employers. The office did not have the extensive state or local arms that USES had to assist in carrying out its new responsibilities and was initially given no new staff capability. Nor was this capacity likely to develop. BAT's constituency was in the Building Trades, Metal Trades, and Printing Trades departments of the AFL-CIO, which was not interested in developing administrative capabilities that might interfere with its apprenticeship functions.[16] Decisions regarding the normal operations of apprenticeship and training were in the hands of local unions and employers, not the agency itself. Within the Labor Department, there was little expectation that BAT would measure up to the its new responsibilities, and within BAT itself the level of enthusiasm was about the same.

The third competitor for the program, USES, was eager to have the main responsibility for administering the MDTA as it was originally conceived. Its local arms, the state employment services, were given responsibility for identifying, screening, and referring trainees, deciding on trainee occupations, and placing enrollees after training.[17] USES had the advantage of independent funding, drawing money from Title III of the Social Security Act, which designated part of the unemployment insurance payroll tax to go toward the maintenance of USES. It could also claim an independent source of power in the Interstate Conference of Employment Security Agencies (ICESA), which was linked to Congress's appropriations committees. In addition, it was close to the chairman of the House Subcommittee on Appropriations, as was the Washington staff of BES.[18] USES was the only nationwide manpower service system in the United States and as such had the greatest potential capacity for administering national manpower policy in every state. The Employment Service, however, like many government agencies, began in the service of one wave of social change and "had turned into a breakwater against subsequent waves."[19] Established as a federal-state employment service by the Wagner-Peyser Act of 1933 to assist the millions of unemployed in the Depression find jobs, it was funded on a fifty-fifty federal-state basis with federal funds coming from general revenues. From the start, the inadequate state resources available during the Depression could not match this, so additional monies were found from sources such as the National Youth Administration and the Civilian Conservation Corps. In 1935 the Social Security Act gave new duties to the service under the new unemployment insurance system and with it new sources of revenue: the employers' tax. During World War II, the Employment Service was federalized, establishing the precedent of 100 percent federal financing. These arrangements were made permanent in a 1949 amendment to the Wagner-Peyser Act, which brought all employment service financing into the social security system through the federal unemployment insurance employers' tax. This linked the Employment Service to the unemployment insurance system, both units under the BES. After the war, a struggle developed between these two separate units of administration—between those concerned with administration of unemployment insurance and those concerned with job-matching functions, the historic role of the employment service. This lack of a clear organizational mission created new functions for the employment service, inconsistent goals, and shifts in the distribution of power.[20] The service, which was originally to have been administered through a strong alliance between the federal and state government levels, had splintered, except during the war years when it was federalized, into fifty autonomous agencies.

The major problem with USES was that it never had a clear sense of organizational direction. Consequently, its goals and functions were in constant transformation. Standing in the way of organizational coherence for the Employment Service was "a lack of agreement, among those whose decisions and actions affect the operations of the Service, as to its necessary and appropriate mission and operational field and status."[21] Specifically, two kinds of problems affected the Employment Service. First, it had traditionally linked employers and employees in the manner of a labor exchange, thus providing a government-sponsored job-matching service. During the 1930s and the postwar period, the labor exchange, as a result of recessions, was faced with low labor demand and a labor surplus. Consequently, the local staffs developed practices of screening the best applicants in order to induce employers to use the service. This practice, known as "creaming," had persisted throughout the subsequent life of the Employment Service. Creaming was a considerable obstacle in the way of transforming USES to meet the new national manpower needs for training and placement of the disadvantaged. The second problem with reorienting USES was the connection between Employment Service personnel and Unemployment Insurance personnel as two units under BES sharing the same funding source in the Social Security employers' tax. Except during World War II and the great inflow of returning veterans in 1946, the workload of local offices was dominated by the administration of unemployment insurance as a result of the recessions of the late 1940s and 1950s. For many periods, therefore, Employment Service personnel were shifted to the unemployment insurance system. This dominance affected the Employment Service at every stage of its development.[22]

The basic obstructions, then, were the funding overlap (through the employers' tax) between USES and the Unemployment Insurance system; the contradiction in the Wagner-Peyser concept of universal service and the needs of the new legislation to target resources to the disadvantaged; the built-in bureaucratic struggle between the service and the administrators of insurance; the autonomy of the state Employment Service staffs; outdated state civil service systems; devolution of manpower training responsibility by the federal government to the states; and the overwhelming role of a "federally subsidized pressure group," the Interstate Conference of Employment Security Agencies (ICESA), in the operation of the national manpower program.[23]

The rerouting of the MDTA meant another shift in direction for

USES in administering the act, one that had little to do with either of its previous roles of labor exchange and administration of unemployment insurance. As the only competitor with a nationwide organizational capacity in place, the service was the logical candidate for administering the program, but its objectives were at variance with the evolving goals of the act. When local employment services were accused of creaming, OMAT, under its budgetary authority, stepped in to take over and establish experimental and demonstration projects aimed at helping the poor. USES's two competitors, BES and BAT, quickly ended its short-lived dominance. In the end, the struggle was resolved by giving USES, under BES, authority for approving institutional training projects, giving BAT responsibility for on-the-job training, and relegating OMAT, which had, in fact, been the agency that enjoyed Secretary Wirtz's support, to the areas of research, demonstration, and evaluation.[24]

In February 1963, five months after becoming secretary, Wirtz brought together training and employment functions in a new Manpower Administration in the Labor Department, with Undersecretary John L. Henning serving as Manpower administrator. The new administration included BES, BAT, and OMAT, yet each bureau continued to control its own budget and appropriations, staff, operations, and organizational identity and independent field structure. Nothing important had changed, and Henning's role was reduced to that of an arbitrator. Soon, though, between these responsibilities and the new ones for the Employment Service created by the upsurge of employment-related legislation in Congress, the need for a full-time Manpower administrator became apparent, and John C. Donovan was appointed in April 1964.[25]

As manpower programs grew in size and multiplied, Wirtz and other key Labor Department officials hoped that the department would be assigned responsibility for their administration, particularly the jobs programs associated with the Economic Opportunity Act. Wirtz was pushing for a $5 billion jobs program in the evolving discussions of the president's antipoverty initiative. He was a powerful advocate and institution builder for the department, working on developing programs to bring them into the Labor Department. Yet the newly created Office of Economic Opportunity (OEO) became the administering agency for much of the new legislation, in particular ending up with the Job Corps on which Wirtz had set his sights. It was felt that the new agency "might not be bound by tradition and might be more creative in carrying out new functions."[26]

When the Neighborhood Youth Corps (NYC) became a responsibility of the Labor Department under the EOA, it was not placed under the administration of the Employment Service; instead, the decision of the Labor Department was to create its first new operating bureau since the Roosevelt administration.[27] The NYC became a separate agency and the fourth operating arm of the Labor Department along with BES, BAT, and OMAT.

Wirtz continued to try over the decade to draw training and work programs under the umbrella of the Manpower Administration and to create, in effect, new government capacities in the Labor Department.[28] His efforts had measured success, but the obstacles confronting him were enormous. The Manpower Services Act, which was first introduced in Congress in 1966 and again in 1967, was defeated each time because of opposition from the ICESA. Wirtz's final attempt at centralizing control over the Employment Service began in 1967, when again it was decided to try to consolidate the divergent field organization and authorities of the department. In the end, the attempted reorganization would bring an angry Wirtz into an astonishing face-to-face confrontation with Lyndon Johnson.

The field reorganization Wirtz sought would have combined the Employment Service and manpower training programs into one unit, placing the whole manpower network under one authority. Continuous discussion, extending into 1968, between top Labor Department officials and top presidential advisers Joe Califano and Jim Gaither led, on October 24, 1968, two weeks before the presidential election, to the announcement by Wirtz of the much-needed reorganization. It drew tremendous fire from the National Governor's Association, prompted by state Employment Service administrators. Johnson himself may have engineered this controversy. Stanley Ruttenberg, Wirtz's Manpower administrator from 1965 to 1969, was convinced that the president was behind the Governors' Conference protest of the reorganization. Wirtz believed Johnson's sabotage of his reorganization initiative was sparked by Wirtz's criticism of the administration's conduct of the Vietnam War at the Democratic Convention.[29] Johnson refused to support the reorganization and, after a heated showdown with Wirtz, he directed the secretary of labor to rescind it. In an extraordinary moment of confrontation, Wirtz refused to revoke his announced reorganization, and Johnson demanded his resignation. Confusion ensued when Wirtz's on-file resignation, which had been submitted to Johnson along with those of other Kennedy appointees when Johnson took office, could not be found. An impasse developed that was broken when, after Wirtz threatened to resign without rescinding the order, his assistants James Reynolds and Stanley Ruttenberg each agreed, if appointed secretary to succeed Wirtz, to rescind the order but warned that they would simultaneously resign on complying with the president's demand. Wirtz remained committed to the reorganization even after intervention by Secretary of Defense Clark Clifford and the deputy attorney general on behalf of the president.[30] The order remained unrescinded and unacted on through the election, and the outcome was left to the Nixon administration, whose labor secretary, George Schultze, pushed through the reorganization as one of his first actions.

Willard Wirtz and fellow reformers in the Labor Department were poorly supported and ultimately could not forge the necessary bureaucratic and administrative capacity for the kind of comprehensive manpower administration envisioned by the secretary. They would have benefited from support outside the Labor Department, as Wirtz said later, in whipping the Employment Service into shape. The department's inability to control the service was explicitly evident at the critical period of 1963–1964 when the Shriver task force was planning the War on Poverty. Recognition of the administrative weakness of the Labor Department was widespread, and this influenced receptivity to the idea of jobs policy in the deliberations of policy makers at the time.

PERCEPTIONS OF THE LABOR DEPARTMENT

Two critical, related concerns confronted the Labor Department and its potential administration of jobs policies for the poor. One was the department's ability to impose organizational control from the top on the nearly independent bureaucratic fiefdoms that were key to manpower policy, and the other was the ability of the Employment Service to redirect its priorities to serve a new clientele. These two concerns, which troubled Wirtz and his top reform-minded officials within the department, also troubled antipoverty policy makers.

The creation of the Office of Economic Opportunity as a separate operating agency in the executive branch to oversee the administration of the EOA and to administer the Job Corps directly was the practical outcome of the struggle over which department, if any, was going to have control of the War on Poverty. An important step in this struggle in the planning stage was the shifting of responsibility in mid-November 1963 from Heller in the CEA to political scientist William Cannon, who was assistant chief of the Legislative Reference Division of the Budget Bureau.[31] Administrative concerns moved to the forefront. Cannon was seeking an organizational form that would reflect the bureau's concern with efficient administration and at the same time foster the innovative goals of the poverty program. He was skeptical of the ability of the old-line agencies to meet these requirements and, in particular, felt that Wirtz and the Labor Department, which he saw as "the real competitor" for the poverty program, were not able to administer it: "Wirtz and [Daniel] Moynihan really wanted to have it. . . . Politically, through its assistant secretary, Sam Merrick, the agency had only gotten a brand new Kennedy program, the Manpower Development and Training Act, in 1962. It wasn't clear that Labor was handling it well at that point, and I think there were concerns about Wirtz' erratic administration. In programmatic and organizational terms it wasn't the logical candidate."[32] Labor's bargaining position for the program was not helped by the lack of accord between Wirtz and Moynihan, who, as assistant secretary of labor for policy and research in the Labor Department, was to represent Labor's interests in jockeying for position in the task force. Cannon remembers that tremendous friction appeared to have developed between Wirtz and Moynihan—with the secretary even banning Moynihan from task force meetings for a period—apparently because Wirtz felt Moynihan had sabotaged the department's interests in negotiations over who got the Job Corps by agreeing "that the Employment Service simply couldn't do an adequate job of recruiting for the Jobs Corps."[33]

Stephen Pollack, who served as counsel to the task force in 1964, also remembered the OEO being set up because the White House felt the old-line departments were not doing enough to make the federal government more responsive to poverty.[34] Christopher Weeks of the Budget Bureau also believed that perceptions of the Labor Department's administrative inefficiency affected task force director Shriver. Weeks had worked with Shriver in the early drafting of the Peace Corps legislation and was asked by him to work on the task force preparing the initial legislation for Congress and an initial budget for the poverty bill. He dismissed as inaccurate the idea that the task force considered and rejected a massive jobs program as too expensive, believing instead that it was rejected because it was not in accord with "the kind of program that Shriver would have had in mind. I suspect, although I don't know this for sure, that perhaps Shriver and the President might have differed somewhat in this respect, because I think the President might very well have thought more kindly towards a public works kind of program than perhaps Shriver did . . . because of his association at one time with the National Youth Administration (NYA) in Texas." Shriver was more influential with Johnson in the early stage of planning and won out in the showdown with Wirtz in March 1964, gaining control of administration of the poverty program. According to Weeks, Shriver

> suspected the U.S. Employment Service and how effective it was working through the state agencies. . . . Shriver is a person who is very much involved, and he wants to damn well make sure that if he's going to give some money to something that he's going to have control over whether it works or whether it doesn't work. And it's true, the U.S. Employment Service does not have very much control over state employment agencies. . . . There was a strong feeling that not only must OEO operate some programs, but that the threat of establishing a new operating agency would have a stimulative effect on the existing agencies and get them to clean up and make their programs more effective in some way, the idea that a little competition certainly won't hurt in government operations as well as in private operations.[35]

Jack Conway, who was active in the task force and had served as initial deputy director of the OEO after Adam Yarmolinsky was sacrificed in a legislative compromise for passage of the EOA, also singled out the Employment Service as a source of the Labor Department's problems in gaining control of the poverty program. Not only did Labor lose out in the struggle for control, but any role it did capture was administered outside the Employment Service because the "Labor Department and the Labor Secretary never ha[ve] been able to control the Employment Service, never move it, never in a sense guide it. It has a life of its own."[36]

Stanley Ruttenberg, whom Wirtz appointed Manpower administrator of the Department of Labor in January 1965 and who served as economic adviser to Wirtz in 1963 and 1964, helped lead the struggle from within the Labor Department to reorient the Employment Service. He pointed out that administrative responsibility of the MDTA was not given to the Employment Service because of its resistance to "dealing with the hard core or disadvantaged individual." Ruttenberg described USES's view of its mission as providing "employers with the kind of workers the employers wanted, so that, in a sense, the employment service screened people out of employment if they didn't meet the specifications and requirements set forth for the employers' jobs." Ruttenberg agreed that the OEO was set up as an independent agency because the Labor Department was too set in its ways to take in the new ideas developing in manpower and antipoverty policy. The OEO helped Labor officials "to bring about an understanding on the part of the Employment Service that they had to get down to brass tacks and deal with the disadvantaged and the long-term unemployed individual because if they didn't, employment programs would be picked up by the Office of Economic Opportunity, by the poverty program, and by the Community Action agencies."[37]

Concerns in the OEO about the administrative abilities of the Labor Department were great and continued after passage of the EOA through the 1965 and 1966 amendment processes when three new programs were being considered. These programs were New Careers, an adult-work program designed to assist individuals in moving out of dead-end jobs and up the career ladder; a second program that later became Operation Mainstream, an adult work program concentrating on conservation and reforestation; and the Kennedy-Javits program, called the Special Impact Program, which was designed to pull together manpower, capital investment, and economic development in urban environments. It was only after strong support from the White House that in 1967 the Department of Labor was able to get delegation of these programs from OEO, to be run by the department along with the Neighborhood Youth Corps.[38] As late as 1967, four years after the creation of the Manpower Administration, the Labor Department was still struggling to establish a manpower identity among policy makers. It argued, according to Ruttenberg, that it was becoming a manpower agency: "We did establish a Manpower Administration. We did have the Employment Service, which was on the move in terms of being changed and reoriented. We did administer the Manpower Development and Training Act and we did have the Neighborhood Youth Corps Program, . . . and therefore another agency running manpower programs would overlap."[39]

Feeling among OEO people was that if Labor administered the programs it "wouldn't be able to run them in an intelligent, modern way. [It would] turn [them] over to [the] Employment Service to run and it would be very bad. And we agreed that we would not administer these programs through the Employment Service. We would expand the Neighborhood Youth Corps Bureau . . . and call it a Bureau of Work Training Program, and that this new bureau, unrelated to the Employment Service, would be responsible for running these new programs." In winning these delegations the Labor Department again had to overcome bias against the Employment Service to obtain the support of the Conference of Mayors and the League of Cities, which were opposed to the delegation on the grounds that the Labor Department was state oriented (through its association with the Employment Service), whereas the legislation, according to the EOA, was federal-local oriented, thereby passing over the states. The argument that the Labor Department was state oriented, according to Ruttenberg, was one of the most difficult problems the department confronted.[40]

SECRETARY OF LABOR WILLARD WIRTZ

Secretary of Labor Willard Wirtz himself was well aware that the Employment Service's intractability was a liability for his department. Indeed, achieving control over the state agencies had been one of his earliest and most important goals, one that was to have been realized through the reorganization of the Labor Department. He also knew that his struggle to orient the War on Poverty to jobs programs was burdened by widely shared perceptions of his limited ability to control USES. Yet Wirtz was also convinced that some degree of the concern over the Labor Department's administrative incapacity was feigned and that Heller and Shriver were using USES as a smokescreen to promote their own innovative ideas for the War on Poverty.

Wirtz believed that the most effective means of eliminating poverty lay in the hands of the Labor Department. He felt that money spent in fighting poverty would do more good invested in jobs programs than in Community Action Programs (CAPS), which he believed were the political outcome of bureaucratic politics in a campaign year. In Wirtz's view, Heller, Shriver, Adam Yarmolinsky, and other advisers to President Kennedy were so intent on finding something new, even if it was just new rhetoric, in a campaign year that "that goal became a larger consideration than the effective appraisal, any responsible appraisal, of the likely results" of community action. Wirtz was highly skeptical about CAPs, feeling the likelihood of their dealing with the poverty problem was insignificant. He thought "we would be most effective in reducing poverty by increasing the number of available jobs" and "had real reservations about whether training was enough at that point." He wanted a massive series of jobs programs to address the structural unemployment he saw as the cause of poverty in the nation at the time. He sought job training in combination with public employment and public works programs—infrastructure work such as building roads, bridges, highways, rapid transit systems, and sewage and water systems—although he was mindful that the high cost of public employment made it politically vulnerable. His reservations about the community action concept also went to "its viability and . . . its sala-bility. I think that it did not help as far as the Congress was concerned," and he was certain jobs programs could have been pushed more effectively with Congress and would have greatly enhanced the War on Poverty's ability to survive.[41] "If the poverty program is to be visible and concrete, if it is to have effects that are immediately recognized among the poor, as well as the community in general, if it is to begin with enough activity as to pick up momentum on its own, there is just one course to follow: The Poverty Program must start out with immediate, priority emphasis on employment."[42] Wirtz stated that "without question, the biggest single immediate change which the poverty program could bring about in the lives of most poor people would be to provide the family head with a regular, decently paid job."[43] The effects of stable employment, Wirtz pointed out, would be felt in future generations, as well as in the present.[44] When male heads of households work regularly "not only does the family get the income necessary for existence, but employment becomes a reasonable expectation for the children. These are the kinds of things that mold children and could conceivably overcome the intransigence of the poverty culture. If children . . . live on the basis of income earned by the father, the assumption that they will do the same becomes an element of their character." Nothing was more important in the president's antipoverty program than to "put people to work," Wirtz said, because without jobs for the poor the ancillary social services, which were also "utterly indispensable," would "have no permanent impact on the problem" and, in the long term, go unnoticed and unappreciated.

Willard Wirtz did not personify the brash shirt-sleeved personal style associated with the New Frontiersmen and Great Society warriors in the Kennedy and Johnson administrations. Not casual or irreverent and not iconoclastic, it is unlikely that the brilliant but serious and iron-willed Wirtz brought a relaxed informal style to his relationships with his bureaucratic peers and subordinates. A liberal New Deal Democrat, a labor lawyer, and a former Adlai Stevenson hand, Wirtz was also an exceptionally dedicated cabinet head who firmly believed the role of government had to be tempered through the exercise of social justice. He was positively vehement when he spoke about the consequences of the unemployment he saw. "Maybe I do get emotional about the unemployment problem," he said in 1962. "Maybe I am over concerned by the fact that there are 4 million people unemployed in this country, people who are denied the essential right to work—using that term in the only true sense it should be. But, I think the situation is so deplorable in human terms that it warrants an indignant intolerance of any explanation for it in terms of any kind of economic analysis."[45]

Wirtz also saw structural unemployment substantially from the vantage point of his job as secretary of labor. The department had a strong tendency to think of unemployment in technological terms, which—in view of the Labor Department's responsibilities—was understandable.[46] The fear was that technological characteristics of structural unemployment made it impossible ever to conquer the unemployment problem by expanded demand.[47] Wirtz did not believe that macroeconomic measures would ever achieve full employment without the addition of structural measures.[48] His job was to deal with the human consequences of economic thinking, which led to concepts like full employment set at a 4 percent level of unemployment. Wirtz "regarded the 4 percent target as a kind of an affront to the labor movement, as unduly conservative, as in effect reflecting callousness toward unemployment." He felt so strongly about the 4 percent goal that he successfully "prevented Lyndon Johnson from ever mentioning a specific employment target," getting him to stand behind the idea that as long as even one unemployed able-bodied man was seeking work, unemployment was too great.[49]

Wirtz also knew that Congress did not like 4 percent unemployment figure any better than he did and that it understood unemployment in the structural terms that affected jobless constituents. When Wirtz said the country was not ready for 4 percent unemployment he meant that congressional members had to face the unemployment statistics in their home districts. Every time the unemployment figures came out, Wirtz had to testify before the Joint Economic Committee, where "there was a real consciousness . . . about the necessity of structural unemployment measures." Wirtz felt that while macroeconomics might be easily understood by highly interested noneconomists, it was "not easy for the country to understand macroeconomics. It was not easy for the country to know anything about the Phillips Curve, and people in general would understand structural unemployment measures much better than they would macroeconomics."[50]

Two struggles for Wirtz during this decade had consequences for jobs policies in the War on Poverty and overall in the period. First, there were Wirtz's conflicts with the Council of Economic Advisers over the meaning and extent of structural unemployment and its consequences. While these debates took place in the world of economic ideas, they were engaged, heated conflicts that "centered on the question of where we were going—where we wanted to go as far a unemployment was concerned." The council had a strong feeling that to shoot for anything below 4 percent was to invite an inflationary problem, which seemed to Wirtz "totally wrong, because that places the burden of trying to temper inflation on the people who are least capable of carrying that burden." The argument between Wirtz and the council on the 4 percent target was fierce. According to Wirtz, "They would tell me that 4 percent was it, and I never could understand that. Because the 4 percent, of course, was a function of their thinking," which included the factor of the relationship between unemployment and inflation. Wirtz found the council's attitude patronizing: "The minute we started talking about structural unemployment, that is structural measures to carry us below the 4 percent, . . . a feeling of condescension settled in." Wirtz felt that Heller and his Council patronized him as if he "just didn't know about the Phillips Curve." [51]

Head-on debates between Wirtz and Heller took place outside cabinet meetings, in committee and subcommittee hearings, in their respective offices, and, when the Shriver task force commenced, in Shriver's office during meetings involving Heller, Shriver, Wirtz, and their staffs.[52]

Personal and heated, the debates would frequently take place as well in meetings in the offices of presidential assistants Ted Sorensen and Bill Moyers. Heller waged war against the structural explanation of unemployment as if he were defending bureaucratic turf himself, which, of course, he was, in fighting off any possible incursions into his hegemony over Kennedy's economic policy. He dismissed Wirtz's and his department's commitment to the goal of full employment with "comparatively little commitment" to the need for structural measures and acknowledged the need for them almost "as an afterthought, with never any real conviction about it."53 Victory in a clash between economic ideas was a key measure of influence for an advisory group like the CEA, which had no operational responsibilities.54

The second struggle for Wirtz was within his own Labor Department. To promote successfully the idea of jobs programs—and thus gain a territorial advantage for his department in the War on Poverty—Wirtz had to be able to get control of USES.55 He thought he would be more successful than he was at both goals. He thought that if there were to be a Job Corps then the Labor Department would operate it as they did the Neighborhood Youth Corps. His expectations were somewhat tempered during his first year of administering the Labor Department, as he grew familiar with his own agency. His territorialism was also tempered by the "realization that I had a very bad horse I was trying to ride—the United States Employment Service." In his struggle to control USES, Wirtz would have welcomed assistance from an outside agency to back up his own efforts. "It wasn't only internal with me," Wirtz said. "I knew I was at a real disadvantage when I went up to the Appropriations Committee because, in spite of good working relationships there, that Employment Service lobby had a hold of that Appropriations Committee in a serious way and, therefore, I would have welcomed some identification of authority outside of the Department which would have forced me to do something."

In spite of his problems with the Employment Service, Wirtz still felt the Labor Department was better able to handle the operational responsibilities of administering a large-scale jobs program at the center of the War on Poverty than could a new set of agencies. He observed that while the incapacity of the Labor Department was used against his arguments for jobs program "every time we got together," there was some question as to how much Shriver and Heller sincerely believed in that incapacity and how much of it was "make weight." While "they had a real good argument," Wirtz felt, "it was not critical to the decisional equation." First, the Employment Service "was in bad shape . . . and it complicated my life and weakened my hand significantly. Second, it was used strongly in argument against my position. Third, I don't believe it affected the attitude of either Sarge, Walter and Adam (Yarmolinsky) or the decision by the president. And because I think those things, I think the thing that affected the balance was their interest in getting in 1964 some new novel approach."

Willard Wirtz's views bring greater dimension to the story of the bureaucratic struggle between Wirtz and Heller. To say that Wirtz was trying to get effective control of the War on Poverty in order to increase the dominion of the Labor Department merely describes a widely recognized feature of governmental and organizational conflict. Yet the content of the struggle among politics, players, and ideas gives this story interest, particularly because in this case it was the fight over ideas that constituted the battleground on which Wirtz and Heller competed administratively and politically. Wirtz's perception and understanding of his struggle with Heller over structural unemployment and his struggle in the task force to promote jobs programs as the main strategy of the War on Poverty bring Heller into the picture as another actor in the territorial bureaucratic struggle involving most especially ideas, the most important measure of influence the CEA had. Recognizing that "in personal terms, professional terms, and governmental terms, Walter and the Council exercised a huge influence on Kennedy," Wirtz needed Heller to accomplish his own goals of departmental reorganization. If there had been consensus between Heller and Wirtz on the structural explanation of unemployment and the need for large-scale interventions like jobs programs, "it would have made a big difference," Wirtz maintained. "If they had gone along a hundred percent on a jobs program and had helped me on breaking that monopoly that the states had—instead of using it as a club to beat my brains out— we could have done a lot more" to face poverty.

Why did Walter Heller refuse to accept the structural theory? A number of explanations are possible. It could have been a result of the politics of gaining hegemony for Keynesian ideas in the Kennedy administration and the council's struggle to win acceptance of the tax cut. Perhaps it was a function of his and the council's conviction that they had nailed the structural argument early on in the Kennedy administration and their resistance to the propositions of noneconomists. Or, as Wirtz suspected, perhaps they were dismissing the structural thesis in the task force period to further their own agenda, which was to come up with a showy innovative domestic program during a campaign period. Yet although Heller and the council dismissed the structural thesis at the time, we know today the structuralists had a good argument explaining the relationship between persistent unemployment and persistent poverty. The larger consequences, as Wirtz and others saw them, were that the War on Poverty was directed away from jobs. In an immediate sense for the Labor Department, Wirtz lost an important potential ally in maneuvering around the state agencies and their entrenched allies in Congress. Pressure could have been brought to bear on USES from spheres outside the Labor Department and Wirtz's efforts to modernize his department and administer jobs policies aggressively could have been realized.

This chapter has suggested that the state structures in place in the Department of Labor in this critical decade of the 1960s had consequences for the fate of the idea of jobs policies as the centerpiece of the War on Poverty. The Department of Labor was plagued by extreme administrative incapacity in controlling the nearly autonomous state agencies that made up the United States Employment Service. In the early transitional phase for the Labor Department, 1963–1964, there was little possibility that Labor Department proponents of jobs programs could have convincingly bargained for control of a major antipoverty program because the capacity of the department to administer it effectively was constrained substantially—virtually prohibitively—by disorganization, lack of coordination, and competing mandates. The administrative shortcomings of the Labor Department were widely perceived and were detrimental to acceptance of the idea of jobs policies among relevant policy makers at a critical period in the planning of the War on Poverty. The organizational problems of the Labor Department officials, and their inability to control key bureaus in the field, were no secret in the government. This had important ramifications for the fate of the War on Poverty.

Thus, in spite of considerable societal pressure, as I will discuss, for a major jobs initiative at the time, a contributing factor in the failure of the idea of jobs policies to achieve central status in the War on Poverty—to overcome the power and persuasiveness of Heller's and the CEA's economic ideas and arguments—was the widespread perception of the administrative incapacity of the Labor Department to administer the kind of large-scale jobs program it proposed. While the idea of jobs policies had a forceful sponsor in Willard Wirtz, the importance and appropriateness of the idea was vitiated by the lack of consensus among experts, its viability was challenged by the administrative failures of the Labor Department, and its fate was sealed by the halting and partial nature of the Kennedy administration's commitment to full economic equality for black Americans.

4. Social Forces, Civil Rights, and the Struggle for Jobs

What's new is that we have the techniques and tools to get rid of poverty. The real question is whether we have the will.
— MARTIN LUTHER KING JR.

Black elites, both in and outside the civil rights coalition, had been calling for jobs as antidiscrimination and antipoverty measures long before the national government began to mobilize for the War on Poverty during the Kennedy administration. Early in the 1960s, black leadership and masses intensified their call for jobs policies and government attention to black employment, potentially setting the stage for a major jobs initiative, had their efforts been credited by the poverty planning network within the Kennedy and Johnson administrations. Black efforts to secure jobs and training accelerated in 1963, parallel to the poverty program initiative, and black efforts to improve their employment situation continued without letup over the decade.[1]

Historically, the government response to the black employment agenda had been largely nonexistent, and what response there was had been halting and incomplete. It was no different in the early 1960s, when the antipoverty initiative got under way. The opportunity to tackle the problem of poverty with jobs programs was present from the outset of the planning for the War on Poverty and was missed for the reasons described in the two previous chapters. As I noted there, the origin of the idea of jobs as the preferred government antipoverty strategy was of central importance to its chances for adoption in the War on Poverty. The previous chapter examined the factors that impeded Willard Wirtz, the chief proponent within the government of the idea of a large-scale jobs program, from realizing his goal. Black leaders outside government, however, had long proposed the idea of government jobs programs and employment strategies as antipoverty measures.

Most work on the origins of the War on Poverty is premised on the idea that the poor, black and white, never asked for it; it sprang from the policy deliberations of elites in the president's office in the Kennedy administration. The instrumental policy decisions that led to the Economic Opportunity Act of 1964, the omnibus legislation for the War on Poverty, emerged from the executive office of the president without consultation or direct input of any kind from the black civil rights leadership or community.[2] Yet, with or without consultation, the evidence that blacks wanted and needed jobs and training was inescapable in 1963. Had they been consulted on the antipoverty program, the black community would have reiterated the case for jobs policies it had been pursuing for decades.

This chapter will show that, parallel to the planning efforts that led to the Economic Opportunity Act, the civil rights movement shifted its focus and widespread social protest aimed at jobs and employment escalated. Government awareness of the grim conditions and consequences of black unemployment that contributed to this protest is evidenced by the president's economic report of 1964 and economic analyses of the period. Finally, the "dual agenda" of the civil rights movement, as it related to the black unemployed, is presented in a history of the black community's own economic analysis and outreach to government, which emphasized the critical need of full employment, reduction of unemployment, job training, job provision, and an end to discrimination in employment. This evidence points to a sharp contrast between the intentions and goals of the black community and those of antipoverty planners in both the Kennedy administration in 1963 and the Johnson administration in 1963 and 1964. Antipoverty planners ignored black efforts to affect government employment policies, as well as the economic focus of the surge of parallel protest activity.

1963: A YEAR OF CHANGE

In 1963 an important shift in focus for the civil rights movement occurred, as organizations began to move economic and employment-related issues to the forefront of the civil rights agenda. During this year of change, the

New York Times documented the shift in month-by-month coverage of black leaders, organizations, and masses as they vigorously pressed for jobs.[3] A consistent theme—the need for employment in the black community— ran through the *Times*'s front pages, editorial pages, and "News of the Week in Review" sections, linking the issue of jobs and the black community.[4]

January–March 1963

While coverage began slowly in the first three months of 1963, the stories were important, directly engaging the need for jobs and pushing the president for bolder domestic policy in this area. As the year began, two stories focused on the joblessness that affected the black community. One was the January 28 front-page story announcing the beginnings of Secretary of Labor Willard Wirtz's plan, described in the previous chapter, to revamp his department to mitigate joblessness among the uneducated, unskilled, and untrained.

Of February's five items, three front-page stories and one editorial concerned the administration's position on the proposed Youth Conservation Corps (YCC), a program to address unemployment among poor unskilled youth. The February 19 editorial praised the president for addressing the problem of youth unemployment but criticized the inadequacy of his proposal given the magnitude of the impending problem, a criticism the *Times* would regularly repeat over the year. "We need much bolder ideas," the editorial said, "if we are to cope with the problem of unemployed young people in the years ahead." A fifth story, "Civil Rights Fight Shifting to the North," related the findings of the U.S. Commission on Civil Rights in a report to the president. Among the conclusions was the need to confront discrimination in employment in the North.

On March 1 a lead front-page story, "President Gives Civil Rights Plan on Vote and Jobs: U.S. Prodding South on Hiring Negroes," announced Kennedy's message to Congress asking for a broad rights measure to protect black rights in voting, schools, and jobs. The story reported the failure in the South of the voluntary approach to improve black job opportunities in industries with government contracts. Civil rights advocates asked for firmer national enforcement of nondiscriminatory clauses of employers doing business with the government. Of the four other March items, two stories, on March 8 and 12, highlighted the centrality of jobs and employment in this period generally, headlining the escalating rate of joblessness (". . . 6.1 Per Cent, Highest Since '61") and the critical need for new jobs ("President Calls Rise in New Jobs Key to Economy"). March 20 and 25, respectively, saw the appearance of another story and an editorial on the YCC. The editorial again praised the idea of the YCC but faulted it for being "far too small," stating that a larger program should be developed and "additional ones devised."

April and May 1963

Coverage doubled in April and May as government-related jobs measures were discussed and black protest groups began to increase pressure for basic rights. In April eight stories and editorials and one letter dealt with employment issues central to the black community. Two of the editorials were concerned with the YCC, criticizing the proposed program as being too modest (April 10) and only "a token program" in size (April 27). Drawing attention to one of "the nation's most pressing problems—the growing numbers of untrained young people who are either idle or in the most menial and poorly paid jobs," the April 27 editorial also called for "a broad national program to develop skills and training—a program far beyond the very moderate proposals made by the Administration." An April 25 article, "Youth-Job Panel Calls for Action," also predicted a grim future for thousands of untrained young people. Another editorial, on April 9, and two stories, on April 7 and 11, concerned the administration's request for an additional $500 million over the $4 billion authorized by Congress in 1962 to strengthen its antirecession public works program to create jobs in communities with high rates of unemployment. The House Appropriations Committee's rejection of Kennedy's request brought a strong and swift rebuke from the president and from the *Times*. The House subsequently reversed the committee's action, approving an appropriation of $450 million. An April 7 editorial further suggested the need for a constitutional right to a job.

Five of the nine stories and editorials in May linked the five-week-long integration drive led by Martin Luther King, Jr., and the SCLC to issues of employment. The May 10 front page story, "Birmingham Talks Reach An Accord on Ending Crisis," mentioned "Job Aid" in a subheading; and on May 11 an article bearing the titled "Birmingham Pact Sets Timetable for Integration" included in its subtitle the phrase "Job Gains in 2 Months." The latter story disclosed that a provision of the agreement was "promotion and hiring of Negroes on a nondiscriminatory basis in stores and industries, hiring of Negro clerks and salesmen within 60 days by the stores and the appointment of a private fair employment committee." On the same front page, "Jobs for Youth Held Need Lest Social Crisis Develop" recounted Undersecretary of Labor John Henning's statement that youth unemployment could develop into one of the most explosive social problems in U.S. history. The May 12 "Week in Review" story reiterated the job-related points of the Birmingham agreement. On May 19, in "Negroes Press Harder for Basic Rights," Anthony Lewis concluded that Birmingham reflected the growing restiveness of the black community and the many additional hurdles blacks faced in their move toward equality. In this context, he pointed out the Labor Department unemployment statistics showing that 12.1 percent of nonwhites in the North and South held menial jobs, if any. A May 22 editorial on ending segregation in schools argued that busing children out of neighborhoods was not the best answer; what was needed was an assault on discrimination in housing and the economic constraints that kept blacks in ghettos. "More and better jobs enable the Negro breadwinner to move out of the slums," it concluded.

June–August 1963

Reflecting the summertime tension that would become a mark of the nation's overheated, overcrowded inner cities as the decade progressed, in June, July, and August *New York Times* coverage expanded to more than four times that of the previous months; June's coverage shot up to thirty-seven items. Many of these were either wholly or partially concerned with bias in hiring on union-related construction projects. There were two series of NAACP-led demonstrations in this month, in Philadelphia and in New York City. On June 1, "Negroes Win Jobs at Philadelphia" announced the hiring accord on city construction projects won by the NAACP in that city. On June 2, Anthony Lewis, in the "Week in Review," cited the Philadelphia mass picketing as a force bearing on the president's impending civil rights bill, describing "the dangerous temper of the

Northern Negro." On June 4, the day Pope John the XXIII died, an editorial, "Desegregating the North," again cited the Philadelphia violence over jobs and detailed how discrimination limited job opportunities for blacks, in spite of fair employment laws, in one-half of the northern and western states. Pointing out the depth of black unemployment, the editorial noted that "automation is cutting deepest into unskilled and semi-skilled jobs that have traditionally been the Negro's chief hope." On June 5, in an effort to head off job-related protests like those in Philadelphia, New York City mayor Robert Wagner moved to guarantee "equal opportunities in city agencies and open up more jobs for minority groups in the private construction industry" by strengthening existing equal opportunity programs. On the same front page, "Kennedy Prohibits Job Discrimination at Federal Projects" told of the president's order to prevent discriminatory hiring practices in federal construction programs. Kennedy also ordered Secretary Wirtz to ensure the admission of young workers to federal apprenticeship programs on a nondiscriminatory basis, and, influenced by the Philadelphia demonstrations for jobs, the president announced an upcoming executive order to guarantee "nondiscrimination in hiring in construction projects, resulting wholly or in part from Federal grant-in-aid programs." June 9's "Week in Review" story about the state of civil rights protest detailed the different black strategies in the North and South, mentioning jobs and black employment. The next day, June 10, "Aides Defy Wagner on Order to Count Negro Jobholders" told of several city agencies balking at Mayor Wagner's directive, questioning its legality. The June 13 lead front-page story was of southern civil rights leader Medgar Evers's assassination. On the same page "Unions Here Get Warning on Bias" cited the city's threat to shut down construction at Harlem Hospital unless the building trades acted immediately to end bias in hiring.5 The June 19, 20, 22, 25, and 26 papers all ran front-page stories on NAACP-led action against discrimination by the city in hiring.6 Another "Week in Review" story told of mass black demonstrations in Birmingham, Alabama, and Jackson, Mississippi, in which increased employment opportunities were a major objective of the campaigns against desegregation.7

Four June stories concerned joblessness among youth. On June 7, "Rise in Teen-Age Jobless Pushes U.S. Rate to 5.9%" related Willard Wirtz's fears that the teenage joblessness situation was "critical" and could develop into "one of the most explosive social problems in the nation's history." On June 9, the lead story in the "Week in Review," "Jobless Youth Major Problem: Decline of Work for the Unskilled Increases Teen Unemployment," analyzed the unemployment problem, detailing the impact of technical changes on the unskilled, especially blacks.[8]

A number of items reported President Kennedy's initiatives and strategies on civil rights or employment-related legislation of special interest to blacks. These included James Reston's June 9 and 12 columns, the first criticizing Kennedy's restraint on the critical issue of the racial crisis facing the country and his leadership failure in conveying the human consequences of racial prejudice, unemployment, and poor education on the black community. Reston did an about-face on June 12, hailing Kennedy's new conviction in federalizing the Alabama National Guard to enforce the U.S. Justice Department's attempts to enroll two black students in the University of Alabama. Reston lauded Kennedy's new and "bolder White House strategy in the field of Negro civil rights, jobs and retraining." He went on to praise the president's receptivity to a broader civil rights program that would "concentrate on finding new jobs for Negroes and training Negroes for skilled labor" and cited the black unemployment rate, which was twice that of the white unemployment rate.[9] On June 12, "President Calls Negro-Job Talks," told of the president's White House meeting with 300 labor leaders on ending barriers in hiring. A June 16 "Week in Review" overview of the past critical week's progress on desegregation noted the disappearance of the lower-paid jobs critical to blacks and the "economic discrimination" that led to disproportionate black unemployment. Anthony Lewis wrote in the same section of the Kennedy administration's newfound energy and commitment to the cause of civil rights. Federal legislation to end discrimination alone, Lewis pointed out, would fall short in eliminating hardcore problems that confronted blacks in the North. "You can desegregate a theatre in Tallahassee much more easily than you can reduce the unemployment rate among the Negroes from 18 per cent to 3 per cent in Chicago," he quoted one federal official as saying. Lewis concluded that the Kennedy administration recognized the need for other federal programs to benefit blacks, above all, "vigorous action to boost the economy and cut unemployment."[10] Four stories and two editorials were directly related to the introduction of Kennedy's civil rights bill to Congress. On June 19, "Kennedy to Offer Civil Rights Plan with Job Training" noted Kennedy's expansion of his civil rights proposals by the addition of large programs—possibly in the neighborhood of

$1 billion—for job training and vocational education.[11] Jobs were called "vital." On June 20, "Kennedy Asks Broad Rights Bill" included the need to halt discrimination in federal jobs and related activities. An editorial on the same day called the civil rights proposal bold and generally good but stressed the merits of considering education and wider job training in separate bills. June 23's "Week in Review" story on Kennedy's civil rights strategy described Kennedy's "broad attack on job discrimination, including $4,000,000,000 in new money for vocational and literacy training and intensified efforts to eliminate discrimination by federal contractors." An editorial read, "The basic need is for an assault on poverty and literacy, coupled with a reassessment of individual attitudes and practices. But the start for remaking this country into a 'land of the free' for all its citizens lies in legislation of the kind the president seeks, to bar discrimination in employment, voting, and access to stores, restaurants and other places of public assembly." Finally, in June 28's headline "Rise in Negro Jobs Linked to Growth," Secretary Wirtz's testimony to the House Judiciary subcommittee on behalf of the civil rights bill was recounted.

The thirty-one stories in July fell into two broad categories: stories and editorials concerning protest activity directed toward the city, the state, or private businesses against bias in hiring and stories about union-related discrimination. In July a wave of sit-ins and other demonstrations in New York and the metropolitan area aimed at exposing unequal job opportunities and breaking down job discrimination. Eighteen stories, four editorials, and one letter to the editor addressed these. Items on July 8, 9, 11, 14, and 15 concerned racial clashes in the Bronx over hiring practices of the White Castle restaurant chain as the picketing, led by the Bronx chapter of CORE, led to violence and a long wave of protest aimed at discriminatory hiring in the area by the building trades. The other items appeared on July 4, 9–13, 16–19, 22–26, 29, and 30. On July 10, "Race Sit-in Begins at Mayor's Office in a Job Protest" was about protest activity by the Joint Committee on Equal Opportunity, a consortium of six organizations: CORE, the NAACP, the Urban League, the Negro American Labor Council, the Workers' Defense League, and the Association of Catholic Trade Unions.

Three other stories dealt with more general union-related themes. On July 22, "A.F.L.-C.I.O. Maps Drive to Combat Discrimination" announced a major new national campaign against racial discrimination to be led by the federation's president, George Meany, and coordinated by Lane Kirkland, his executive assistant. On July 27, "New U.S. Directives Bar Discrimination in Apprentice Plan" concerned strict new procedures issued by the Labor Department's Bureau of Apprenticeship and Training to prevent bias in union-management apprenticeship programs. Finally, on July 31, "Building Trades Press Equality," announced the establishment of a top-level national committee to deal with racial discrimination by labor and management in the construction industry.

August's forty-five items fell into three general categories.[12] The largest consisted of twenty-one stories and editorials on black protest activity related to jobs, labor bias, and discrimination in hiring on construction projects.[13] The majority of these stories concerned protest against the construction industry in the New York area. Increasingly intense and violent demonstrations were aimed at unions, who largely controlled hiring in that industry, for barring or limiting black membership, and for discrimination against black youths in apprenticeship programs.[14]

The next largest category, sixteen items, concerned jobs, job training, and economic factors at issue for blacks. Three items concerned the need for fair employment practices protection, in particular the August 1 editorial, "Equality in Jobs," commending the administration's decision to incorporate proposals for a Federal Fair Employment Practices Commission into its omnibus civil rights bill. The *Times* agreed with Kennedy's June message to Congress that "the eradication of job bias is an essential element in making equality real for Negroes." Pointing out the income gap and limited job opportunities that confronted blacks, it concluded that the nation owes blacks legal protection against discrimination by employers and unions and "also owes him and all its other citizens a full-employment economy, so that the road to more jobs for Negroes is not the ouster of whites." The *Times* lead editorial on August 3, "Jobs and the Jobless," urged Congress to act to improve job opportunities for the jobless. The editorial noted that the economy was not expanding fast enough to provide work to all who needed it and projected the need for "at least 25,000 jobs a week for the next decade, just to keep pace" with young new entrants and more to offset the shrinkage resulting from automation and technological change. "The success of our efforts to wipe out economic discrimination against the Negro will be determined, as much by our ability to speed the creation of jobs, as it will be by legislative prohibitions against bias." In an interesting twist, the August 7 article, "House Votes Job Training: Civil Rights Rider Beaten," told the story of a House contest that resulted in the defeat of an antisegregation amendment proposed by Republicans and of the overwhelming approval of a bill that would more than triple federal aid to vocational education. Northern and southern Democrats voted together to defeat a Republican-sponsored amendment that would have denied federal aid to state-run job-training schools practicing racial segregation. In a bitter three-hour debate, the House saw the uncommon sight of a black member arguing against a civil rights measure, and many white members arguing emotionally for it. There was no debate on the main bill, which added $180 million in three years to federal government support of vocational education, at that time $57 million per year.

An August 10 editorial, "Training for Jobs," applauded the House vote to triple vocational education for providing "an essential foundation rock in a structure of increased job opportunity for youngsters in an automated industrial society. The principal gainers will be Negro and Puerto Rican youths, who have been at a particular disadvantage through racial discrimination and inadequate skills." Three items on August 18 related to jobs for blacks. "City Job Registry to Aid Nonwhites" announced the opening of seventeen offices at which black and Puerto Rican applicants for jobs in the construction industry could register, and "Struggle for Jobs," in the "Week in Review" section, raised the issue of employment discrimination. An August 20 story and an editorial the next day also dealt with the city job registry for minority youth. "Economic Factors Underlie Negro Discontent," also in the "Week in Review" on August 18, analyzed how the elimination of jobs resulting from automation intensified employment discrimination against black workers. Examining the dimensions of the black community's "profound economic crisis," the article concluded that the Kennedy administration's increases in vocational education and manpower retraining programs might not "make much of a dent. To redeem large masses of unskilled, uneducated workers who have become virtually unemployed and to prevent hundreds of thousands of children from poor families from falling prey to the same ills is going to take far more work and money than the country has grasped, many Negro leaders believe."[15]

The final category in August comprised six stories and editorials concerning the August 28 March on Washington for Jobs and Freedom. Among these were James Reston's column on the day of the march pointing out that:

> Congress has scarcely noted the full objective of the protest. The demonstration was not designed merely as political agitation for the passage of President Kennedy's civil rights legislation, but was officially titled the "March on Washington for Jobs and Freedom." The jobs part of it may prove to be tougher in the end than the freedom, for the Negro leaders are not only asking for equal opportunity in the field of civil liberties, but for preferential treatment on jobs.

Reston quoted A. Phillip Randolph, the march's director, who emphasized that "getting jobs away from whites to give to Negroes was no solution to the problem. A vast increase in the economic growth of the nation was needed to wipe out unemployment for all, and only special training and treatment for Negroes would enable them to work effectively in an automated society." Noting that the demand for unskilled labor was falling off at a quicker pace than training and education could equip people for skilled jobs, Reston pointed out that "already some of the President's advisers are insisting that only an ambitious public works program, on top of all the other tax, training and relief programs, will really deal with Negro unemployment in the cities." The August 29 lead story, "200,000 March for Civil Rights in Orderly Washington Rally: President Sees Gain for Negro," told of the historic demonstration for "a full and speedy program of civil rights and equal job opportunities."[16] Finally, an August 30 editorial called the march "the most impressive demonstration of its kind in America's history" and urged that redress of the marchers grievances become a national priority.

September 1963

In September coverage fell dramatically to six stories and two editorials, eight items in all. One reason for the decline in stories related to jobs was that protest activity began to focus on segregation in education. There was also a cessation of demonstration activity generally at this time because of "the amount of energy and funds expended by the various civil rights organizations in carrying out the March on Washington for freedom and jobs" and because the coffers of the organizations had been temporarily drained by the fines, jail sentences, and bail bond fees that had resulted from it.[17] Among the items were three that dealt with the march. On September 1, a large story in the "Week in Review" described the march as a symbol of the intensified drive for black rights.[18] On the same day, Claude Sitton, in the "Week in Review" story "After the March on Washington—New Drive For Negro Rights," noted that the march clarified for more Americans than ever before what freedom and equality meant to blacks. The demonstration, Sitton said, underscored the multiplicity of issues that at times tended to undermine the unity of the movement. The chief national problems, as seen by blacks, included "discrimination in hiring, education and housing." "We want employment," Sitton quoted Roy Wilkins, president of the NAACP, "and with it we want the pride and responsibility and self-respect that go with equal access to jobs. Therefore, we want an FEPC (Fair Employment Practices Commission) bill as a part of the legislative package."[19] A September 2 editorial, "View from Lincoln Memorial," urged that the aims of the march become a reality. "The specific aim of the March was to demonstrate for jobs and to influence Congress to pass a strong civil rights bill," it said.[20] Finally, a September 27 editorial criticized the president for oversimplifying and exaggerating the case for the tax cut and its effect on unemployment. The young and unskilled among minority groups and women may require "special treatment" rather than the general stimulus of tax reductions, the editorial read.

October 1963

The fifteen items in October concerned three general themes. Eight items dealt with the impending civil rights bill, in particular its FEPC section. Half of the October items in this category were highly favorable editorials urging the adoption of a strong civil rights bill with a forceful FEPC provision. An October 4 editorial, "Still Too Many Jobless," said unemployment remained unconscionably high and indefensible in light of the national commitment made by this country after World War II to conduct its economy under conditions of full employment. The editorial said that passage of the administration's tax bill was one step toward fulfilling this "ignored pledge" of full employment but also necessary were measures from the Youth Employment Act to the creation of an FEPC to put the jobless back to work. On October 6, another editorial, "Moving Ahead on Civil Rights," noted that the "the most comprehensive civil rights bill ever to receive serious Congressional consideration" had emerged from subcommittee "vastly stronger" than the original draft sent to Congress by the president in June. Crucial in the new bill was provision "for creation of a Fair Employment Practices Commission, with power over discrimination by both employers and unions." The October 17 editorial "How Strong a Civil Rights Law?" addressed the dilemma the administration found itself in because of the House Judiciary subcommittee's approval of a civil rights bill that the White House considered "too strong to have any realistic chance of passage." Warning that the worst strategy for the administration would be to retreat before the battle began, the *Times* urged that the bill not be weakened too much and, in particular, that the FEPC provision receive strong backing. On the thirtieth, the lead editorial, "Forward Step on Civil Rights," applauded the compromise civil rights measure "for emerging from committee in such good shape" and noted that it went "beyond the administration's proposals in establishing a Fair Employment Practices Commission," if with restricted powers.

The other four stories concerning the civil rights bill related its progress and how the FEPC provision fared in Congress.[21] Also in October were two stories and one editorial on job opportunities in the South. On the twentieth, "In the South: Main Emphasis Is Shifted from Demonstrations to Political Activity" said that "more and more the objectives include full participation in political life and improved job opportunity" and noted that the theme of the Student Nonviolent Coordinating Committee's upcoming conference in Washington reflected the switch. "Negroes Get Better Jobs at U.S. Steel in Alabama," on October 25, and an October 31 editorial, "Corporate Race Relations," concerned the opening up of jobs to blacks in Alabama plants and urged the corporation to use its economic influence to go beyond its hiring policy and do more to erase racial tensions.

Two stories that dealt with giving special consideration to blacks in New York City made up the third category: on October 28, "Preferment for Negroes Is Sought By Board Here"; and, on October 29, "Wagner Says City Has Not Discussed Negro Preferment."[22]

November 1963

Eleven items in November fell into two general categories. The largest category contains six items: three editorials and three letters to the editor concerned with Appalachian poverty.23 A theme consistent to all of them was the need to bring the level of unemployment down, the need for jobs in these areas, and the need to bring the issue of the unacceptably high level of unemployment to the forefront of the administration's deliberations on public policy. The second category, of five items, concerned jobs. A November 16 headline, "Kennedy Calls Jobs Vital, Outranking Civil Rights," announced Kennedy's message before the leaders of American labor at the convention of the AFL-CIO, telling them that providing jobs was the "most important issue in the country, more important than civil rights legislation or education." The president said that civil rights legislation was important, "but to make that legislation effective, we need jobs in the United States." The lead editorial the same day, "Priority for the Jobless," twitted the president for having reiterated the same theme since his 1960 campaign—that joblessness was the most pressing domestic issue facing the nation—and failing to present and back a comprehensive and convincing program to do something about it. Criticizing the hollowness of his tax cut in the face of swelling unemployment, the *Times* said there was nothing "in the President's listing of other specific goals that had the sweep of Mr. Wirtz's plea for a 'war on ignorance' that would make education America's largest economic enterprise, and that would assure to every child the right to schooling from first grade through college." A November 17 editorial, "Jobs and Taxes," noted that the president's goal of tax reduction was a good idea but that Kennedy had not fought hard enough to keep intact other key reforms, such as his requests for public works. On November 18, a letter to the editor from Walter Heller, the chairman of the Council of Economic Advisers, defended the council from the *Times*'s October 31 claim that, whereas the CEA had previously "belittled the issue of structural unemployment," it had now come to recognize the need for "special measures" to cope with it. Heller asserted that the council had repeatedly stressed the need for measures to improve the "mobility, education and skills of the labor force."

Finally, on November 24, an analysis of the great domestic issues confronting new president Lyndon Johnson, "Key Domestic Problem for

Johnson—Civil Rights," noted that blacks were economically submerged and the recent picketing for jobs in the North.

December 1963

In December, most of the nine *Times* items were concerned with the related themes of job training, works projects, public works, and the new president's attack on poverty. Among them was a December 2 editorial, "Retraining the Unemployed," that again restated the *Times* position, repeated regularly over the year, that special obstacles blocked access to jobs for the hardcore poor.[24] On December 6, "U.S. Work Projects Urged by Wagner to Aid Jobless" announced Mayor Wagner's proposal that a national works program, along the lines of the Works Progress Administration of the Depression era, be established to meet the challenge of hardcore unemployment. An editorial by James Reston on December 20, "On Exploring the Moon and Attacking the Slums," pointed to the dilemmas confronting the new president as he made policy decisions shaping national choices. Reston noted the renewed interest in jobs, education, and poverty and the reemergence of a kind of New Deal rhetoric and commented that concentrating education and economic relief where it was needed fit into the president's approach to most problems.[25] "President to Ask Rise in Spending for Human Needs," on December 29, announced the initiation of Johnson's antipoverty program, noting that the program "will have modest beginnings." An editorial on December 30, "Assault on Poverty," reported the introduction of the program and said, "The imperativeness of action has been underscored by Secretary of Labor Wirtz's year-end warning that changing technology is condemning more and more workers to a 'human slag heap.' The United States, with profits, wages, and total production at record heights, nevertheless finds 'a separate nation of the poor, the unskilled, the jobless' growing inside its borders."

Over the year 1963, then, unemployment and civil rights were clearly dominant domestic themes in *New York Times* coverage, and, as the analysis above has shown, civil rights was also linked to employment for blacks regularly and frequently in this same period. The theme of joblessness, for the nation as a whole and for the hard-core unemployed, was con-

78 SOCIAL FORCES, CIVIL RIGHTS

stantly emphasized on the front pages and in the editorial sections of the *Times*. The black community offered a defining case of hard-core unemployment; no group experienced higher unemployment or experienced it more persistently, thus remedies addressing hard-core unemployment were especially important to blacks. Although coverage began slowly in January, February, and March, these stories were significant in that they directly and regularly linked the need for employment and training to minorities and especially minority youth and insisted that the president address the problems of unemployment of young people with more aggressive, forward-looking domestic policy. In April and May, coverage doubled as black protest activity increased, as did discussion of government-related jobs measures. In June, July, and August, coverage increased more than fourfold. This bulge was caused by two factors. First, blacks were applying pressure on the federal government to get a strong civil rights measure passed, one that had a jobs-related component, and, second, blacks were putting pressure on cities and states to hire blacks—evidenced by the CORE- and NAACP-led demonstrations—and to address discrimination in hiring. After the August 28 march on Washington there was a falloff in coverage, although it was still substantial. As mentioned above, civil rights organizations were temporarily exhausted by the drains on their resources from mobilization for the march, and their attention was turned to the issue of integration in education, particularly to Alabama and the confrontation with Governor George Wallace there. Other prominent themes in September, October, and November were the Birmingham bombing killing four black children, the tax cut, difficulties in passing the civil rights bill, and, internationally, the coup in Vietnam and the Foreign Aid Bill. Then, on November 16, 1963, a large front-page headline announced "Kennedy Calls Jobs Vital, Outranking Civil Rights as the Most Pressing Need Facing the Nation." This was a week before the president was killed, ten days after he had tentatively decided to push a poverty reduction program as part of his 1964 program and three days before he gave Walter Heller the go-ahead on the poverty program. Furthermore, the initiation and exploration of a possible program on poverty had been going on at least since February or March of 1963.[26] In addition, the *Times* editorial writers had been hounding President Kennedy throughout the year to do something significant about the jobs situation and, in fact, had been pressing the issue during his entire administration. Jobs measures were also extremely popular in Congress, as the votes for public works and vocational education showed.[27] Finally, public attitudes were highly favorable toward the proposition that blacks should have equal opportunities for jobs, having grown steadily since World War II from 42 percent of the population in 1944 to 83 percent in 1963. The proportion of those in favor would reach 87 percent by 1966 and 95 percent by 1972. As Paul Burstein and others have found, public opinion seems to have been the primary reason Congress acted on the Equal Opportunity Act of 1964, having first passed equal employment legislation in that year when the percentage of the public in favor of it, and the intensity of their concern, reached historic highs.[28]

What this analysis points to is the salience of jobs and employment issues to black Americans who pressed their own jobs agenda in Washington and at local government levels everywhere. This played a dominant role in the headlines of the day, reflecting the change in the course of the civil rights movement. Connecting the proposed antipoverty agenda to the demonstrated need for jobs among the lowest-paid and most unemployed group in the nation was inescapable for government antipoverty planners. Mentions of poverty per se had been infrequent and generally limited to Appalachia. Yet there was a pronounced emphasis on the need for employment in the nation generally and especially in the black community.

BLACK UNEMPLOYMENT AND POVERTY IN THE SIXTIES

The scarce official information that existed only served to reinforce Secretary of Labor Willard Wirtz's view of the necessity of jobs and training in the regular labor market for the black poor. As chapter 2 showed, there were direct differences in the fall of 1963 between economists in the CEA and the structuralists centered around the Department of Labor on unemployment and how it related to poverty. Just what was the official picture of poverty confronting the antipoverty policy makers who made decisions about the outlines of the War on Poverty, and what were the human dimensions of unemployment in this decade? Although Robert Lampman's single report served as a guide for the antipoverty policy makers, other official sources of information on unemployment and poverty were available at the time.

One source of information, the 1964 *Economic Report of the President,* put together by Walter Heller and the Council of Economic Advisers, documented the magnitude of poverty in the nation as it was understood at the time. Over nine million families had money incomes below $3,000 in 1962; 5.4 million families (seventeen million people) had incomes below $2,000 in 1962; five million "unrelated individuals" had incomes below $1,500; and three million of these had incomes below $1,000. The profile of poverty among nonwhites revealed that, while 22 percent of the poor were nonwhite, almost half of all nonwhites lived in poverty.[29] The official picture, however, failed to demonstrate the extent of the consequences of poverty and unemployment for the black poor.

Labor market expert Charles Killingsworth's structural interpretation of black unemployment illustrated why black employment was affected so adversely and demonstrated the causes of black disadvantage in the labor market in the 1960s to be more complex than the usual explanations of racial discrimination and lack of education.[30] Killingsworth's analysis also strengthens the argument that a large-scale jobs program to address unemployment was particularly warranted to deal with the special problems of joblessness in the black community. Wartime production conditions, in the period from 1940 to 1953, generally acted to the advantage of black workers, who were able to move into available positions in heavy industry in the industrial Northeast and Midwest. Changes in production techniques and government on-the-job training made it possible for workers with little skill and education to benefit from the increased demand for labor. When World War II ended, consumer demand and industrial renovation enabled many blacks to hold on to jobs, especially in the heavy manufacturing sector, when veterans returned to reenter the labor force. Although the boom slowed at the end of the decade, the Korean War to some degree revived the conditions of the early forties.

Killingsworth cites four factors that had serious consequences for black employment in the postwar period. First, after the end of the Korean War, the drop in defense spending eliminated many of the less skilled jobs in manufacturing that blacks had held. Second, although defense and space exploration raised government spending in the 1950s, the ensuing jobs were very different from the low-skilled jobs in defense-related industries during WWII, requiring special construction and engineering and scientific expertise.[31] Third, the job mix also changed in the nondefense industries, with a downturn in the number of blue-collar jobs, especially low-skilled jobs, and a rise in white-collar jobs. Fourth, plant de-centralization meant that new plants were built away from the former centers of manufacturing in the north-central and northeast markets and near the new markets in the South and the West.[32] And, while employ-ment was rising in newly emerging service industries, these sectors were growing less quickly in the older industrial centers of the country, where black job seekers had relocated.[33]

Unemployment was catastrophic in American urban ghettos in the sixties. Among young black males, it had begun to climb dangerously in the 1950s. By March 1964, when President Johnson proposed a nation-wide War on Poverty to Congress, the official unemployment rate for black males was 9.3 percent, as against 4.7 percent for white males—nearly twice as high, which was the usual ratio for the decade. This offi-cial rate did not take into account the differential effects of labor force participation factors on black males, in particular, the fact that when un-employment was high, as it was for black males, the scarcity of jobs dis-couraged many would-be workers from job seeking, thereby removing them from the statistics of those "actively seeking work" and consequently from official government employment statistics. This hidden unemploy-ment must be accounted for to obtain a realistic view of black unemploy-ment. Taking it into account, the adjusted rate of black unemployment in March 1964 was 13.5 percent, as Killingsworth has shown: in other words, the true black rate of unemployment was nearly three times the white rate.[34] An official rate of unemployment for white workers of 4.7 percent was close to the Council of Economic Advisers' definition of full employment, which they targeted at 4 percent. But such a rate tolerated an official unemployment rate among all nonwhites of 8 percent and an average rate of unemployment, in the midsixties, of nearly 25 percent for young black males and 33 percent for females.[35] Arthur Ross has shown that in 1964 a total of 811,000 blacks were out of work and that if their unemployment ratio had been 4 percent, the number would have been 332,000.[36] One in four black workers was unemployed at times in the six-ties, the same devastating rate that the nation experienced in the Depres-sion. Moreover, the trend over the decade deteriorated for black youth. In June 1966, a record-breaking month in which the American economy pushed out two million extra jobs, the unemployment rate among black eighteen- and nineteen-year-olds rose to 32 percent, exceeding the previ-

ous June's percentage by five points.[37] By the end of the decade, the unemployment rate for nonwhite youth would be higher than it had been in
1964. Nonwhite female unemployment ratios were close to those of nonwhite males when considered by age, except those for teenagers, which
were consistently and considerably higher for females. Although hidden
unemployment among nonwhite females was difficult to measure, it was
understood that it was considerable among teenagers. While rates for
white teenage females had risen in the sixties, those of nonwhite teenage
females had fallen dangerously in the fifties and sixties, and their reported
rate of unemployment was the highest of any group by age, sex, or color.
By the end of the sixties, it had reached 30 percent.[38]

Another characteristic of the employment picture faced by a large
portion of the black community was the dead-end job opportunities available to the poor. The ghetto labor market could look to low-wage jobs
that offered neither opportunities for advancement nor security, where
work conditions were demeaning and layoffs were customary, and where
few skills and little education were required.[39] The job-training and educational programs we did have in the sixties did little to improve the economic status of the black poor. Brown and Erie have concluded that, conceived as they were with little attention to the low-paying, menial job
opportunities awaiting participants in these programs, these programs
served as de facto income maintenance programs rather than as avenues
to compete in the primary labor market.[40]

What did this mean for black workers?[41] Median income for black
families in 1960 was $3,233, compared to $5,385 for white families. Professional, managerial, and technical jobs were held by 23 percent of the
white workforce, as against 6.7 percent of the black workforce, most of
whom were found in black schools, businesses, or construction. Eighty
percent of black workers were in semiskilled, service, and unskilled jobs,
as against 40 percent of white workers. In white- and light-blue-collar occupations (computer operators and secretaries, for example), 13 percent of
black workers were employed, compared to 36 percent of white workers.

THE DUAL AGENDA

These employment and economic issues were major and longstanding concerns of the civil rights organizations that for decades had been seriously

involved in bringing the case for jobs and training to the attention of official Washington. As Charles V. Hamilton and Dona Hamilton have shown, civil rights organizations persisted as far back as the 1920s in asking government to intervene in helping those left out of the market system, systematically confronting government with a "dual agenda" of civil rights and social policies, in pursuit of the economic and jobs-related goals of their black constituents.[42] The fear of the larger black organizations was always that blacks would be relegated to the secondary economy if they did not receive the training and education essential to participation in the regular labor force. These concerns were borne out by the course of government cash assistance programs for the poor, such as Aid to Families with Dependent Children, and the absence of the very work and education initiatives they sought. Government response to even prominent black leaders was so perfunctory and unresponsive to the black agenda it was ludicrous at times.[43]

What follows is an overview of the position of the larger black organizations concerned with employment-related issues. Considered are the National Urban League (NUL) and the National Association for the Advancement of Colored People (NAACP), as well as other civil rights leaders and organizations such as A. Phillip Randolph, the Congress of Racial Equality (CORE), and the Southern Christian Leadership Conference (SCLC). The relationship of these organizations to organized labor is also taken up, as is the shift in focus of the civil rights movement in the sixties, as economic and employment-related issues began to more to the forefront of the civil rights agenda.

National Black Organizations

Two organizations, the National Urban League and the National Association for the Advancement of Colored People, had long recognized the centrality of jobs for black Americans. Both organizations, before and after the Depression, sought government action in the provision of jobs and income security to black workers.[44] Both believed that jobs and job opportunities were essential to the well-being of black Americans. And both sought a government role in prohibiting discrimination in the workplace.

The National Urban League was founded in 1911, uniting three philanthropic organizations concerned with the social and economic problems that confronted blacks who had migrated to northern cities.[45] Funded primarily by employers and wealthy philanthropists and considered a conservative organization in comparison with the more protest-oriented NAACP, the goal of the Urban League and its local chapters was to improve job opportunities of black workers in industry. The league believed that improving the caliber of black labor would lead to its acceptance by white employers. To this end, it organized and trained black workers, acted as an employment agency, and established relations with employers to facilitate their acceptance. By the 1920s and 1930s, a number of local leagues had been established, and the organization instituted an annual Negro Industrial Week to bring black labor to the attention of industry. In 1930 its Negro Vocational Opportunity Campaign brought vocational guidance, a new activity for the league, to high school and college youth.

Founded in 1909, the NAACP dealt with labor problems in the context of discrimination, protesting against discrimination by government, unions, and private employers. This continued until the 1930s, when economic issues became more crucial. Like the NUL, the NAACP communicated unsuccessfully with the AFL on matters of discrimination, doing so by addressing specific isolated complaints about employment, since its principal activities were concerned with voting, segregation, and lynching.

Critical economic issues became more important to the NUL and the NAACP with the crisis of the Depression. In 1932 black unemployment was nearly 50 percent, and many blacks who held on to their jobs were working at half their former wages; 40 percent of black workers in the 1930s earned less than $200 a year.[46] The NUL and the NAACP interceded on behalf of black workers to get a share of federally financed public works jobs, and the NAACP carried out a major campaign to protest exploitation and exclusion of black workers in specific New Deal construction projects. The Joint Committee for National Recovery, a coalition of twenty-two organizations, was the vehicle through which the NAACP and the NUL acted on discrimination in employment during the early New Deal. This coalition was formed to address the displacement of black workers, especially in the South, through the implementation of the National Recovery Administration's (NRA) fair practice codes.[47]

The policy preferences of the NAACP and the Urban League concerning major employment-related laws also indicated their concern with the economic situation of the black community. Examination of these organizations' historical positions toward legislation demonstrates a consistent preference for measures that would provide working income rather than charity or relief.[48]

The National Labor Relations Act of 1935 (the Wagner Act) placed the weight of government behind workers' rights to join unions and to participate in collective bargaining. This act was a key piece of legislation for the American labor movement, legitimating unions in the United States. Both the NAACP and the league opposed features of the bill that legalized closed shops, and the league testified against it.[49] Their fear was that "since many black workers were excluded from unions, thousands would be shut out of employment."[50]

Another landmark piece of legislation, the Social Security Act of 1935, established the basis for the American welfare state. Although it was hailed as a universal social policy designed to protect against wage loss resulting from unemployment, old age, prolonged disability, or death, the bill was not, in fact, universal: it excluded domestic and agriculture workers, shutting out two-thirds of the black labor force.[51] The Urban League and the NAACP had both testified in favor of the coverage of all workers.[52]

During World War II, employing the threat of direct action, a significant accomplishment in the area of employment came about largely because of the efforts of A. Phillip Randolph; this was the establishment of the Fair Employment Practices Commission (FEPC). The imposing founder of the first major black trade union, Randolph had been a longtime advocate of jobs, having fought the Pullman Company for twelve years to gain recognition for his Brotherhood of Sleeping Car Porters.[53] The socialist group around Randolph and Chandler Owen, who edited the monthly New York magazine *The Messenger* between 1917 and 1928, sought to establish links between black workers and the white labor movement.[54] In 1941, threatening a mass march on Washington of ten thousand blacks protesting discrimination in the defense industries and the armed services, Randolph pressured President Roosevelt to issue Executive Order 8802, which stated, "There shall be no discrimination in the employment of workers in defense industries or government because of race, creed, color, or national origin," temporarily establishing the wartime FEPC. Although the march was canceled when Roosevelt reluctantly complied, it signified the centrality of economic problems to the black community. Although the FEPC did not lead to large-scale employment of blacks, it was precedent setting in the defense industries for two reasons: for the first time, economic discrimination was considered a denial of civil rights, and the federal government had assumed a role in eliminating discrimination in employment. In the post-WWII period, it became the basis for fair employment practices laws in a number of states and for federal contract compliance committees. The FEPC was also responsible for the issuing of court degrees against job discrimination and for the establishment of the Equal Employment Opportunity Commission under Title VII of the Civil Rights Act in 1964.

The league and the NAACP were impressed with the original 1945 Full Employment Act, which was intended to achieve the goals of national production, purchasing, and employment in a comprehensive way, and testified in support of it. The act would have been of enormous consequence to black workers given their disproportionate rates of unemployment and vulnerability to economic recessions.[55] A right to employment and full employment were to have been government responsibilities, but the right to a job was considerably weakened in the 1946 act that passed.

Before the Depression, direct action techniques began to be employed by groups largely outside national organizations such as the NAACP and the league. These "Don't Buy Where You Can't Work" campaigns were boycotts of white-owned establishments within the black community refusing to hire black employees. Originating in Chicago by the local Urban League in 1927, such methods were extended to New York (by the Muslim Sufi Abdul Hamid), Washington (by the New Negro Alliance), and to Richmond, Cleveland, and elsewhere by the NAACP branches. The Congress of Racial Equality (CORE), formed in 1942, had been concerned, in the 1940s and 1950s, largely with desegregating public accommodations and had pioneered the direct action tactics that were successfully employed in the sit-in movement in the South in the sixties.[56] By the late 1950s CORE began to make use of direct action techniques to address job discrimination. In 1962 the organization began to stress going beyond token representation in employment of blacks and raised the issue of special compensation to redress the effects of past discrimination, although this issue originated with the Urban League. By 1963 employment had become the principal focus of most of CORE's activity.

Martin Luther King, Jr., formed the Southern Christian Leadership Conference (SCLC) in 1957 to coordinate black protest activity in southern cities. Although its initial focus was on the opening-up of public accommodations, most spectacularly in the 1955–56 Montgomery Alabama bus boycott, it too turned to direct action campaigns against job bias in the South in the sixties. In particular, in 1962 in Atlanta the SCLC adopted the successful "Operation Breadbasket" campaign, which had originated in Philadelphia in 1959. The campaign, which would move to Chicago with King in 1966, successfully opened up white-collar sales and clerical positions in 1963.

Organized Labor

The discriminatory practices of organized labor often forced black organizations and workers into paradoxical relationships with industrial employers in these early years. In 1918 the NUL and the NAACP together addressed the issue of industrial employment with Samuel Gompers and other AFL representatives. Again, in 1920 and 1925, there were communications between the league and the AFL concerning discrimination, but little of substance resulted. Discrimination in the unions often required the NUL to recommend inconsistent strategies to local chapters, which placed workers in contradictory relations with unions and employers. While the position of the national office of the league was that black workers should join unions and not serve as strikebreakers, local chapters could recommend that workers work with unions, refer black workers to serve as strikebreakers, or be neutral.

In 1935 the emergence of the more radical Congress of Industrial Organizations (CIO) was the occasion for the NUL and the NAACP to re-examine their positions toward organized labor. Organized along industrywide lines rather than by craft, the CIO's racial policy was broader than that of the AFL.[57] The league organized workers councils in over a hundred cities to introduce the principles of trade unionism, and some black workers in these councils gaining admittance into AFL craft unions. Black elites, however, were divided on the CIO, feeling that its radical objectives would harm the larger goals of the civil rights organizations. In this period of potential transition, the NAACP, which had begun to develop a precedent-setting judicial strategy against labor union discrimination, backed away from this approach to concentrate its resources on the campaign against school desegregation. It eventually came to incorporate the tactic of alliances with industrial unions and, in the post–World War II period, established a labor department within the organization, which exposed discrimination in business and government employment.

Beginning in the 1940s, the NAACP labor department pressured government and firms with government contracts for policy changes to benefit blacks. The NAACP sought legislation to aid black workers and fought against discrimination in government agencies. It worked with other organizations to have state and municipal fair employment laws passed. It also interceded with the government on behalf of migrant agricultural workers. At the end of the decade, the labor department was reorganized with three goals in mind: the elimination of bias in hiring, training, and promotion; equal rights for blacks in trade unions; and union backing for the NAACP's civil rights agenda. The NAACP also filed complaints with President Eisenhower's Committee on Government Contracts to attack bias among employers and in unions.

Civil rights organizations and leaders viewed employment-related issues as essential concerns, devoting scarce resources—time, money, and attention—to pursuing economic and employment-related goals for their black constituents. As demonstrated next, these critical issues of jobs and employment gained momentum early in the 1960s as concrete economic demands and goals were increasingly incorporated into the agenda of the civil rights movement.

SHIFT IN THE CIVIL RIGHTS MOVEMENT IN THE SIXTIES

As shown above, by 1963 employment had become an important focus of black protest as movement activity shifted from a principal emphasis on segregation and constitutional issues to a more pronounced concern with economic equality. The NAACP, the Urban League, and CORE were all addressing employment issues by this time. Over the decade they would continue to pressure the Kennedy and Johnson administrations to address black employment. This section illustrates some important organizational initiatives that emerged from the black community beginning in this period that reflected their judgment that jobs were central to full racial equality.

Originally, the 1963 March on Washington for Jobs and Freedom was to bring attention to the need for black employment. The march was conceived by A. Phillip Randolph, and it was largely planned and coordinated in less than sixty days by his deputy director, Bayard Rustin, working out of a Harlem walk-up office owned by the Friendship Baptist Church.[58] The march was premised on the notion that, considerable progress having been made on the moral question facing blacks, it was time to bring pressure to bear on the jobs question.[59] Over 200,000 mostly black marchers converged peacefully on the capital on August 28, in the largest protest of its kind that Washington had ever seen, demonstrating for quick and full action on civil rights and equal job opportunities. At a ten o'clock private meeting with Labor Secretary Willard Wirtz on the morning of the march, Martin Luther King pressed for jobs for black youth. He expressed no interest in discussing the upcoming civil rights bill and, in fact, deflected Wirtz's efforts to discuss the act, choosing instead to push for the summer jobs component of the Labor Department's two-part program.[60]

In June 1963, in an aggressive new posture, Whitney Young and the Urban League issued a leading policy statement—a "Domestic Marshall Plan"—focused primarily on employment. The league, which had come under Young's direction in October 1961, called for a "conscious, planned effort [to] bring qualified Negroes into 'entrance jobs' in *all* types of employment, to upgrade them and aid them to qualify for advancement, and to place them in positions of responsibility, *including the full range* of management positions."[61] The plan called for a massive effort of crash programs to be sponsored by government and the private sector to eliminate the economic, educational, and social gap between blacks and whites, to end poverty, and to restore urban life.[62] Young propelled the league into tackling the emerging new issues surrounding the civil rights movement. His new focus was on compensatory employment to help unemployed and deprived blacks overcome the consequences of past discrimination. The league maintained that for blacks to be able to make use of new opportunities, special efforts had to be made in employment and manpower training, among other areas. It had redirected its energies to improving job opportunities with employment programs such as the National Skills Bank, On-the-Job-Training (with the Department of Labor), the Broadcast Skills Bank, the Secretarial Training Project.

Not only had employment become a central focus of black organizations by 1963, over the decade these organizations would continue to pressure government to respond to black joblessness. In 1966, for example, responding in part to Johnson administration cutbacks in the War on Poverty, the A. Phillip Randolph Institute issued a "Freedom Budget for All Americans."[63] First proposed by Randolph during the White House Conference on Civil Rights, the budget was put together by Bayard Rustin, who oversaw the work of a mixed black and white group of economists and policy analysts that included John Kenneth Galbraith, Michael Harrington, Leon Keyserling, Vivian Henderson, and Tom Kahn.[64] It was backed by a coalition of civil rights, religious, and labor leaders and sought $185 billion in federal outlays between 1967 and 1975. Among other programs, the Freedom Budget called for jobs projects and job training to achieve full employment for the employable, a minimum wage of $2 an hour by 1968 or 1969, and guaranteed income for the jobless.[65]

Also in 1966, recognizing that the civil rights coalition had run its course, Martin Luther King began to change his emphasis, moving increasingly to explicit class-based analyses of economic issues that confronted blacks and poor whites. The ghetto revolts outside the South called into question the utility of King's nonviolent strategy and his role in the leadership of the civil rights movement. In this new territory, King and the SCLC faced a series of problems—poverty, joblessness, and housing—that seemed to lie beyond the methods they had successfully promoted in the early days of the struggle in the South. Their decision to address them signaled a deeper—and riskier—analysis of the fundamental economic causes of racism.[66]

In this period, King spoke of restructuring society, of rebuilding America's cities to benefit the poor, of nationalizing industries, and of a guaranteed annual wage.[67] In his work in Chicago, Cleveland, and Detroit he made demands for jobs, open housing, citizen review of police and housing boards, and economic boycotts of business.[68] He spoke of creating a new coalition, of eliminating the barrier of racism to forge bonds of economic interest between black and poor whites. King's vision of the future rested on the "macroeconomics of 'total, direct, and immediate abolition of poverty.' "[69] "Poverty is not new," he said. "What's new is that we have the techniques and tools to get rid of poverty. The real question is whether we have the will."[70]

Two years later the Poor People's Campaign was for King a step in his plan to create a new coalition to wage the struggle for economic rights.[71] SCLC staff completed plans for the Poor People's March in mid-February

1968. At its heart was the SCLC's proposal for a $12 billion Economic Bill of Rights. Originally proposed by A. Phillip Randolph, the bill guaranteed employment to all who could work, incomes to those who could not, a federal open housing act, and enforcement of integrated education.

Toward his goal of building a broad coalition, King also turned to union organizing and strikes, carrying the SCLC campaigns into Atlanta; Memphis; Detroit; Birmingham; St. Petersburg, Florida; and Charleston, Georgetown, and Florence, South Carolina.[72] King was assassinated in Memphis on April 4, 1968, and consequently never completed his plans to create an economic class coalition that cut across lines of race. His decision to concentrate on socioeconomic issues at the end of his career cost him the support of the federal government, the business community, a large part of organized labor, and much of the older civil rights leadership.[73] Indeed, the decision may have cost him his life.

Near the end of the decade, the need for jobs in the black community was a leading finding in the report of the President's Commission on Civil Disorders, the Kerner Commission, on March 1, 1968. The report called for public jobs to supplement new and existing jobs in the private sector. It sought increased federal efforts for jobs and job training and in education and housing and recommended strong civil-rights enforcement.[74] Appointed by President Johnson in 1967 to study the conditions that underlay the summer riots that destroyed large parts of the nation's ghettos, the commission found that pervasive discrimination in employment, housing, and policy was the product of underlying white racism in American society.[75] By 1968 Johnson, so embittered by the public enmity against him, turned his back on his own commission, refusing to accept its report publicly.

Between 1963 and 1968 were five years of astonishing transition, as large parts of the American public moved from openness and embrace of the federal role as agent of social change to resentful anger and rejection. In 1963, however, politics, the policy-making agenda, and social protest had converged to create a window of opportunity for desperately needed employment programs to address what was called the "Negro job crisis." While blacks did not ask for a War on Poverty, they were asking for jobs and employment programs and particularly for national government attention to black unemployment, which was catastrophic in 1963. Blacks had already been seeking government assistance for jobs and employment programs for decades, and the importance of the jobs agenda is borne out by the fact that they never retreated from this issue for the duration of the sixties. But this critical need for adult employment programs remained unmet by the Economic Opportunity Act.

Why would the jobs agenda and the antipoverty agenda not be joined in the minds of policy planners, especially since the issue had been linked for them by a forceful advocate in the Labor Department, Secretary Willard Wirtz? A greater irony lies in one of the chief criticisms of the War on Poverty, especially among its liberal critics, which is the backlash it engendered from white working-class Americans who, regarding it as a black program, resentfully rejected it, Johnson, and the Democratic Party by electing Richard Nixon president in 1968.

The inability of the structuralist argument to gain hegemony provided one important explanation for the fate of the jobs agenda, as shown in chapter 2. Governmental leaders consistently refused to acknowledge the pressures, lobbying, and demands from the African American community for jobs and incorporate them into public policy, refusing to address the critical employment gap of black Americans and choosing instead to rely on macroeconomic remedies to stimulate the general economy that were consistent with Keynesian economic philosophy as it was understood and practiced by the Council of Economic Advisers.[76] In chapter 3 a second reason for the failure of the jobs agenda was proposed. This was the perception of the Labor Department's inability to implement and oversee successfully the large-scale jobs programs sought by its secretary, Willard Wirtz. To understand this failure further, it is necessary to consider the dilemma in terms of the government's will to respond to the black community.

APPENDIX: *NEW YORK TIMES* COVERAGE OF ECONOMIC AND EMPLOYMENT-RELATED CIVIL RIGHTS ACTIVITY IN 1963

January

"Negro Equality in Jobs Is Asked: Governor of North Carolina Sets Up State Panel to Fight Discrimination," January 19, 1963, sec. A, 1.

John D. Pomfret, "Wirtz to Revamp Labor Programs to Assist Jobless: Will

Reshuffle Agencies to Meet Challenge of Technological Changes," January 28, 1963, sec. A, 1.

February

John D. Pomfret, "Kennedy to Push Aid to Idle Youth: Backers Hope for Action by This Session of Congress—2 Work Corps Planned," February 12, 1963, sec. A, 1.

Marjorie Hunter, "Civil Rights Fight Shifting to the North: Report to President Cites Menial Status to Negro and Curbs on Housing," February 13, 1963, sec. 1, A.

Marjorie Hunter, "President Calls for 2 Work Corps to Aid Idle Youth: Asks Congress to Create Groups for National and Hometown Projects," February 15, 1963, sec. A, 1.

"End of Fairy Tale," February 19, 1963, sec. A, 6.

Joseph A. Loftus, "Five Cabinet Members Back Youth Conservation Corps at Senate Hearing," February 27, 1963, sec. A, 1.

March

Claude Sitton, "President Gives Civil Rights Plan on Vote and Jobs: U.S. Prodding South on Hiring Negroes," March 1, 1963, sec. A, 1.

John D. Pomfret, "Jobless Rate Up to 6. 1 Per Cent, Highest Since '61," March 8, 1963, sec. A, 1.

John D. Pomfret, "President Calls Rise in New Jobs Key to Economy," March 12, 1963, sec. A, 1.

C. P. Trussell, "Youth Conservation Corps Approved by Senate Panel: Subcommittee Votes 120 Million on Plan to Provide Jobs on Public Projects—G.O.P. Fights Drive for Passage," March 20, 1963, sec. A, 1.

"Youth Corps," March 25, 1963, sec. A, 6.

April

Marjorie Hunter, "Kennedy Assails Vote to End Fund on Public Works: In Appeal to House, He Calls Committee's Rejection of Plan 'Most Unfortunate,' " April 7, 1963, sec. A, 1.

Untitled editorial, April 7, 1963, sec. 4, 12.

"Need for Public Works," April 9, 1963, sec. A, 30.

"Young Men Wanted," April 10, 1963, sec. A, 38.

John D. Morris, "House Votes Works Plan; Backs President, 228–184," April 11, 1963, sec. A, 1.

John D. Pomfret, "Youth-Job Panel Calls for Action: Report to President Warns Hundreds of Thousands Face Grim Futures," April 25, 1963, sec. A, 1.

Letter from Harrison J. Goldin, New York, April 26, 1963, sec. A, 34.

"Opportunities for Youth," April 27, 1963, sec. A, 24.

Arnaldo Cortesi, "House Holds Up Bills on Transit and Youth Jobs: Democratic Leaders Fear Strain on Party Discipline in Close Floor Fights," April 29, 1963, sec. A, 1.

May

"Senate Bars Cuts in Kennedy Plan on Public Works: Votes 60–26 to Reject G.O.P. Move to Trim 200 Million from 450 Million Fund," May 2, 1963, sec. A, 1.

Claude Sitton, "Birmingham Talks Reach an Accord on Ending Crisis: Dr. King Accept Pledges from Whites After Cutting Demands of Negroes," May 10, 1963, sec. A, 1.

John D. Pomfret, "Jobs for Youth Held Need Lest Social Crisis Develop," May 11, 1963, sec. A, 1.

Claude Sitton, "Birmingham Pact Sets Timetable for Integration: Big Downtown Stores Agree to Desegregate Facilities in Next 90 Days, Job Gains in 2 Months," May 11, 1963, sec. A, 1.

"Still the Forgotten," May 12, 1963, sec. 4, 10.

"A Truce Is Reached in Birmingham, But the Threat of Turbulence Remains," May 12, 1963, sec. 4, 12.

"Aiding the Jobless," May 17, 1963, sec. A, 28.

Anthony Lewis, "Negroes Press Harder for Basic Rights: Birmingham Reflects Their Growing Restiveness and the Many Hurdles in the Path Toward Equality," May 19, 1963, sec. 4, 10.

"Moving Children Not the Answer," May 22, 1963, sec. A, 40.

June

William G. Weart, "Negroes Win Jobs at Philadelphia," June 1, 1963, sec. A, 1.

"Desegregating the North," June 4, 1963, sec. A, 38.

Anthony Lewis, "Kennedy Weighs New Rights Law: Strong Action Could Jeopardize His Programs in Congress," June 2, 1963, sec. A, 1.

Charles G. Bennett, "Wagner Directs Agencies to Push Minority Rights: Greater Housing Integration and More Job Openings Sought in New Order," June 5, 1963, sec. A, 1.

Tom Wicker, "Kennedy Prohibits Job Discrimination at Federal Projects," June 5, 1963, sec. A, 1.

Eileen Shanahan, "Rise in Teen-Age Jobless Pushes U.S. Rate to 5.9%: Wirtz Fears an 'Explosive' Buildup—Total of Unemployed in May was 4,100,000, an Increase of 0.2%," June 7, 1963, sec. A, 1.

Tom Wicker, "President Says Racial Barriers Imperil Schools: Also Asserts Economic Lags Harm Education and Asks Action in Both Areas," June 7, 1963, sec. A, 1.

"Our Excluded Youth," June 8, 1963, sec. A, 24.

Anthony Lewis, "Campaign for Integration: Major Battle Looming in Congress," June 9, 1963, sec. E, 3.

Letter from R. E. Planas, East Orange, N.J., June 8, 1963, sec. A, 24.

John D. Pomfret, "Jobless Youth Major Problem: Decline of Work for the Unskilled Increases Teen Unemployment," June 9, 1963, sec. E, 8.

James Reston, "Kennedy's Uncertain Approach to Racial Crisis," June 9, 1963, sec. E, 12.

"What on Rights?" June 9, 1963, sec. E, 1.

Emanuel Perlmutter, "Aides Defy Wagner on Order to Count Negro Jobholders," June 10, 1963, sec. A, 1.

"President Calls Negro-Jobs Talks: He Will Meet 300 Labor Leaders Tomorrow on Ending Barriers," June 12, 1963, sec. A, 1.

James Reston, "Kennedy and King Canute of Alabama," June 12, 1963, sec. A, 42.

Samuel Kaplan, "Unions Here Get Warning on Bias: Screvane Threatens to Halt Work at Harlem Hospital After Picketing There," June 13, 1963, sec. A, 1.

Samuel Kaplan, "City Halts Work at Site In Harlem," June 14, 1963, sec. A, 1.

Anthony Lewis, "Kennedy Presses G.O.P. to Support Civil Rights Drive," June 14, 1963, sec. A, 1.

Marjorie Hunter, "Marchers in Capital Hear Washington Will Get a Fair Housing Law," June 15, 1963, sec. A, 1.

Anthony Lewis, "Washington: Kennedy Commits Administration to Determined Effort to Improve Conditions," June 16, 1963, sec. E, 3.

"President Moves in Racial Conflict," June 16, 1963, sec. E, 1.

E. W. Kenworthy, "Kennedy to Offer Civil Rights Plan with Job Training," June 19, 1963, sec. A, 1.

Philip Benjamin, "N.A.A.C.P. Accuses City of Job Bias," June 20, 1963, sec. A, 1.

"The Civil Rights Message," June 20, 1963, sec. A, 32.

Tom Wicker, "Kennedy Asks Broad Rights Bill as 'Reasonable' Course in Crisis; Calls for Restraint by Negroes," June 20, 1963, sec. A, 1.

Charles G. Bennett, "Wagner to Help Negroes Get More Building Jobs," June 22, 1963, sec. A, 1.

Marjorie Hunter, "Negroes Inform Kennedy of Plan for New Protests," June 23, 1963, sec. A, 1.

"Kennedy Acts on Civil Rights," June 23, 1963, sec. E, 1.

"Land of the Free," June 23, 1963, sec. E, 8.

Charles G. Bennett, "Negroes Here Ask a Job-Quota Plan: Seeks a Fourth of Work Let by City—Say 'Dikes Will Break' Without Action," June 25, 1963, sec. A, 1.

Peter Kihss, "Negroes Find Bias on Appointments," June 26, 1963, sec. A, 1.

C. P. Trussell, "Aid for Distressed Areas Revived by Senate, 65–30," June 27, 1963, sec. A, 1.

Richard P. Hunt, "Governor Speeds Projects to Open Jobs to Negroes," June 28, 1963, sec. A, 1.

E. W. Kenworthy, "Rise in Negro Jobs Linked to Growth: Wirtz Tells House Unit End of Hiring Bias Hinges on Increase in Employment," June 28, 1963, sec. A, 1.

"Murphy Rejects Racial Pressure," June 29, 1963, sec. A, 1.

Fred M. Hechinger, "Jobs and School," June 30, 1963, sec. 4, 7.

July

Letter from Martin Panzer, Great Neck, N.Y., July 1, 1963, sec. A, 28.

"Bigger Pay, Less Building," July 2, 1963, sec. A, 28.

Milton Honig, "Racial Job Clash Erupts in Jersey," July 4, 1963, sec. A, 1.

"Bronx Youth Is Wounded in Second Racial Clash," July 8, 1963, sec. A, 1.

"The Bounds of Protest," July 9, 1963, sec. A, 30.

Peter Kihss, "Governor's Office Here Is Besieged as Sit-Ins Spread," July 10, 1963, sec. A, 1.

Peter Kihss, "Race Sit-In Begins at Mayor's Office in a Job Protest," July 10, 1963, sec. A, 1.

"Bronx Hoodlumism," July 11, 1963, sec. A, 28.

Clayton Knowles, "City Panel Gives Job Racial Plan," July 12, 1963, sec. A, 1.

Letter from Claire Gallant Berman, N.Y., July 13, 1963, sec. A, 16.

Letter from Robert Grookins Gore, N.Y., July 13, 1963, sec. A, 1.

Martin Arnold, "Police Ask Clergy to Help in Bronx Racial Disputee," July 14, 1963, sec. A, 1.

"CORE Plans Fight on Latent Racism," July 15, 1963, sec. A, 1.

Martin Arnold, "42 Rights Pickets Arrested by City," July 16, 1963, sec. A, 1.

Martin Arnold, "Accord Reached on Harlem Hiring," July 17, 1963, sec. A, 1.

Samuel Kaplan, "Unions Reject Racial Plan of Mayor's Action Panel," July 18, 1963, sec. A, 1.

Samuel Kaplan, "Governor, Mayor Take Steps to End Race Bias in Jobs," July 19, 1963, sec. A, 1.

"The Negro Quota," July 19, 1963, sec. A, 26.

Charles Grutzner, "Skilled Negroes in Demand Here," July 21, 1963, sec. A, 1.

Arthur Krock, "Kennedy and Civil Rights," July 21, 1963, sec. E, 9.

Emanuel Perlmutter, "Unionists Soften Stand on Negroes," July 22, 1963, sec. A, 1.

John D. Pomfret, "A.F.L.-C.I.O. Maps Drive to Combat Discrimination," July 22, 1963, sec. A, 1.

Peter Kihss, "200 Racial Pickets Seized at Building Projects Here," July 23, 1963, sec. A, 1.

Peter Kihss, "143 More Seized in Protests Here," July 24, 1963, sec. A, 1.

Peter Kihss, "5 Racial Pickets Get 30-to-60-Day Jail Terms," July 25, 1963, sec. A, 1.

Peter Kihss, "Rockefeller Bars Negro Job Quota; Hails Union Plan," July 26, 1963, sec. A, 1.

John D. Pomfret, "New U.S. Directives Bar Discrimination in Apprentice Plan," July 27, 1963, sec. A, 1.

Peter Kihss, "Negroes to Push Picketing in City in Drive for Jobs," July 29, 1963, sec. A, 1.

Peter Kihss, "Pickets Arrested for Blocking Way to Mayor's Office," July 30, 1963, sec. A, 1.

Peter Kihss, "Wagner Extends Civil Rights Talks on Job Practices," July 31, 1963, sec. A, 1.

John D. Pomfret, "Building Trades Press Equality," July 31, 1963, sec. A, 1.

August

Letter from J. C. Michael Allen, August 1, 1963, sec. A, 26.

Homer Bigart, "Near-Riot Flares in Race Protest at Project Here," August 1, 1963, sec. A, 1.

"Equality in Jobs," August 1, 1963, sec. A, 26.

Homer Bigart, "7 Pickets Seized for Blockading Governor's Door," August 2, 1963, sec. A, 1.

John D. Pomfret, "Employment in July Set a Record of 70.8 Million," August 2, 1963, sec. A, 1.

Homer Bigart, "Wagner's Panel on Hiring Negroes Notes Progress," August 3, 1963, sec. A, 1.

Letter from B. Russell Brinley, White Park, Fla., August 3, 1963, sec. A, 16.

"Jobs and the Jobless," August 3, 1963, sec. A, 16.

John D. Pomfret, "Labor Bias Rules Won't Be Delayed," August 3, 1963, sec. A, 1.

"Progress Towards Equality," August 3, 1963, sec. A, 16.

"Jim Crow on the Job," August 4, 1963, sec. E, 2.

E. W. Kenworthy, "Rights Bill: The Arguments in Congress," August 4, 1963, sec. E, 10.

"Domestic Peace Corps," August 5, 1963, sec. A, 28.

Homer Bigart, "Building Trades Accused Snub of Racial Groups," August 6, 1963, sec. A, 1.

Homer Bigart, "Negroes Call Off Brooklyn Pickets As Governor Acts," August 7, 1963, sec. A, 1.

Letter from Roger Starr, New York City, August 7, 1963, sec. A, 32.

UPI, "House Votes Job Training: Civil Rights Rider Beaten," August 7, 1963, sec. A, 1.

Homer Bigart, "Picketing Goes On As Leaders Spurn Rockefeller Acts," August 8, 1963, sec. A, 1.

Letter from Lawrence Plotkin, New York City, August 8, 1963, sec. E, 26.

"Accord Reached at White Castle," August 9, 1963, sec. A, 1.

John D. Pomfret, "N.A.A.C.P. Offers a Pact to Builders to Calm Protest," August 9, 1963, sec. A, 1.

John D. Pomfret, "Building Groups to Train Negroes," August 10, 1963, sec. A, 1.

"Training for Jobs," August 10, 1963, sec. A, 16.

"Balance Sheet on Civil Rights," August 11, 1963, sec. 4, 1.

Milton Bracker, "White Castle Pact on Recruiting Ends Picketing by CORE," August 11, 1963, sec. A, 1.

Claude Sitton, "Gains on Civil Rights Whets Appetite for More," August 11, 1963, sec. 4, 8.

Milton Bracker, "500 Nonwhite Applicants to Test Building Job Pact," August 12, 1963, sec. A, 1.

Homer Bigart, "City Urges Unions to Favor Negroes," August 15, 1963, sec. A, 1.

C. P. Trussell, "Home Peace Corps Backed in Senate by a 47–44 Vote," August 15, 1963, sec. A, 1.

Homer Bigart, "Union Chief Sees Reverse Job Bias," August 17, 1963, sec. A, 1.

Milton Bracker, "City Job Registry to Aid Nonwhites," August 18, 1963, sec. A, 1.

John D. Pomfret, "Economic Factors Underlie Negro Discontent," August 18, 1963, sec. A, 1.

"Struggle for Jobs," August 18, 1963, sec. 4, 8.

"CORE Expects Agreement on Jobs Here in 2 Weeks," August 19, 1963, sec. A, 1.

Homer Bigart, "Minorities Job Plan Starts Slowly Here," August 20, 1963, sec. A, 1.

"Census of Skills," August 21, 1963, sec. A, 32.

Cabell Phillips, "Kennedy Opposes Quotas for Jobs on Basis of Race," August 21, 1963, sec. A, 1.

Letter from Jerome Gotkin, August 25, 1963, sec. 4, 12.

James Reston, "Washington: The White Man's Burden and All That," August 28, 1963, sec. A, 1.

Nan Robertson, "Capital Is Ready for March Today: 100,000 Expected," August 28, 1963, sec. A, 1.

Jack Roth, "Governor Heard at Pickets' Trial," August 28, 1963, sec. 4, 12.

"Equality Is Their Right," August 29, 1963, sec. A, 28.

E. W. Kenworthy, "200,000 March for Civil Rights in Orderly Washington Rally: President Sees Gain for Negro," August 29, 1963, sec. A, 1.

"Equality Is Their Right," August 30, 1963, sec. A, 20.

Hendrick Smith, "Leaders of March Pledge Widening of Rights Drive," August 30, 1963, sec. A, 1.

September

"For Rights: The March and After," September 1, 1963, sec. 4, 1.

Claude Sitton, "Status of Integration: The Progress So Far Is Characterized as Mainly Tokenism," September 1, 1963, sec. E, 4.

"City Aide Confident Unions Will Accept 600 Negroes Soon," September 2, 1963, sec. A, 1.

"View from Lincoln Memorial," September 2, 1963, sec. E, 8.

Margaret Weil, "Rights Groups Plan March on City Hall for Jobs Sept. 29," September 8, 1963, sec. A, 1.

Martin Arnold, "Non-Bias Job Plan Here Draws 2,600," September 14, 1963, sec. A, 1.

George Cable Wright, "Negro Job Quotas Urged in New Jersey," September 25, 1963, sec. A, 1.

"The Tax Bill," September 27, 1963, sec. A, 28.

October

"Still Too Many Jobless," October 4, 1963, sec. A, 34.

"Moving Ahead on Civil Rights," October 6, 1963, sec. E, 8.

C. P. Trussell, "Job Training Bill Passed by Senate," October 9, 1963, sec. A, 1.

Anthony Lewis, "Robert Kennedy Tries to Prevent Rights Deadlock," October 16, 1963, sec. A, 1.

"How Strong a Civil Rights Law?" October 17, 1963, sec. A, 34.

"Moves on Rights," October 20, 1963, sec. E, 3.

Claude Sitton, "In The South: Main Emphasis Is Shifted from Demonstrations to Political Activity," October 20, 1963, sec. E, 3.

Letter from John C. McCabe, New York City, October 21, 1963, sec. A, 30.

David R. Jones, "Negroes Get Better Jobs at U.S. Steel in Alabama," October 25, 1963, sec. A, 30.

Anthony Lewis, "Halleck Pressed for Commitment on a Rights Bill," October 25, 1963, sec. A, 1.

Sydney H. Schanberg, "Preferment for Negroes Is Sought by Board Here," October 28, 1963, sec. A, 1.

Clayton Knowles, "Wagner Says City Has Not Discussed Negro Preferment," October 29, 1963, sec. A, 1.

"Forward Step on Civil Rights," October 30, 1963, sec. A, 38.

"House Unit Votes Bipartisan Plan for Civil Rights," October 30, 1963, sec. A, 1.

"Corporate Race Relations," October 31, 1963, sec. A, 32.

November

"Mountains of Misery," November 4, 1963, sec. A, 34.

Letter from Franklin D. Roosevelt, Jr., Washington, D.C., November 11, 1963, sec. A, 30.

"Two Worlds at Home," November 14, 1963, sec. A, 34.

John D. Pomfret, "Kennedy Calls Jobs Vital, Outranking Civil Rights as the Most Pressing Need Facing the Nation," November 16, 1963, sec. A, 1.

"Priority for the Jobless," November 16, 1963, sec. A, 26.

"Jobs and Taxes," November 17, 1963, sec. 4, 8.

Letter from Walter W. Heller, Washington, D.C., November 18, 1963, sec. A, 32.

"Priority in Kentucky," November 21, 1963, sec. A, 38.

Letter from Gunmundar Arnason, Reykjavik, Iceland, November 24, 1963, sec. E, 8.

Anthony Lewis, "Key Domestic Problem for Johnson—Civil Rights," November 24, 1963, sec. E, 5.

Letter from Joseph E. Moody, Washington, D.C., November 30, 1963, sec. A, 26.

December

"Retraining the Unemployed," December 2, 1963, sec. A, 36.

John D. Pomfret, "Johnson Appeals for Aid of Labor and Businessmen," December 5, 1963, sec. A, 1.

Clayton Knowles, "U.S. Work Projects Urged by Wagner to Aid Jobless," December 6, 1963, sec. A, 1.

Eileen Shanahan, "Jobless Rate Up to 6-Month High; 5.9% Out of Work; 3.9 Million Unemployed Last Month—Level Is Near that of November '62," December 7, 1963, sec. A, 1.

"Situation on Rights," December 8, 1963, sec. 4, 8.

James Reston, "On Exploring the Moon and Attacking the Slums," December 20, 1963, sec. A, 28.

"Civic On-Job Training," December 26, 1963, sec. A, 26.

Eileen Shanahan, "President to Ask Rise in Spending for Human Needs: Wide Attack on U.S. Poverty Will Be a Key Feature of Budget for 1964–65," December 29, 1963, sec. A, 1.

"Assault on Poverty," December 30, 1963, sec. A, 20.

5. Governmental Will: The Limits of Noblesse Oblige

For all its carping about the work ethic, white society has consistently turned a deaf ear to the desperate pleas for jobs that emanate from the black community.
— STEPHEN STEINBERG

It is difficult to overstate the political, social, and economic disadvantages confronting the position of African-Americans.
— ROBERT LIEBERMAN

In 1963 why did policy makers fail to pick up on the ample cues available to them on the centrality of jobs to the black agenda? This chapter argues that it was an example of the historical pattern of governmental failure to put institutional weight behind legislation that would grant substantive economic rights to blacks. Jobs and job training, the means to economic parity they had sought for so long, would have been a genuine step in this direction. This chapter demonstrates that while the governmental will to take decisive steps to address the expressed needs of the black community was absent in the critical Kennedy phase of the War on Poverty, it was potentially present when Lyndon Johnson stepped into the presidency. President Kennedy's slow pace on civil rights and his resistance to the movement's agenda are examined through content analysis of the *New York Times* for the year 1963, as well as close reading of available oral history records of the civil rights leadership in the period. During this year civil rights leaders and the *Times* openly and relentlessly needled Kennedy about his slowness and lack of resolve in publicly undertaking the black agenda. On the other hand, when Johnson stepped into the presidency, his immediate embrace of the civil rights agenda, the steps he took, and their pace were received enthusiastically by civil rights leaders and repeatedly lauded by the *Times*.

The chapter also explores the racial attitudes and assumptions of the liberal policy makers who fashioned the Economic Opportunity Act and the political constraints they confronted as they shaped legislation to embody the goals they sought. The failure to heed the black community's pressure and protest urging acceptance of the black jobs agenda has to be understood also as a failure of nerve, an issue of governmental will. The inherent difficulty of explaining the broad exclusion of important black voices in governmental antipoverty policy making—none of the civil rights leaders was involved in formulating the War on Poverty—is compounded by our incomplete understanding of the racial motivations of the planners. Equally difficult to understand were the impact of the civil rights movement and the social unrest of the period on their policy-making agenda.[1] Keeping in mind the improbability of uncovering concrete evidence of unconcealed racial prejudice among these liberal policy makers, one aim of this chapter is to demonstrate racial resistance sufficiently with the available evidence.

Critics have used the term "institutional racism" to identify influences of governmental discrimination and racism that contributed to resistance to the black economic agenda. Stephen Steinberg has delivered incisive and harsh criticism on the failures of liberal policy makers and academics, most recently in *Turning Back: The Retreat from Racial Justice in American Thought and Policy*.[2] Yet whether or not the charge of institutional racism appropriately explains racial bias in government institutions and policy, it remains an ill-defined and polemical term. In recent years, more precise scholarship has emerged, isolating the role of race in the determination of public policy, thereby bringing greater explanatory power to the subject of race and racial considerations in the making of antipoverty policy. Robert Lieberman's analytical approach in *Shifting the Color Line: Race and the American Welfare State* is an example of such work that explicitly depicts the facts of racial bias and their consequences on institutional results in New Deal Social Security legislation.[3] Both Steinberg's and Lieberman's methods and styles of analysis have merits; drawing on these analyses will help establish how race was a factor in the determination of public policy at the origins of the War on Poverty. Looking back today, the irony is how far the War on Poverty was from being the program sought by blacks.

KENNEDY AND JOHNSON AND RACIAL EQUALITY

President Kennedy's characteristic ambivalence and reluctance to commit his administration resolutely to the cause of civil rights rankled the black leadership. His ambivalence was well documented by the *New York Times* in 1963. In the 1960 presidential campaign, Kennedy had been quick to speak out against President Eisenhower for his failure to sign an executive order against bias in housing, promising with the "stroke of a Presidential pen" to wipe out discrimination. Yet his own slowness in implementing a five-month-old executive order eliminating bias in housing was, the *Times* said, "bound to strengthen doubts in the Negro community about the sincerity of those who advocate moderate measures to end discrimination."[4] Although he asserted that the civil rights issue was of great moral concern to him and would receive the full weight of his authority as president, in fact, for most of his administration, the civil rights movement received only late and limited attention and then only when it confronted the terrible violence in the South.

While the Democratic platform of 1960 had promised concrete civil rights legislation, in his first two years Kennedy offered mainly verbal support for civil rights. In 1961 the violent attacks on the Freedom Riders created a shocking climate of public opinion in the North. Freedom Rides—the integrated bus rides that began in the North and went into southern states, initiated by CORE and then led jointly by the Student Nonviolent Coordinating Committee (SNCC), CORE, and the SCLC—tested Kennedy's conviction and placed the Justice Department in the position of having to enforce the law of the land. Kennedy was forced to act by mobilizing the National Guard and applying pressure on state officials to control violence against the riders. Movement hostility deepened with the failure to protect the Freedom Riders, and the experience of the rides produced anger, frustration, and continued disillusionment with the federal government. The fact that the government only acted when faced with brutal violence increased their distrust.

Both the president and Robert Kennedy had urged civil rights leadership to pursue a southern voter registration strategy, where they believed the federal government's clearest legal authority lay, as an alternative to confrontational freedom rides, sit-ins and demonstrations. Attorney General Robert Kennedy suggested at one point to SNCC and CORE representatives that by refocusing on voter registration, they might be able to get tax exemption status from the government.[5] Although the government promised protection to the organizations, in reality the Justice Department did not uniformly guarantee the safety of the SNCC workers who carried out the southern campaign. To civil rights participants, the FBI appeared to be in collusion with the local white power structure. Moreover, Kennedy's judicial appointments, four southern judges of widely known segregationist opinion, were an embarrassment to a liberal administration.[6] His attempts to redirect the civil rights agenda away from the demonstrations that discomfited the administration seemed self-serving to movement militants and aroused suspicion.

Attitudes hardened over time among activists who experienced the consequences of Kennedy's vacillation and lack of resolve.[7] Illustrative was Attorney General Kennedy's failure to intervene in the trumped-up charges against four SNCC leaders in Americus, Georgia, and his refusal to block the indictments of the so-called Albany Nine. Such federal government responses sharpened activists' distrust and led seasoned young activists, like SNCC's John Lewis, to sound a dissenting note in the 1963 march on Washington, asking, "Which side is the Federal Government on?"[8] Taylor Branch says the Albany Nine came to be "almost a watchword for bitterness" and an utter "refutation of Pollyannaish Camelot" to civil rights veterans, as the full weight of the U.S. Attorney's office came to be used against the movement.[9]

By the end of May 1963, after national outrage at the Birmingham spectacle of snarling police dogs attacking marchers, fire hoses trained on children, jails overstuffed with thousands of protesters, and massive demonstrations tying up the city's commercial areas, a change in the administration's mood was apparent, and the president agreed to press for civil rights legislation. By June 1963 pressure from the black leadership, repercussions from large-scale southern demonstrations, and concerns over black extremism had moved the president, a large part of the Congress, and the nation to the realization that the country was faced with a national crisis, an impending black revolt. A "new official attitude" changed the administration's priorities to forcing a major bipartisan effort, but it remained to change this new attitude into policy and legislation.[10]

Leaders of the civil rights movement had long been highly critical of Kennedy and his failure to commit to the black community, his lack of moral passion in getting behind the civil rights agenda, and his feet dragging on issues that concerned them. Kennedy's laxity here was in contrast to Lyndon Johnson's aggressive style. Everything in Johnson's background and personality had made the vice presidency a nearly unbearable limbo for the wily southern politician. Taylor Branch has described Vice-President Johnson as having been "lifted from the torpor of the vice presidency" by the racial crisis confronting the Kennedy administration, when he was "suddenly in demand again as the Senate architect of the only two successful civil rights bills since Reconstruction."[11] Although he was a southerner, Vice-President Johnson's direction of the President's Commission on Equal Employment Opportunities had shown the civil rights leadership his sincere belief in the goals of the commission. Roy Wilkins observed that the vice president "began to emerge during the Kennedy Administration wholly unexpectedly and to the delight of the civil rights forces . . . ; he took a very personal concern on the fair employment business. He used the inevitable telephone . . . and he called all manner of people—unions and employers all over the country on the matter of increasing their employment of Negroes."[12] Bayard Rustin said that Johnson was "deeply concerned" in this work and was "tremendously beneficial" to the cause of civil rights in those days.[13] Whitney Young was impressed with Johnson's role in heading up the commission, "with what he said, and the kind of people he was getting around him, and the determination that he exhibited to make this a much more effective commission and to really do something."[14]

In their retrospective assessments of the two presidents, the black leaders saw Johnson as credibly committed to the black community and to the cause of civil rights and believed he was dedicated to eliminating racism, as evidenced by his bold approach in securing passage of the Civil Rights Act of 1964. Johnson was a New Dealer whose formative experience was running the National Youth Administration (NYA) in Texas during the Depression. His background (southern and poor), his temperament (compulsive, energetic, driving, and manipulative), and his experience (a political genius and expert at congressional politics, a consensus seeker) uniquely shaped him for a black political agenda that included civil rights and jobs.

Urban League director Whitney Young felt that while President Kennedy did not have confidence in the country's support for the passage of civil rights legislation, President Johnson did, and he further believed that, as a southerner, Johnson was better able to understand the American people, and blacks in particular. Where Kennedy was preoccupied by concerns that the march on Washington in August 1963 would get out of control and jeopardize the chances of the Civil Rights Act, Johnson was far more encouraging.[15]

Bayard Rustin too credited Johnson's administration as far more committed to the black struggle for civil rights than any previous or subsequent administration. Kennedy's administration was "horribly overrated," in Rustin's view: "I don't know what John Kennedy did on domestic questions that is so great," but "Johnson was the best we've ever had."[16]

CORE's James Farmer recognized Johnson's "strong belief" in civil rights and his sincere—"almost passionate"—commitment and ability to push legislation that Kennedy could not.[17] Johnson's record on civil rights, before Vietnam intervened, "was excellent—the best of any president so far."[18] Johnson had freely used the power of the office to bring pressure to bear to get the legislation passed, a failure for which Kennedy had been routinely criticized. Johnson was "the first Southern President since . . . Andrew Johnson," in Farmer's assessment, who "wanted to go down in history as a person who really accomplished something in civil rights for blacks."[19]

The NAACP's Roy Wilkins observed that Johnson would go down in history, more than any other president, "as the man who when he got in the most powerful spot in the Nation . . . committed the White House and the Administration to the involvement in getting rid of the inequalities between people solely on the basis of race." Johnson did what Kennedy would not do, Wilkins said, "when the chips were down he used the great powers of the presidency on the side of the people who were deprived." To Wilkins, Johnson was absolutely sincere on issues of race and opportunity. He felt that Johnson's background equipped him to understand poverty, to understand people, and to understand the limitations race placed on minority people in the United States. Kennedy, in contrast, did not seem to act on civil rights from conviction but was pushed by events to respond. Wilkins felt the Kennedy administration did not move fast enough on civil rights legislation in part, he believed, because Kennedy, unlike Johnson, did not know how to manipulate the government. What was needed to get civil rights through was "precisely the qualities that Lyndon Johnson later exhibited, and which only Lyndon Johnson could have, by reason of his experience and his study and use of the materials of government."[20]

The *New York Times* was also attuned to President Kennedy's lack of obvious commitment to the black community, giving the struggle national prominence and significance with regular front-page coverage.[21] Throughout his administration, the *Times* badgered the president on its editorial pages to get behind civil rights and to use the weight of his office to support the struggle as a matter of national purpose.[22] The paper noted that the president's program in civil rights had been "relatively modest," focusing mainly on efforts to speed up litigation for black voting rights in the belief that blacks would be able to ensure their own rights by voting. Blacks were critical of the president, the *Times* said, for going easy on civil rights legislation out of fear of jeopardizing his legislative program. Black leaders said, "that lack of vigorous leadership from the White House is one reason for the slow pace of integration."[23] James Reston urged the president to take greater efforts to persuade moderates in the South of the necessity for desegregation, saying "the President has not used anything like his full influence in this field." A "Presidential swing through the South," Reston said, would be of great help and ought to be "as important as the President's forthcoming tour of Europe."[24]

The president was criticized repeatedly in the *Times* for temporizing on a critical national problem, for "standing too far from the battle, for resisting emotional commitment." While he said that he would enforce the law, his critics pointed out that he had yet to make "a simple, emotionally direct statement that it is outrageous to refuse service to a human being because of the color of his skin."[25] The *Times* criticized the president for failing to demonstrate his wholehearted commitment to civil rights as a moral, issue, not just as a political one. His postponement of civil rights legislation for a week in early June and his decision to depart for Europe "at a crucial stage in the mobilization of national opinion in support of a strong program" were particularly unfortunate.[26] Great presidents, said the *Times*, regarded the office as a "moral compass helping to guide the people on the great issues of the day." Kennedy, it urged, "as the man charged with supreme responsibility for the enforcement of Federal law," should personally accompany two black students attempting to enroll in the University of Alabama as "a presidential gesture" on civil rights, "the great domestic issue of this day."[27] Kennedy's failure to get into the battle left a vacuum that had been filled by extremists on both sides of the issue, said Reston.[28] High criticism of the Kennedys also

marked Robert Kennedy's confrontational New York meeting with prominent blacks to obtain their views on northern desegregation, which had received front-page coverage on May 25 and Reston's attention on June 7.[29]
Calling the president ineffective, Reston challenged him to wrest opportunity from the racial crisis and exercise decisive leadership. Something
was wrong with his domestic leadership, Reston said, something was missing "in his speeches, in his press conferences, his trips and his timing." He
approached race intellectually and failed to grasp it emotionally or to "appeal to the spirit of the whole nation." This had the effect of distancing
potential support for civil rights, because people "do not quite believe in
him enough to support him openly."[30]

The events of June 11 and 12, 1963, marked a turning point in Kennedy's public posture toward civil rights, as the *Times* noted. He assigned
federal troops to the campus of the University of Alabama in a smooth
operation to enforce the enrollment of two black students there, forcing a
confrontation with Governor George Wallace; he appeared on nationwide television the same night telling the nation it faced a "moral crisis"
in race relations and committing the nation to action in support of the
black cause. The assassination of Medger Evers hours after the Kennedy
speech underscored the perception of the civil rights leadership that Kennedy's action was late, arriving when the costs to the black community
were great. The *Times* quoted Washington NAACP official Clarence
Mitchell as being representative of the thinking of the country's blacks.
Evers was dead, Mitchell said, "because the Government of the United
States follows a policy of too little and too late in safeguarding the rights
of colored citizens in the South," a view that was widely held in the black
community.[31]

After Kennedy's assassination, President Johnson moved into office,
bringing at last a sense of governmental direction and commitment to the
civil rights agenda. Immediately after the assassination, Johnson demonstrated his commitment, calling key black leaders within hours of assuming
the presidency and meeting with the top civil rights leadership—Martin
Luther King, Jr., Roy Wilkins, and Whitney Young, among others—within
days.[32] Johnson felt that congressional inactivity in 1963 had "resulted
from lack of firm, determined, unrelenting leadership," and he intended
to provide it.[33] Appearing before a joint session of Congress, five days after Kennedy's death, Johnson pledged the nation's commitment to the

"earliest possible passage of a civil rights proposal that would remove every possible trace of discrimination and oppression" in the nation.[34]

Throwing his full weight behind the civil rights bill, Johnson did what few presidents have done, or been able to do, directly challenging the House Rules Committee by openly backing a discharge petition to pry the bill from the committee's dead hand.[35] There could be "no more dramatic sign" of the president's "determination on this vital issue" than his willingness to confront the congressional establishment by "openly backing the circulation of a discharge petition," said the *Times*.[36] Knowing from his three decades in the House and Senate how odious such pressure from the president was to congressional leaders, Johnson stepped in to fill the government leadership vacuum in civil rights. The sparseness of Congress's record on minority rights had been often attributed to the "fact that the weight of the White House has seldom been brought fully to bear in civil rights debates."[37] Johnson did precisely that in immediately filing the rarely used discharge petition to move the civil rights legislation before Christmas.

Before Johnson's first State of the Union address, there was "something of the zeal and rhetoric of the old New Deal days coming back into the pre-budget debate." James Reston said that the president's cabinet spoke more of jobs and education than it had in months, commending Secretary Wirtz for publicly expressing what President Johnson had been saying in private. Schools were not preparing people for the jobs that needed to be done; job needs had changed. Wirtz pointed out at the University of Michigan that there were, "no longer enough unskilled jobs to take up the school's failures." Reston noted the increasing talk in the administration about emergency measures to attack poverty, "having a special program of education and public works." This was not new, Reston pointed out, but such measures happened "to fit President Johnson's approach to most problems."[38]

While the Kennedy administration had been unforthcoming on civil rights until the issue was inescapable and had ignored the opportunity to address the pressure for jobs coming from the black community in planning for the War on Poverty, Johnson was credibly committed to racial equality and had established good, in some cases warm, relations with the black leadership. He had been predisposed to helping the poor get on their feet and help themselves most of his life, and "nothing in politics appealed more to him than marrying his ambition to help for the poor."[39] His first government job was heading up the National Youth Administration (NYA) in Texas.[40] This experience had left an indelible impression on the young Johnson, who, at age twenty-eight, was the program's youngest state director. He seized on his job with unshakable conviction and fierce commitment to results. He pushed himself—and everyone who worked with him—to the maximum. Working sixteen to eighteen hour days, seven days a week, week after week, Johnson sought to motivate his coworkers "with a sense that they were making history—that they were reaching out to desperate young people whose lives would be profoundly affected by what the NYA did."[41] As vice president, he had wanted President Kennedy to propose government jobs programs for blacks along with the Civil Rights Act.[42]

There is little doubt that Johnson would have liked an antipoverty program centered on jobs measures had it been presented to him as the strong consensus of the task force.[43] In fact, according to Johnson aide Bill Moyers and to Walter Heller, Johnson thought it *was* organized around jobs programs. Adam Yarmolinsky recounts his conversation with Bill Moyers shortly after the bill was passed in August 1964: "I was saying something about community action grants to private agencies. Bill said: 'What do you mean private agencies. None of this money is going to go to private agencies.' And I said, 'My God, Bill! What do you think we have been doing!' He said, 'The president doesn't think that. The president thinks this is like NYA!' Of which he was the administrator."[44]

Walter Heller, when interviewed by Nicholas Lemann years later, also observed that President Johnson was under the impression that the attack on poverty was to be organized around jobs measures similar to the National Youth Administration program he had headed up in Texas during the Depression. Heller said that Johnson envisioned "visible accomplishments." "He had this sort of concrete idea. Bulldozers. Tractors. People operating heavy machinery."[45]. Johnson was also extremely suspicious of the idea of community action when it was presented to him as inchoate, untried, and diffuse. Community action to Johnson did not seem to contain any political capital for legislators in their home districts and had the potential—in its structural separation from city, state, and local political chains of command—to create political resistance. Johnson aide Horace Busby says Johnson finally accepted the idea of community action because it was linked to the Kennedy people and because, had he not done so, he would have been seen as unintellectual and uncommitted to the causes of race and poverty.[46]

Walter Heller, however, refused to accept the structuralist thesis of the need for jobs measures to eradicate hardcore unemployment, although Wirtz continued to struggle for jobs measures in the task force. As I have argued, there was not a firm consensus on jobs in the task force because the die was cast early on in the Heller phase of planning. Had Heller's 1963 poverty planning committee under Kennedy accepted the need for large-scale jobs programs—forcefully advocated by Wirtz—as the central antipoverty strategy, the idea could have come through the Shriver task force to be presented to President Johnson with strong consensual backing.

RACE, INSTITUTIONAL RACISM, AND PUBLIC POLICY

Three questions guide us through the difficult task of deciding what kind of cues race provided as planning for the War on Poverty evolved: What role did race play? What is institutional racism? Why did an antipoverty initiative arise in the first place?

Retroactively, some scholars and students of the civil rights era have argued that the poverty program was undertaken as a political response to emerging black needs in society, a response to real or anticipated urban unrest, or as a means to secure the Democratic black vote.[47] In a series of books and articles detailing the efforts of social groups and movements to bring about responsive public policy, Frances Fox Piven and Richard Cloward have been strong proponents of such views. They argue that the War on Poverty was a political necessity, created, on the one hand, to drain off rising discontent in much the same way the 1935 Wagner Act was passed to circumvent building labor unrest and the growing appeal of radical unionization initiatives and, on the other hand, to consolidate a necessary Democratic voting constituency. But this view is not consistently borne out by the historical record or by the conflicting assessments of the antipoverty policymakers themselves.

Daniel Patrick Moynihan, Hugh Heclo, Charles V. Hamilton, and Ira Katznelson set the context for understanding the approach to poverty and policy in the United States. Moynihan posited a small policy world of pragmatic and calculating elites seeking showpiece domestic legislation.

Heclo described policy outcomes as an accident of political conjuncture. New Kennedy people came into government with fresh approaches, and innovative ideas were put into circulation. In part they were motivated by a desire to move the government forward, responding to the dearth of initiatives in the second Eisenhower administration. So motivated, Kennedy and his advisers were concentrating on his second term and shaping a bigger mandate in the 1964 election to give him the leverage he wanted to move forward. Despite his awareness of the need to shore up the black urban Democratic vote, Kennedy's political concerns were more focused on the conservative vote than on the black vote in this period. His incipient concerns about the black vote were tied to his need to increase his Democratic support in Congress in order to go further in the next administration and tighten up the Democratic urban constituency. There was no real threat to a Democratic black vote in 1963 or in 1964 once radical Republican Barry Goldwater received the Republican nomination, shutting out moderates Nelson Rockefeller, Henry Cabot Lodge, and William Scranton.

Charles Hamilton provided a cautionary reminder that the American ethos permitted opportunity, not redistribution. Inevitably, some would seize opportunities and succeed, and some would fail. Inequalities in American society are fair, insofar as the opportunity for mobility is present. Therefore, it never was intended by these policy makers to eliminate poverty. Indeed, from its inception, the War on Poverty was never framed around the idea of economic redistribution. In June 1963 economist Robert Lampman, responding to an early request from Walter Heller for help in shaping the antipoverty initiative, cautioned Heller that "probably a politically acceptable program must avoid completely any use of the term 'inequality' or the term '*redistribution* of income or wealth.' "[48] The planners' thinking emphatically did not include concerns of restructuring society. The poverty program was not redistribution oriented but directed toward providing services. The services were new, to be sure, but the service orientation was carried over intact from the fifties. The idea was to foster initiatives to promote opportunities (hence the name Economic Opportunity Act) for the poor to take advantage of the expanding economy that existed, preparing people for available jobs. And, of course, with an expanding economy the issue of redistribution could be sidestepped. The Kennedy initiatives in the War on Poverty were packaged in the rhetoric of a new era, the "New Frontier," but the idea of placing the interests of any group, and certainly in 1963 not a politically secured group like the black community, over mainstream interests was plainly not the priority.

While all these views are valid, so too is Ira Katznelson's notion of silences, which speaks not only to the inherent economic limits of American policy making but also to the role of race and the racial motivations of the planners as well. For just as economic options such as redistribution were not thought, so too full racial equality (especially in the economic sphere) was not thought, even by well-intentioned liberals.

The Policy Makers

Although in the end the formulation of the Economic Opportunity Act of 1964 bridged two presidencies and was shaped by hundreds of policy actors, its important dimensions were first conceived by key individuals in the Kennedy and Johnson subpresidencies—as discussed in earlier chapters—and by the Shriver task force, which formalized the ongoing work on antipoverty strategy. Sargent Shriver picked up the initiative after February 1, 1964, when Johnson announced his appointment heading up the War on Poverty, designating Shriver as special assistant, to report directly to the president. Although Shriver had vigorously objected to Johnson's insistence that he lead the task force—preferring to continue angling for the vice presidential slot—the appointment pleased Johnson for a number of reasons. Shriver, who had successfully headed up the Peace Corps and was still its director when Johnson strong-armed him into taking over the War on Poverty leadership, had direct positive leadership qualities. In particular, he had the ability to muster and disperse the necessary forces to get an antipoverty bill enacted in Congress. He was a capable speaker and lobbyist and was skillful at identifying the needs of his audience with the aims of his program.[49] Like Johnson, Shriver was a master of face-to-face persuasion.[50] This was a key consideration since, even though Johnson would have a Democratic congress after 1964, the first since 1936, votes for the antipoverty program were still going to be hard to come by. In addition, in Johnson's mind, Shriver, who was brother-in-law to both President Kennedy and Attorney General Robert Kennedy through his marriage to their sister Eunice, became his own co-opted Kennedy appointee, a competition that was never far from his thoughts, especially before the transition to his own presidency, which he sought—and got—in a 1964 electoral landslide.

The Task Force

The use of task forces for domestic policy innovation was one of the chief administrative legacies of the Johnson presidency. While Kennedy had used the task force in the transition period to his presidency and sporadically thereafter, it became a central feature of domestic policy making in Lyndon Johnson's White House.[51] Through his wide use of task forces Johnson replaced the previous process of legislative program development, in which agencies and departments produced proposals that were first submitted to the BOB and the White House staff and then to the president. Johnson knew from his congressional and legislative branch experience the limits of traditional legislative methods in generating new and innovative ideas.[52] He believed the mandate of the 1964 election, not just in his presidential victory—his 61 percent of the vote was the greatest victory of any presidential election in modern history—but in the great change in the composition of Congress as well, was evidence of the nation's wish for and acceptance of representatives and policies that would confront the serious domestic problems ahead.[53] As a means of finding innovative answers and approaches to these problems, the instrument of the task force was indispensable.

Given the pressures with which the task force had to contend to pull together a new and unique program for a new president and administration thrust into office by a catastrophe many Americans felt was equal in magnitude to the Depression and World War II, it is little wonder that chaos and sheer confusion characterized its day-to-day operations. The task force was literally homeless for its first months. It started out temporarily on the fifth and twelfth floors of the Peace Corps building, moved from there to the old Court of Claims Building at the corner of Seventeenth Street and Pennsylvania Avenue, and was hastily evacuated from there to the old hospital building on Virginia Avenue and C Street one afternoon when the foundations of the building were rendered unstable by the nearby construction of the New Executive Office Building. The task force's planning and operating funds were no steadier at the outset. Everything—people, office space, typewriters, supplies—was borrowed from other departments; scrounging "was an important part of the operation." Nevertheless, ad hoc as its arrangements were, the task force could count on sufficient White House support that, no matter how reluctant the existing departments were to relinquish them, it got the staff it sought.[54]

There seems to be virtually universal agreement among former members of the Shriver task force on the exhilarating environment of that fluid working policy group. The task force is described as chaotic, eclectic, open, free flowing, unstructured, enthusiastic, heady, optimistic, highly charged, rushed, panicked, and intellectual, as an "idea-filled experience," "full of turmoil and creativity." Decision making was characterized by confrontation and conflict; ideas were hotly exchanged and fought over.[55]

Membership in the task force was in constant motion. While some members would have ongoing identification with particular projects under way, others would be asked to participate, spend a period of time involved in the workings of a group—often guided by no more direction than their own interest—return, or perhaps not return. Many participants describe their experience as literally wandering from room to room until a meeting, discussion, panel, or working group caught their attention and they would link up with that activity. The individuals involved were experts such as income distribution specialist Robert Lampman, who had produced the original working papers on poverty for Walter Heller; academics such as political scientist William Cannon and Harvard's Daniel Patrick Moynihan; bureau leadership and personnel such as Willard Wirtz (Labor), James Sundquist (Agriculture), Anthony Celebrezze (HEW), William Cohen (HEW), and Harold Horowitz (HEW); lawyers from the Justice Department, such as Norbert Schlei, who drafted the legislation; labor organizers and community activists such as Jack Conway and Richard Boone; journalists and writers such as Paul Jacobs and Michael Harrington; and great numbers of young people drawn from across the government who, attracted by the energy and agenda of the task force, would come to work there after a full day's work at their agencies. While a clear-cut division of labor on the task force is indiscernible, many staffers and participants have described it as roughly divided into theorists and problem solvers—people who did intellectual work and those who specialized in implementation. Norbert Schlei, for example, was a lawyer from the Justice Department who had drafted a lot of legislation. He was brought over to the Task Force because he was thought of as "someone who could get a lot of people together and draw on their ideas and put it together into a piece of proposed legislation with the backup paper and documentation."[56]

Shriver, who never envisioned running the day-to-day management of the task force and by all accounts would have been terrible at it appointed Defense Secretary Robert McNamara's special assistant, Adam Yarmolinsky, as his number-two man, and it was Yarmolinsky who actually ran the task force operation.[57] Shriver needed a second in command like Yarmolinsky. The men had two radically different styles. Shriver was enthusiastic, charming, and persuasive.[58] His manner was intense, personal, and uneven. Shriver generated explosions of innovative ideas but had little patience or ability to sift the good ones from the bad. His working technique was open and fluid in the extreme, and he disliked fixed organization.[59] The chaotic ways of the task force reflected his own personal style. He was not a methodical administrator, working in "bursts of tremendous creativity and energy."[60] In contrast, Yarmolinsky, as sharp and thorny as Shriver was charming, kept everything on track, supplying precisely those elements that Shriver lacked. He was the key figure in developing the legislation and the program, pulling together the staff, and picking up the pieces strewn by Shriver's erratic command.[61] With the very disruptive exception of a long absence resulting from a serious automobile accident, Yarmolinsky was always there. He headed up working sessions, deciding with Shriver what direction the task force efforts would follow, gave assignments, provided continuity and follow-up, called meetings—often at midnight—and, all in all, ran the whole program.

There exists no better example of the liberal impulse that drove policy makers in the frenzied atmosphere of the task force than Adam Yarmolinsky. He had come to the Kennedy administration through the Defense Department, which, under Robert McNamara, was staffed with a self-consciously brainy and technocratic corps of experts mined from the Rand Corporation. Yarmolinsky had been influential in several ways at the Defense Department, but in particular he was instrumental in declaring segregated facilities—bars, restaurants, taverns, and other facilities—off limits to military personnel in the South. The policy created an uproar in southern congressional districts because of the prevalence of military bases in the South and the numbers of commercial establishments that had grown up around them.[62] At McNamara's suggestion, Shriver brought Yarmolinsky over to run the task force as his chief assistant.

Shriver's chief assistant has retroactively described the initiative that fueled the Kennedy administration's adoption of civil rights and the anti-poverty program as "99 & 44/100 percent noblesse oblige," reflecting his measure of the essential fairness and the essential limits (and perhaps essential purity) of the liberal worldview.[63] A program to aid the poor was something appropriate to do, and it made sense, in particular since the companion legislation to the Economic Opportunity Act, the tax cut won by the CEA in 1963, would not benefit the poor who did not have enough income to pay taxes.[64] To the extent possible, given the competing pressures and constraints, an antipoverty initiative reflected a vision of what seemed right and what ought to be done and what could be done. As Martin Rein has said, there was a desire to do something that would help the blacks, but "the acceptability of a war on poverty (it barely passed the strongly Democratic congress) is in doubt, the acceptability of a program to aid blacks is in doubt. Yet the desire to do something is there."[65] Good intentions aside, we are still left with the question of why they seized on an antipoverty initiative instead of jobs programs, which is what blacks had been seeking for decades and concertedly in this period.

INSTITUTIONAL RACISM

> But when it comes to "institutional racism" (which a hell of a lot of people—liberal and conservative—don't want to admit to) the standard of proof is always going to be exceptionally high.
> —CHARLES HAMILTON

Why is it so difficult for scholars to talk about institutional racism? Comparatively little scholarly research exists on the subject, and much of it is dismissed in academe as unserious.[66] One of the many consequences of the long silence between Daniel Patrick Moynihan's "Report on the Negro Family: The Case for National Action" (interpreted widely in the black community as an attack on black families, culture, and adaptation) and William Julius Wilson's *The Truly Disadvantaged* twenty-two years later was the closing off of frank discussion about key aspects of the relationship among racism, culture, and public policy.[67] Although much heated rhetoric filled the interregnum, two-way analysis of institutions and their policy outcomes was absent. Such outwardly self-induced censorship took a burgeoning discussion of institutional racism off the agenda as well. The problem presented by this absence of systematic intellectual vetting—which includes research, debate, refereed publication, criticism, and rebuttal—is the difficulty of knowing what institutional racism is, much less identifying how it operates in the creation of public policy.

Stokely Carmichael and Charles V. Hamilton, who, in *Black Power*, gave the phenomenon its name in 1967, provided the original statement on institutional racism.[68] Racism, according to the authors, can be either overt or covert. It can be a product of individual acts of violence or discrimination—by whites, for example, against blacks, as when black churches are bombed or black families who move into white neighborhoods are harassed and threatened. A second type of racism, though, is less overt, more subtle. This institutional racism is embedded in "the operation of established and respected forces in the society" and includes those political, economic, and governmental practices and institutions that operate to preserve racial inequalities.[69] Institutional racism does not necessarily stem from individuals' intentional motivations to maintain the racial status quo, but the very fact of the deeply embedded racial inequalities that remain unaddressed by government is evidence that it exists. In Carmichael and Hamilton's formulation, the consequences of persistent poverty, including the gross economic, educational, health, income, employment, and housing inequities that characterized ghetto communities, were in and of themselves evidence of institutional racism.

It is these consequences of institutional racism that induced sociologist Stephen Steinberg to excoriate liberal-minded social scientists and policy makers for their temporizing on the race issue over the last half century. In *Turning Back: The Retreat from Racial Justice in American Thought and Policy*, Steinberg argues that the failure to remedy the consequences of the economic and social inequalities of race derives from the hypocrisy and faint-hearted commitment of liberal policy makers and social scientists genuinely to transform black-white power relations. "Blacks have had to overcome not just the vicious opposition of their political enemies," he reminds us, "but the well-intentioned counsel of 'friends' who, whether inspired by utopian ideals or swayed by practical politics, actively discouraged the aggressive pursuit of civil rights."[70] Of the many arguments Steinberg makes, two in particular are relevant here. First, he uncovers and traces the liberal tendency in the post–World War II period to ignore, deflect, and/or marginalize black efforts to press their own agenda forcefully and in their own terms in the realms of civil rights, scholarship, public policy, and employment. Second, he unflinchingly confronts the phenomenon he calls "Occupational Apartheid" as "the essence of racial oppression" in the United States.[71] American apartheid lies in "a racial division of labor, a system of occupational segregation that relegates most blacks to work in the least desirable job sectors or that excludes them from job markets altogether."[72] While his discourse on the dual labor market is not unique, Steinberg effectively demonstrates the disagreement between white and black scholarship and interpretation of the economic effects of racism and the priority of employment in furthering full citizenship for the black community. Whereas liberal social science scholarship has treated "discrimination as a by-product of racial prejudice, and therefore focused on rooting out prejudice rather than addressing the issue of employment discrimination directly," in contrast, "employment discrimination has always been in the forefront of black thought and politics" (as I demonstrated in chapter 4).[73] Steinberg's criticisms of the failure to validate the black economic agenda is not limited to liberals; even leftists, he points out, have been reluctant to confront the job discrimination that has resulted from working-class racism. Nor were the confrontational academic politics of the 1960s better able to address and specify concrete solutions for employment segregation, choosing instead to offer biting but purposeless condemnations at high levels of abstraction of "racist society" and "the system." Steinberg similarly challenges liberal governmental policy makers for consistent failure to promote the black economic agenda effectively. As Steinberg says, "[For] all its carping about the work ethic, white society has consistently turned a deaf ear to the desperate pleas for jobs that emanate from the black community."[74]

Yet while Steinberg's unflinching challenge to the complacency beneath the liberal worldview and his hard-hitting, no-nonsense criticism are refreshing counterpoints to self-serving liberal apologetics ("99 & 44/100 percent noblesse oblige"), his own critiques tend to rail against "the system" broadly and polemically, and his candid condemnation of liberals is not altogether fair, not reasonably taking into account the political facts and factors with which the liberal racial agenda had to contend. Robert Lieberman's methods in his work on race and the American welfare state balance both the broadness and the polemics that accompany claims of institutional racism and the apologetics of liberalism. Looking at the critical juncture in U.S. state development when the primary institutional structures of the welfare state were created by the Roosevelt administration in the Social Security Act of 1935, Lieberman—whose concern is to explain how African Americans were disadvantaged in the political calculations that attended the birth of the welfare state—concentrates on the structural conditions that underlay the choices political actors were able to make in devising old age insurance. He explicates the "institutional rules, norms, and other patterns of political life" that condition the choices political actors make. Lieberman notes, for example,

> the committee structure of Congress and the seniority system; the two-thirds rule for Democratic presidential nominations; the one-party South; the policy legacies of mothers' pensions and unemployment insurance; among others. Taken cumulatively, these factors privileged certain interests at the expense of others; in particular, they tended to privilege the power of Southern whites, who held the keys to power in Congress and the Democratic Party. Thus the strategies of all the players in the Social Security Act drama were shaped by a context largely dominated by a group for whom preserving racial domination was paramount.[75]

As Lieberman demonstrates, it is difficult to overstate the political, social, and economic disadvantages confronting African Americans attempting to further their interests in the establishment of social security legislation, which initially excluded the majority of black workers because they were employed primarily in the agricultural or domestic sectors of the workforce. Lieberman points out that only one (northern) member of Congress was black; southern blacks were disenfranchised and exerted no political influence over their region's representatives; the power of northern blacks over their elected representatives was curtailed by their limited participation and influence in urban politics; and, without the backing of a valued voting constituency, elite organizations such as the NAACP wielded little effective power over legislative struggles. In the end, the Social Security Act of 1935 left out agricultural and domestic workers.

Lieberman delineates the role played by race in the politics of social security legislation. He reveals the causes and consequences of racial politics in 1935, detailing the conditions, factors, assumptions, and deals that shaped political decision making—all disadvantaging the black agenda. Not only does his analysis corroborate the existence of institutional racism and the way it is embedded in "the operation of established and respected forces in the society," it confirms the inherent limits of liberalism.[76] His methods can be drawn on to explain black disadvantage in examining the assumptions and decisions that attended political decision making in planning the War on Poverty legislation.[77] Borrowing from Steinberg's confrontational mode of bringing the racial treason of liberals to light and Lieberman's method of bringing out the facts of institutional failures to back up racial goals, we can return to the task force and its policy makers equipped to discern the workings of institutional racism at the origins of the War on Poverty.

"DO-GOODISM"

It would be difficult to exaggerate the disadvantage faced by blacks in securing the important jobs and employment policies commitment they sought from government. Still, difficult as it was, the black agenda was better situated in 1963 than it had been in 1935 and would be better still in 1964. Not only was congressional representation greater, the southern bloc's stalemate of progressive legislation in the Senate was harder to come by, since aroused public opinion favored an end to the suppression of civil rights and civil liberties in the South. Another plus was the election of two liberal Democratic presidents, one of whom ostensibly supported their agenda (Kennedy) and the other of whom did so (Johnson). The Johnson election had also brought, in particular, the House majority position so sorely needed by the Democrats. In addition, the strength and cohesiveness of blacks in and around the civil rights movement was of another order of magnitude from their collective strength in 1935. In the South, their voting participation had risen to about 40 percent, and far more blacks were living, and voting, outside the South since their WWII exodus seeking employment in northern cities. Even though life in the North was virtually segregated, at least blacks could take advantage of the wartime need for manpower, and they could also vote, so their electoral strength was greater.[78] Furthermore, 1963 and 1964, as I have shown in this book, saw the coming together of a domestic initiative bridging the administrations of two presidents that could have had major consequences for black Americans. Yet in spite of this more favorable position in the legislative scheme, the fact was that the seniority system was still in place and southern feudal control of key committees remained. Even more important, though, was how these factors affected the decision making of the individuals who would be the champions of their agenda—in the present case, liberal policy makers in the Shriver task force—and compromised their conception of the possibilities and paths to racial inclusion. While the fluidity and openness of the task force permitted consideration of a wide range of policy ideas, in the end the War on Poverty legislation would have to be passed on Capitol Hill. In particular, this was the concern of Shriver, whose job it was to push the legislation through.

A number of political, racial, and budgetary issues were faced by Shriver, Yarmolinsky, and working members of the task force in formulating the Economic Opportunity Act and by the Kennedy administration in introducing the antipoverty program in the first place. Most of these issues were linked in one way or another. In looking back, a prime consideration is to what extent the War on Poverty was conceived out of noblesse oblige and to what extent it was a political necessity. Answering this question entails looking at both administrations, since the impulse for the poverty program came from Kennedy's administration and its shape and agenda were formulated in LBJ's. Johnson also could have rejected the Kennedy initiative, a choice he did not take, instead making it bigger and showier, as if it were a political asset, not a liability. The poverty program for Johnson was not a political necessity but a political choice. In the case of Kennedy, political necessity could have meant he had to stabilize the black vote for his party to get reelected, since his 1960 presidential contest against Nixon had been stunningly close, or it could have been that the black vote was especially important so he would gain the mandate he did not have in his first administration to get his programs passed in Congress and move the nation forward. Incorporated in the following discussion of these issues is also consideration of numerous competing arguments that have been offered to explain why the idea of jobs policies veered off course in 1963. These include the cost of proposed jobs programs, political deals made by both Kennedy and Johnson to get prized bills through Congress, and the high bureaucratic stakes involved. Moreover, jobs proposals cost too much money; President Johnson was loath to renege on the budget deal he cut with Senator Byrd to get the 1964 tax cut; and the structural liability in the internal disarray in the Labor Department vitiated its sponsorship of job training programs.

COUNTING THE VOTE

The first requirement of any legislation is that it be passed in Congress. For Sargent Shriver, this was the paramount political goal. In the Johnson White House the legislative agenda was chiefly handled by White House legislative aides Michael Manatos—as liaison with the Senate's Democrats—and Henry Wilson—the House congressional liaison head—both under Lawrence F. O'Brien, the president's special assistant for congressional relations. In shepherding a bill successfully through the congressional voting process, attention is keenly focused on one factor: head count. While concerns about the legislative viability of the War on Poverty bill were ever-present as the shape and content of the legislation were hammered out, it was not until the task force had a specific bill in its hands that the salience of the head count came into play. The fate of the Economic Opportunity Act could not have been in better hands than those of Shriver, O'Brien, Manatos, and Wilson; and it could not have found better presidential stewardship than Johnson's. In the Senate, Democrats outnumbered Republicans 67 to 33; in the House, 258 to 177. Mike Manatos, who acted as the sole White House Senate liaison in both the Kennedy and Johnson presidencies, credits Johnson's extraordinarily successful legislative record to two factors: the plain fact of the numbers in the Democratic Senate and House after the 1964 election and the instinctive feel for politics and numbers of both Larry O'Brien and President Johnson. Johnson's, O'Brien's, and Manatos's instincts seem to have dovetailed into shared recognition of the essential need for personal contact with legislators, presidential availability for personal meetings with legislators, persistence, and energy. In particular, presidential availability seems to have been a critical factor in gaining successful head counts. Manatos recounts how in the Kennedy and Johnson years, any senator who wanted to see the president could do so readily: the presidents were available to any member of congress without formality or delay. Furthermore, in the case of Johnson, his incredible energy, stamina, attention to detail, and extensive congressional experience were incalculable assets in achieving his legislative goals. "Lyndon Johnson knew exactly what was going on all the time," said Manatos. Johnson also benefited in the Senate from shared recognition and respect for "his knowledge of the government and the whole area of government," even among the Republicans who opposed him. Moreover, Johnson was so thorough in his knowledge of legislation, and so interested in even the smallest piece of legislation. As long as it was on [his master] list, he wanted you to go out and win it. He'd go over the list with you and say, "Well, what are we doing about this? Where are we here, and where are we there? What are we doing?" As a consequence, you'd sometimes get sixty, seventy, eighty bills on that list, and he knew them all. He knew just exactly where they were, and he'd follow them.

Johnson's attention to detail was so great that Manatos would try to stay away from giving him an explicit head count because "if I told him we were going to win a vote by 56–44, and we won it by 58–42, well, he'd say, 'You know, Mike, you were two votes off.' "[79]

As for the Economic Opportunity Act, getting the legislation passed in Congress entailed dealing with the southern question. How would they get the proposed bill past the fiefdom of the southern Democrats? One brilliant maneuver was Shriver's convincing Democratic Congressman Phil Landrum of Georgia to cosponsor the bill in the House Education and Labor Committee, which was under the chairmanship of the flamboyant and headstrong congressman Adam Clayton Powell. Landrum, a highly respected and powerful representative, had been chosen to introduce the bill and be its floor manager. A leading southern Democrat, he was the most powerful southern congressman on the committee. Securing his sponsorship meant there would not be any Democratic opposition to the bill.[80]

Shriver's strong personal advocacy in support of the bill and his establishment of a new pattern of personal diplomacy in pushing for its passage had the adverse effect of tying the bill's success to his continued involvement with the poverty program. He did not want to take on the role of director of the OEO. He had been literally bullied by Johnson into running the task force and did not want to continue as the program's director. Shriver's interests at the time were in the vice presidency, and he saw his job as head of the task force as limited to putting together the legislation and getting it passed.

Shriver saw his role from the beginning as the salesman. And very early in the program—as some of you who were involved will remember—Shriver went up, started going up on the Hill at 9 o'clock in the morning and not coming back till 7 or 8 o'clock at night, or not coming back at all. . . . He was thinking not only of having to sell it in order to get the votes this time—and parenthetically, the count was very close and until the very end our best count was against us by a small margin—[but also to] have the kind of program that will produce results next year [for reauthorization].[81]

Shriver was so thoroughly focused on getting the legislation through that he met personally with every single member of the Senate and House in lobbying for its passage. Although in the end he did run the OEO, before the legislation's passage he expected that someone else would head up the program. He had no deputy director at the time, although it was widely assumed that Adam Yarmolinsky would move into the position of director if he did not become Shriver's deputy director after passage of the act. A cruel irony of the bill's passage, and one that—it was widely agreed by members of the task force—would go on to have negative consequences for the outcome of the poverty program under the OEO, was that Yarmolinsky was sacrificed by Shriver, at the insistence of the southern bloc, to achieve passage of the Economic Opportunity Act. When it came down to the crucial vote, the cost of the southern votes—which came "like a bolt out of the blue"—was that Yarmolinsky would have no involvement in the poverty program. In addition to his role in integrating southern military facilities, Yarmolinsky's background drew southern hostility.[82] His mother, Babette Deutsch, was a well-known communist; he was Jewish, an intellectual, and Ivy League educated (at Harvard), all factors certain to be a magnet for southern ire in 1964.[83] Getting the votes necessary to pass the bill required jettisoning the program's most expert and effective potential administrator.

THE PROBLEM OF RACE

In terms of race, for the most part, if not wholly, the task force was headed up and staffed by individuals who could be described as politically liberal, progressive, or radical, so whatever racial tensions were present in the policy-making environment—and there were many—internal liberal versus conservative rifts did not produce them. In both the Kennedy administration's committee under Walter Heller and the Johnson administration task force, race may have been explicitly in the minds of policy makers in a variety of ways. There was a desire to help racial minorities but uncertainty as to how to do this, and there was worry about the overt racial prejudice of the blacks' enemies (the southern bloc) defeating liberal efforts to help them; there was concern about locking up the black vote for the Democratic Party; there was fear that blacks would jeopardize their own well-being if they continued to push stridently for inclusion; there was fear that a white conservative backlash might threaten Democratic electoral fortunes or Democrats' ability to propose progressive legislation.

The problem of race ran in a number of directions. Would blacks hurt their own agenda if they did not cool off and slow down their increasingly aggressive insistence on civil rights and jobs? Or, for Kennedy, would they hurt his agenda to get reelected with the mandate he needed to pursue his programs in his second term? Or was racial disturbance the reason that Johnson enacted the poverty program in the first place, as Piven and Cloward have argued? Yet Kennedy's concern about the urban black vote (there was no insecurity about the southern black vote) logically would have been to increase his mandate for his second term, so he could move the nation forward, passing the legislation he sought. There was nowhere else the black urban vote was going to go in 1963. If blacks needed to be appeased for other reasons, for Kennedy, it was because of his fears that civil rights legislation would be endangered by aggressive black activity; in particular, he was highly concerned that the August 1963 march on Washington—which turned out to be a picnic—would threaten passage of the Civil Rights Act. For Johnson and the Shriver task force, in spite of Piven and Cloward's arguments, concerns about urban unrest in 1964 do not seem to have the importance it did for Kennedy.

Without doubt liberal policy makers in both administrations wanted to construct a poverty program that would benefit blacks but to do so without creating a controversial race-based subsidy sure to draw fire from any number of directions and, in particular, to alienate Southern whites. Republicans could make it an inflammatory issue in the election, and the southern bloc would readily vote down an explicitly race-oriented program that would provide means for economic independence to very poor southern blacks. This would have the effect of weakening the iron hand Southerners had over their black workforce. Therefore, the Economic Opportunity Act did not highlight race. It was in no way what we would call today a targeted program. The anticipated benefits for northern urban ghettos were not discussed in its promotion; concentration instead was on rural and Appalachian areas as the prototype.[84] This is borne out by the documentary evidence.

Although it is clear that policy makers took efforts to downplay the issue of race, it is less clear why they did this. Were they thinking of the viability of the poverty program in Congress, or were they seeking a way to dispense a handout to blacks to tighten their electoral grasp on the black vote? Both arguments have been made. David Zarefsky points out that, because the Democrats had won the 1960 election by a slim margin, the black urban vote had gained in importance, as Democrats sought to solidify the loyalty of urban blacks. He makes the point that one way to do this was to assure them of federal largesse, yet in such a way that whites not be alienated. So, "programs in aid of the poor must mute the question of race, translating it into terms which would command biracial support."[85] Yet Zarefsky also notes the lack of clarity as to how aware of or how motivated by these electoral concerns members of the Johnson administration were. And the documentary evidence confirms just how ambiguous this issue is as former participants directly contradict one another on the point.

What is at issue here is, did the presidential administrations—and it is Johnson's that is most relevant—want the poverty program to have (as Moynihan in his book, *Maximum Feasible Misunderstanding*, quotes Johnson as saying) immediate programs for Negros and want them to be visible, and, if so, why? Shriver also announced from the beginning of his association with the task force that he wanted a program that "would move fast, be visible and have an impact."[86] According to Piven and Cloward, both at the Brandeis conference and in their writings on the subject, the president's insistence on a visible, high-impact program of special benefit to blacks stemmed from his concerns about the black vote and the 1964 election, as well as about potential urban unrest and how that would affect the election. Adam Yarmolinsky denies that Johnson's and Shriver's wishes for high-impact programs were a result of the '64 election but claims that they were necessary "in terms of the impact on the first session of the succeeding Congress," so that when the second-year appropriations for the poverty program came around, Congress would not cut it off.[87] Shriver's evaluation of the potential for the salability of community action programs in Congress was "it will never fly."[88] His meaning, according to Yarmolinsky, was that they could not possibly survive the second-year appropriations process.[89] "That it will not accomplish enough to give the program the momentum it will have to have to survive, specifically. And he was thinking—now, everybody bases his decisions on his primary experience. Shriver's primary experience at that point was the Peace Corps. And he was thinking if the Peace Corps had started off this way, we wouldn't have gotten the second year's appropriation. So he wasn't thinking about electoral impact."[90]

Most direct participants in both the Kennedy and Johnson phases of the antipoverty initiative acknowledge awareness of the events taking place in society in 1963, in particular insurgency among blacks, but viewed them as part of the contextual environment rather than as dynamic causes for their particular legislative agenda. (Evidence for the validity of this view might be in the fact that they seemed to miss entirely the content of much of the black protest, which was focused on jobs and employment policies.) So, for example, William Capron relates:

> I think that certainly in the minds of a few of us, the reelection campaign of '64 was in our heads. We knew that it would be death—I think we thought, I shouldn't say we knew—we thought that it would be death to bill any kind of program as a help-the-blacks program. But that doesn't mean that we didn't realize that this program was very important in terms of the black vote, just to make that perfectly clear. Now, we did not articulate it that way. We used Adam's phrase . . . in January of '64 several times pointing out that most of the poor aren't black and most of the blacks aren't poor.[91]

Although they were aware of the political liability of a black-oriented program—it was a risk to be cushioned to the greatest extent possible—it also brought political benefits. But since in this case the costs might well have exceeded the benefits, why would they go on to focus on a poverty program? William Cannon's answer is that they were "responding to a program that the president [Kennedy] felt that he wanted to do and could stand on politically."[92] The president, according to Capron, "was persuaded politically that, having made his major '63 domestic program a tax cut which helps the middle and upper income people, that the next piece had to be something to help people that didn't have enough income to pay taxes. And that's the way it was put directly by Heller—just as simple as that."[93] Fred Hayes, who worked in the U.S. Housing Department and in the OEO during the period, expands Capron's account of motivation with

> one basic underlying factor. . . . On the political aspect, it seems to me, of both the poverty program and the civil rights program—and even to some extent the programs that were distinctly urban—is that the administration, I think realistically, really regarded them as things that, in terms of congressional attitudes, were political liabilities not advantages. You know, there really is some commitment of soul, some kind of responsibility for being the more left of the two political parties, something in the way of real social conscience.[94]

Furthermore, Hayes points out, on the poverty program itself, not one mayor in the country, with the possible exception of Jerome P. Cavanagh in Detroit, asked for the program or expressed confirmation to the administration that they needed it for their black constituencies. "They didn't see this constituency as a basic problem in their own political situations. And in the Congress, the presumption, I think, is of a hostile response on practically everything of this kind."[95]

For Adam Yarmolinsky, virtually the only important motivation was noblesse oblige.

> I can't tell you how strongly I feel—I've tried to analyze the factual basis for my feelings, but it comes out of three years of experience—that the stance of the Kennedy administration on civil rights was 99 & 44/100 percent noblesse oblige and that there was no concern whatsoever about holding on to the black vote, about an upsurge of revolt of the masses, that this was entirely a matter of "this is what we've got to do because we're good fellows and we're doing it as fast as we can; we've got to make them slow down because if they go too fast they will negate the gains that we're trying to help them get for themselves." . . . The [Kenneth P.] Kenny O'Donnells of this really cared [that] the most important thing was to make sure that the president could go on and do what he had to do in his second term. Let me just expand this a little bit more. We're aware of the fact that President Kennedy came in without a strong mandate in '60, and a lot of people felt that it was terribly important not that he should continue in office for a second term but that he would have a firm mandate, a big mandate, in '64 so that he could really do the things that he wanted to do in order to move the

THE LIMITS OF NOBLESSE OBLIGE 131

country ahead. But even the people who felt this most in their bones and were most political [Kenny O'Donnell, Lawrence F. O'Brien] were just not worried about [the black vote]. There was no place that the black vote could go. They were worried—and they were worried more than I was worried so I'm more sensitive to it—about the right. That was where the danger was. . . . But the concern that all of ourselves as liberals had were of moving the country at all. Well, the blacks, my goodness, there was just no worry about them at all.[96]

According to Yarmolinsky, concerns that policy makers had about the effects of black insurgency were focused on blacks' own interests in Congress, not the Democratic vote. "There was no concern that I'm aware of that black militancy would take white votes away from the Democrats because . . . there was no feeling of identification with the blacks. The blacks were 'they' not 'us.' "[97] Moreover, the issue of urban riots in summer was not a concern in the Kennedy administration and not a reality until summer of 1964, so the idea of backlash had not emerged yet.

THE PROBLEM OF MONEY

Johnson's first battle with Congress was driving through the Kennedy tax cut. His chief adversary in that contest was Senator Harry Byrd, chairman of the Senate Finance Committee, who adamantly resisted proposals for a federal budget in excess of $100 billion, including the proposed Kennedy budget of $101.5 billion, the first peacetime budget to exceed $100 billion. After wrangling with the Finance chair for months, Johnson reduced the Kennedy target and shaped his own budget—getting it down to $97.9 billion—to satisfy Chairman Byrd, opening the way for congressional action on the tax cut. "Now you can just tell all your friends that you forced the president of the United States to reduce the budget before you let him have his tax cut," he complained to Byrd.[98] The Johnson budget planned to use existing funds and reroute agency appropriations to pay for the new poverty program, and the only new appropriations in the first year (approximately $500 million) were for CAPS. The fact of such parsimonious funding for the first-year appropriation of the poverty program is generally attributed to Johnson's budget deal, and it is frequently argued that, because of this deal, proposals for costly jobs programs were turned away. Yet if the problem was that jobs cost too much and were therefore unviable in the first year, it is also the case that Johnson did not consider the first year as the defining one but as a period in which the program would gain acceptance, especially if it was visible and producing results.

THE PROBLEM WITH LIBERALS

In spite of the ubiquity of evidence of every kind on the prominence of jobs programs on the black agenda, in both the Kennedy and Johnson administrations the subject of jobs programs for black constituents was notable as the dog that didn't bark. And, as is shown by the great pains to which liberal policy makers went to disguise racial concerns, in fact, their cloaking of race in return for safe passage of legislation reified and perpetuated the racial status quo, consigning blacks, as Stephen Steinberg describes it, "to a twilight zone where they are politically invisible."[99] There was debate and argument among bureaucratic chieftains, in particular Wirtz and DOL representatives and allies, about who was going to have the territorial advantage in the poverty program, who would run the Neighborhood Youth Corps, the Job Corps, but outside Wirtz, there was little acknowledgement of the need for employment programs (especially for blacks), or their superiority as antipoverty measures (generally), or of the fact of building social unrest focused specifically on jobs for the black community. Liberal policy makers in 1963 and 1964 did not even hear the calls for jobs. In the scores of oral histories and documentation, there is never a mention of the strong desire expressed by the black community for large-scale jobs-training programs and jobs to meet the Negro job crisis in the way that the New Deal jobs programs were enacted to meet the jobs crisis of the Depression.

Certainly, race was a factor. But, in the Brandeis conference transcript— the only available explicit discussion of the role of race that occurs on the subject among principals and between principals and academic specialists— and other archival materials, retrospective assessments are both unclear and contradictory. The fact of race, the fact that race is an issue, is discussed, but an unambiguous assessment of its impact is impossible. Piven and Cloward's argument for calculated political motivation anticipating or responding to racial protest and disruption is the most analytically coher-

ent argument. Neither of them, however, was directly involved in the task
force, and, like many of their arguments, the interpretation of events they
present serves their hypothesis—in this case, on the efficacy of mass unrest in bringing benefits to disenfranchised people—not the experience of
the task force.

WHY AN ANTIPOVERTY INITIATIVE AT ALL?

Setting aside causal factors such as political needs for domestic programs
or social rest—which both Kennedy and Johnson sought—and leaving out
pure chance, could the antipoverty program have been motivated by, as
Yarmolinsky puts it and seems to believe, "99 & 44/100 percent noblesse
oblige"—in essence, "do-goodism"? Looking back today, it is not easy to
imagine a world in which a minority agenda would be taken on not from
direct political necessity but out of fairness or do-goodism. We wrestle
with the same dilemma when we ask why the framers drew up the Constitution. More than enough calculation was present to cast doubt on the
federalists' attention to the constitution project in 1789. This was a plot
to secure their financial interests, their landed assets, their regional hegemony, a means to shut out ordinary folk from self-determination in governing, to tamp down more radical insurgency. Yet we know, intuitively
as well as from documentary evidence, that it was not only self-regarding
impulses that forced the constitutional moment. Whatever else they were,
these impulses drew on something beyond narrow self-interest and political calculation, although there were plenty of both. Likewise, in addition
to calculation, were such motives at work in the machinations of the liberal framers of the Economic Opportunity Act? In 1963 young people
were not flocking to the task force from scores of agencies—and working
two jobs and eighteen-hour days—because they wanted to effect a marginal increase in Kennedy's black vote from 69 to 80 percent; they were
doing so because they sensed some larger purpose behind the poverty
program initiative. To argue that pure political necessity caused an activity
like this misses the point, according to Daniel Fenn:

> You had a certain kind of group of people there with a certain view of the
> world and a certain view of what was right and what ought to be done. I re-
> member developing a specialized program to put a half a dozen blacks in

visible top agency line position—not in the civil rights division and not in staff positions . . . and we undertook this not because there was any great demand for it from the black community, not because people were saying, "Hey, listen, gee, the 1962 election" or "we've got a black constituency in the cities" or something like that, but at least in our view because, damn it, it was just something that ought to be done and something that hadn't been done. . . . I think that we're straining when we're trying to see a direct political cause for each one of these steps that were taken. These were the kind of people to whom this sort of program would appeal as something which was appropriate and would make sense.[100]

Was political calculation or noblesse oblige behind the impulse to develop a poverty program in 1963? Both may have been involved, but there are obvious and timeless limits to do-goodism. Noblesse oblige can bring about good, often to great effect. Among its shortcomings, however, is the irrefutable fact that the status quo must not be tipped. Would seizing on costly jobs and training programs and making them available to the black poor have been controversial? Possibly, but how much more controversial could the cost problem have been than community action? Benefits versus detractions were bandied back and forth throughout the task force period. Would jobs programs have threatened the status quo? Certainly. The southern bloc would resist challenges to its hegemony over black labor from measures to give blacks an independent base for earning. Labor would resist it. Yet the point is also that the problems created by jobs programs were not irresolvable; certainly, they were no more formidable than CAPS turned out to be. Nonetheless, they are not heard or thought of— outside of Wirtz's attempt and ultimate failure to move jobs to the center of the poverty legislation—because of a lack of political will. Governmental will called for programs, budgetary commitment, and direct acceptance of racial work issues—not political suicide, but political courage. At the heart of institutional racism is the lack of political courage.

Given the limits and contradictions of the evidence available and discussed up until now, an unambiguous charge of institutional racism still remains difficult to make. In the absence of the essential standard of proof of institutional racism, we may rely on our common sense and general knowledge or—in legal terms—judicial notice, "accepting as fact what is general wisdom and accepted knowledge."[101] And from what we know, and what we sense in the American political system, we must inevitably recognize that its bias is, as Henry Cohen tells us, the maintenance of tension: recognition of the delicacy of the social, political, and economic fabric, the need to proceed cautiously so as not to develop rents in that fabric, the concern with a balancing of equities. That balancing is a political task.[102]

WAS THE WAR ON POVERTY A BLACK PROGRAM?

Were Presidents Kennedy and Johnson racist because their administrations failed to get behind critical needs of politically marginal black constituents? Not necessarily. Kennedy's foot-dragging on civil rights may be evidence of institutional racism in Carmichael's and Hamilton's terms, although his political skills were not so confidently held as were Johnson's. Further, Kennedy, unlike LBJ, faced a conservative Congress after winning with the narrowest of margins. But both presidents were also capable pragmatists. Even given his contradictions, Johnson, certainly in the eyes of black Americans, demonstrated more commitment to racial equality and had more political skill at handling Congress. Having experienced deep poverty himself, he was keenly ambitious and able to take the necessary steps to incorporate blacks into full economic citizenship. At the same time, Johnson was a consummate pragmatist who had to contend with Senator Harry Byrd and his budget deal. Therefore, the case is also that high-level commitment by Johnson was still constrained in placing the government resources required to further the black jobs agenda. Does that make LBJ equally culpable of institutional racism? Or is his culpability greater since he, unlike Kennedy, did have the political skills and political will? We have to factor in Johnson's political sense of timing since, although he recognized the political risks of altering mainstream economic opportunities to advantage the poor, he was a skillful judge of the political moment. He *would* get his poverty program; it *would* make him a hero for his time. He was confident that he would get it through Congress and seasoned enough to know, as he told his aides, that he did not have to get it in one big bang.[103] Although the initial appropriation of new money for the EOA was modest, the premise was that once a national commitment had been made, they could go on from there:

This was the first year, after all, and we set something in motion. What we were concerned with then was getting a national commitment to an objective. At that point you don't quibble very much about the specific content of the program. In fact, the more conservative and cautious you are, the more likely you are to get the commitment. But we felt that once the act was passed and the OEO was in being, and the President's leadership at that time on these matters was superb, that these other problems would work themselves out.[104]

Lyndon Johnson's will and goals would have been better served if the structuralist economic argument had prevailed early on and if the poverty program had been organized around jobs. If Wirtz had won his battle with Heller over the economic definition and consequences of long-term unemployment, if he had been better able to administer the transition he sought at the DOL (and gotten the help he needed from the CEA in seizing hold of the department), Lyndon Johnson would have pushed longer and even harder for a jobs-centered War on Poverty. His formative experience at National Youth Administration, his desire to go beyond the unfinished New Deal agenda, his commitment to bringing blacks and browns into the economic mainstream, public receptivity to both an antipoverty initiative and work-related programs, the popularity of work-related legislation in Congress, and his monumental need for recognition and acclaim that would burnish his legacy all pointed to a showpiece poverty program promoting employment with the Johnson imprimatur.

Blacks recognize the governmental will problem better than white liberals do. They also recognized the important distinction between Kennedy's perpetuation of and Johnson's potential to challenge institutional racism. In the Kennedy administration, black allies were sparse. In the Johnson administration, black allies were misplaced at the very top of the political heap when they were needed in the bureaus.[105] Blacks may have had the heart of the president, but the details that would have transformed a potential Johnson-level commitment to racial and economic equality into an antipoverty program with impact were in the hands of the fainthearted liberal policy makers who formulated the poverty program. The interests, thinking, and position of black elites on employment reflected important social forces that were brought to bear on antipoverty policy making in the Kennedy and Johnson administrations. Yet these demands and the strenuous pressure for jobs emerging from the black community were not incorporated into the planning initiative. They were not heard. In the absence of concerted jobs efforts, the black hard-core poor were not going to be helped substantially by the macroeconomic techniques proposed by Heller and the Council of Economic Advisers, who themselves recognized this in offering a service-oriented War on Poverty. The structuralist argument, also recognizing this, diagnosed it as central to the problem of poverty, identifying the extent, depth, and consequences of black unemployment.

Aware of the need to know more about the connection between unemployment and poverty, an issue that had been unsuccessfully thrashed out between Heller and Wirtz at the Joint Economic Committee in 1961 (see chapter 2), in March and April 1964 the task force again turned to Robert Lampman for firmer analysis of this relationship. Lampman remembers the conflict between the Labor Department and the CEA at that time as being particularly sharp, a great deal of tension between people who believed in community action and those who sought the direct creation of jobs, the conviction on Labor's part that the CEA was wrong, Heller and his council's displeasure that they were always out of step with the Labor people, and competition between proposals to increase government spending and Heller's tax-cut proposals.

> Wirtz and other people in the labor movement were very critical of Heller and the Council of Economic Advisors and their emphasis on the tax cut as a way to solve the unemployment problem. There was a big argument about whether the high unemployment of that period was due to structural causes or to cyclical causes. Heller of course argued that it wasn't mainly a structural problem but that it would all melt away rapidly if you got the tax cut in place. Well, I don't think Wirtz ever believed that for a minute. . . . And a lot of other people thought—for example, Galbraith thought—the thing to do would be to not cut taxes but increase government expenditures for programs like job creation and public works and more education and so on.[106]

As he had done before, Heller dismissed the structuralists' claims, or, to the extent he acknowledged them, he did so weakly. Either he did not find them compelling enough to warrant important government jobs intervention or found them an unacceptable threat to his Keynesian agenda to effect a tax cut.

Antipoverty planners were aware of the political climate in which they worked in 1963. It was the year of headline civil rights campaigns in Birmingham, the horrific bombings in that city, the march on Washington, and increasing insurgency focused on jobs and employment in the nation's northern cities, all events pushing home the need for jobs and training in the black community. Antipoverty planners were also aware that the debilities that accompany poverty—unemployment and poor health, nutrition, housing, and education, for example—were more pronounced among blacks even though they did not constitute a majority of the poor population.[107] Oral history records also document policy makers' awareness of active pressure from the black community.

Yes, antipoverty planners' concerns with the acceptability of an antipoverty program did constitute institutional racism as they played politics by dancing between the need to do something because it was right, the need to aid blacks because of increasing pressure coming from the black community, and the need to maintain the black vote, their apprehensions about the 1964 reelection campaign, and their fear "that it would be death to bill any kind of program as a help-the-blacks program" (bowing to what Lieberman calls parochial pressure).[108] These inescapable contradictions of liberal policy making are the content of institutional racism.

Yet between 1961 and 1963 civil rights and related issues affecting the black community received high support in the country.[109] It was national public opinion that helped to turn around the intransigence of southerners with regard to integration and voting.[110] Moreover, the War on Poverty would not have had to be billed as a black program if the program had been centered on jobs programs along the lines envisioned by Wirtz. Johnson had the votes he needed to pass legislation embodying work-oriented programs, and the votes would not have been as hard to come by had jobs measures been at the heart of the legislation rather than social services and controversial, poorly understood community action programs. Conservatives in Congress liked jobs measures and understood structural explanations of unemployment.

Antipoverty planners could have produced a critical program for black Americans and directed the War on Poverty to the catastrophic need for employment in the black community. There was ample evidence in the period of the need for employment initiatives to aid black unemployment and underemployment. There was significant confirmation that jobs were critical from within government in the advocacy of jobs programs by Willard Wirtz and the structuralists in the Labor Department. Confirmation of the need for jobs also came from active protest outside government by the larger black community and from black organizations and their leadership, who had been writing letters, calling for jobs legislation, and negotiating government attention to black unemployment all along.

No, the War on Poverty was not a black program, if such a program was intended to provide the means of economic equality to the black community in 1963. Jobs programs would have constituted a genuine black War on Poverty. As it turned out, the War on Poverty was a program designed by liberals to get across some measure of relief to a constituency seen as "them." It was not an extension of whole-hearted attempts—community action rhetoric aside—to further blacks' own efforts to enter into mainstream economic life. Whether the liberal impulse was do-goodism or calculation is not, on the whole, important. Such as it was, with social service and community organizing programs at its center, the War on Poverty was an offense and detrimental to African Americans, none of whom were present at its creation. Yes, it was perceived as a black program by the white middle and working classes. Yes, liberal Democrats were certainly repaid for their perceived preferential treatment of black Americans by the electoral backlash that installed a Republican president in office for—but for the Carter years—the next five electoral cycles. The influence and viability of liberal Democrats in their party itself were also diminished, as evidenced by the rise of a centrist Democratic Party, the hegemony of the DNC, and the election of Bill Clinton in 1992. Tragically, the greatest cost has been borne by the black community.

Accordingly, what continues to stand out sharply is how limited and equivocal have been the commitments of our presidents to full racial equality. Lyndon Johnson, paradoxically a southerner, remains an exception to this as a president who was paternalistic but credibly committed to effecting economic change for black Americans. Had there been consensus on the technical causes of unemployment and the way it related to poverty, and had the Labor Department been able to administer a large-scale jobs program—crucial "ifs," to be sure—by 1964 Lyndon Johnson was in place as a president who could have seized on the idea of jobs and reversed the historic pattern of government failure to put institutional weight behind legislation that grants substantive economic rights to black Americans.

6. Ideas and Government Policy Making

Tout commence en mystique et finit en politique.[1]

While, as the previous chapters have shown, explanations for the failure of large-scale jobs initiatives reside in the realms of politics, institutional relations, personalities, events, and social forces, there is also the crucial context of the ideas in which policies must find form. This chapter considers further the importance of the prevailing Keynesian economic notions in the early 1960s and the way these framed the idea of jobs policies, undermining their appeal as the preferred government antipoverty strategy during this period.

As this book has shown, three sets of factors—economic, political, and social—together diminished the likelihood that jobs policies would be the central strategy in the War on Poverty. These were the lack of technological consensus early on about the relationship between unemployment and poverty, the incapacity of the Labor Department to administer the type of jobs programs it was advocating, and the incomplete commitment by government—especially during the crucial Kennedy years—to addressing the explicit calls for jobs measures that were especially critical to the poorest part of the black community. Of these factors, however, the most decisive was the lack of consensus in the Kennedy administration on the economic problem of unemployment and its relationship to poverty, which led the administration to accept the particular combination of Keynesian economic ideas that was used to define and frame the problem of poverty. Clearly, these specific ideas were deeply consequential to the War on Poverty.

We are accustomed to considering contextual ideas as underlying or background factors, not direct causal influences on policy making, and relatively little attention has been paid to why specific ideas matter.[2] But ideas can—and do—change the frame of reference through which people see objective situations.[3] It is not enough, however, to recognize that ideas are important to the formation of policy; most people would agree that ideas are significant. A firmer structure must be imposed on the relationship between ideas and public policy.[4] If "we cannot say why one set of ideas has more force than another in a given case, we do not gain much explanatory power simply by citing ideas."[5]

The previous four chapters provided structural analyses of the influence of the idea of jobs policies in three decisive political arenas in which it competed, identifying and examining the critical factors that affected its success, and showing how the structural context of ideas in the period of the War on Poverty shaped—both positively and negatively—the outcome of public policy. Jobs policies failed to find form in public policy as the centerpiece of the War on Poverty because of what happened in these three arenas. Each was important, but not equally so. How, then, can we extrapolate from the story of the idea of jobs policies—the right idea at the right time—to learn what causes specific ideas—such as the economic ideas in the Kennedy administration—to become dominant and eclipse other, more appropriate sets of ideas?

THE FIRST POLITICAL ARENA

The first arena (examined in chapter 2) was the broad realm of economic ideas in which governmental and nongovernmental experts participated. Jobs programs were an answer to the kind of structural unemployment at the heart of the hard-core poverty that hit the black community particularly hard. Willard Wirtz and other structuralists in the Kennedy administration correctly diagnosed this problem and sought to address it through jobs programs; specifically, through formulating the War on Poverty as a larger-scale effort of government jobs programs. But Wirtz's understanding of the extent and consequences of structural unemployment was not shared by Walter Heller and the Council of Economic Advisers, who were the formative influences in conceptualizing antipoverty policy in the Kennedy administration, so that there was a critical lack of expert consensus on this key issue.[6] Their economic definition of poverty and their economic understanding of the way it related to unemployment were ultimately to have the greatest consequences for the War on Poverty.

The idea of full employment was defined in numerous ways. It was often considered in relation to inflation, and it was permitted to fluctuate in the 4 to 7 percent range, accepting as natural an unacceptably high rate of unemployment. Yet, as Willard Wirtz and the structuralists around him argued, there was—and is—no natural rate of unemployment. Economic assumptions, which rationalized high levels of unemployment, were disputable and were necessitated by structural changes in capitalism, reified in the idea of the Phillips curve (and illustrated by the James Tobin quotation that serves as the epigraph to "Unemployment in the Kennedy Administration" in chapter 2), or were the product of wrongheaded economic thinking.[7] Anything greater than 2 percent, which, it has been argued, would represent genuine frictional unemployment—that is, a function of workers changing jobs—was mistaken economics and would not address the kind of hard-core poverty present during this period.

Full employment had become a leading issue since the end of World War II. The Employment Act of 1946, which started out, more ambitiously, as the Full Employment Act of 1945, recognized for the first time an explicit government role and relationship in employment and unemployment.[8] Underlying the act was the fear of the consequences of falling from the full employment of the war years. The law stated that "it is the continuing policy and responsibility of the Federal Government to use all practicable means consistent with its needs and obligations and other essential considerations of national policy with the assistance and cooperation of industry, agriculture, labor, and State and local governments to coordinate and utilize all its plans, functions, and resources for the purpose of creating and maintaining . . . conditions under which there will be afforded useful employment, for those able, willing, and seeking to work, and to promote maximum employment, production, and purchasing power."[9] The act was a departure from past national policy, but it did not represent as great a shift as had been hoped by some proponents of the original 1945 act.

The idea of full employment and a right to employment have been constrained here in the United States.[10] Originally, under the Full Employment Act, a right to employment and full employment were to have been realized through a "National Production and Employment Budget," which Congress was to receive from the president at the start of each session. By taking into account estimates of the size of the labor force, along with the gross national product (GNP) required to employ that labor force fully and the anticipated GNP, the budget was supposed to close any gap preferably by encouraging appropriate action by the private sector or, if necessary, by federal investments or expenditures.[11] The 1946 act was a compromise bill from the Conference Committee on the original 1945 bill, which had passed the liberal Senate in a 75–0 vote. It was defeated in the less liberal House, which countered with the Employment and Production Act of 1946, jettisoning the ideas of a right to employment and national responsibility for full employment.[12]

The Employment Act of 1946 was modeled somewhat on an essay about postwar employment written by economics specialist Leon Keyserling in 1944.[13] With regard to managing employment and economic policy, Keyserling describes the act as a combination of the confusion of the New Deal and the purposefulness of planning during the Second World War. It was to have been a great planning statute providing through the instrumentality of the president's economic reports to the Congress a "great white state paper on economic affairs." The administration, with the assistance of the Council of Economic Advisers and the Joint Economic Committee, was to coordinate the overall national economy in the way the budget process sought to coordinate federal expenditures. "The Employment Act of 1946 was designed to provide the counterpart of the federal budget in the larger field of all of our economic policies." The original intent was that the act "as never before should set forth a completely integrated evaluation of all important national policies affecting the American people and affecting the American economy." Spending, taxing, social security, housing, monetary, farm, international economic, and basic regulatory policies would be integrated into the economic report. Such policies would be directed toward goals of national production, purchasing, and employment. This was consistent with Roosevelt's postwar rhetoric in the 1944 reelection campaign calling for postwar planning and full employment.[14] Ideas like these drew on the wartime work of the National Resources Planning Board and represented "the outer limits of the ongoing political conversation about the future of the welfare state."[15] While fears of unemployment had fueled the Employment Act of 1946, the postwar economic boom pushed these fears into the background, and, as noted previously, it was not until the early Kennedy years that unemployment again loomed large.

The practical definition of unemployment, the tolerance of levels of unemployment that permitted 4 percent of the workforce to be unemployed, and the reliance on particular macroeconomic measures such as the tax cut were all products of the kind of applied Keynesianism of the Kennedy period. This was, according to some analysts, a mistaken application of Keynes that consequently closed off the opportunity for government spending on a large scale, which could have opened the way to a jobs program.

Keynesianism has been frequently misrepresented in this country, and this was the case in the Kennedy administration. Two general issues are involved in this misrepresentation. First, in the United States an incomplete kind of Keynesianism was practiced as understood and implemented by the council under Heller; thus, with no full commitment to planning and government deficit spending in place, the full impact of Keynesian measures has never been realized here.[16] In the Kennedy economic program, as chapter 2 explores, the idea of government spending was shut out by the council's championship of fiscal stimulation measures. Second, Kennedy and his political advisers (Ted Sorensen, Bill Moyers, and Pierre Salinger, for example) misunderstood and resisted the new economic practices. Nor was this just a misunderstanding, as Kennedy's dual set of beliefs and the political constraints he faced played a role as well (see "The Competition of Economic and Political Ideas" in chapter 2).

The case of the tax cut, and the ideas underlying it, is instructive. Leon Keyserling believed that the tax reductions of 1964 were the most egregious mistakes of economic policy made by this country since World War II, making the level of public income incompatible with the priorities and needs of the nation. As a technique to stimulate the economy, tax reductions were the wrong choice. The economy could also have been stimulated by public spending or by splitting it equally between spending and tax reductions. In Keyserling's view, the Kennedy and Johnson economists found it politically easier to get reductions and so chose that route. Tax reductions were the path of least resistance, although, as mentioned earlier, it was not an easy task for the council to convince Kennedy of the need for them. Tax reduction combined with increased public spending was a more logical distribution, says Keyserling, and would have been doable if the president had been willing "to get his nose bloodied a bit." Worse still, according to Keyserling, was that the council started to rationalize its strategy in economic terms, "developing on a nationwide basis spurious economic rationalizations for a wrong policy which befoul[ed] the whole stream of economic thinking." The council's view that tax cuts and increased spending were equally applicable as Keynesian tools to stimulate the economy was flatly wrong in Keyserling's view.[17] To say that the decision to choose a tax cut over public spending did not make a difference overlooks what a federal budget is all about: "The federal budget is not primarily to fight inflation or deflation. . . . [It] is to allocate to the public service what the nation needs and can't do privately. . . . Tax reduction never cleared a slum."

Keyserling considers the misguided War on Poverty a classic example of the consequences of misinterpreted and misapplied Keynesian techniques, standing Keynes on his head. An appropriate economic analysis of poverty at the time would have moved production of income to the center of any antipoverty program. With 40 percent of U.S. poverty a result of unemployment, and 20 percent more attributable to inadequate pay, a poverty program should have "meant the creation of a job program, not job training without jobs at the end of the trail; not asking people on every street corner what they think they might do to get jobs, but a fundamental federal underwriting in the final analysis." A guaranteed federal job program meeting the needs of the public sector was what was needed. Indeed, this would be the finding of the Kerner Commission near the end of the decade. "Jobs are the big thing. How did the President's economic advisers forget it? How did the economic reports forget it? How did the war on poverty forget it?"

The practical effect of the tax cut as a particular Keynesian technique chosen to stimulate the economy was in its consequences for the poor—in particular, the black poor who would have benefited not from tax cuts but from increased public spending through large-scale government job provision and training programs. "It was noted by some commentators and particularly some spokesmen for the poor and particularly the blacks, . . . in 1963, that the tax cut directly didn't do a damn thing for poor people because they didn't have any taxes to be cut."[18] A second practical effect was to close off an obvious means for Johnson to raise revenue for large-scale jobs programs: new taxes. President Johnson would be less open to Shriver's and Wirtz's proposals for new taxes to support jobs programs when at the same time he was cutting costs across government in an effort to keep his budget under $100 billion to counter the image of profligate Democratic spending and pushing Kennedy's tax cut bill in Congress.

While Johnson's deal with Harry Byrd to keep the budget under $100 billion supposedly constrained his ability to commit the large sums that jobs policies would have entailed initially, Johnson, whose 89th and 90th Congresses passed more domestic legislation than any since the New Deal, had more than enough political skills to effect any number of compromises. What is more Johnson—who had built his legislative career through his genius for bargaining and compromise—did not view the Economic Opportunity Act, the first phase of his War on Poverty, as the decisive moment in the establishment of his domestic policy agenda. As he told Richard Goodwin in March 1964, "I'm going to get my War on Poverty. Of course, we can't have it all in one gulp. We'll have to make some concessions, make a few compromises—that's the only way to get anything. But that's this year. I have to get elected, and I don't want to scare people off. Next year we'll do even more, and the year after, until we have all the programs."[19]

THE SECOND POLITICAL ARENA

In the second arena, I have argued that the fate of jobs policies was influenced by lack of administrative ability in the Labor Department to manage large-scale jobs programs effectively (chapter 3). I introduced the administrative problems of the Labor Department in the theoretical context of how historical bureaucratic arrangements affect the acceptance of policy ideas. This thesis about state capacities, however, requires further elaboration of how it applies to the case study of the Labor Department at that time.

Many of the key figures in the formation of the Economic Opportunity Act felt that jobs policies represented the central idea of the War on Poverty. But who would administer jobs programs, and how large and what kinds of jobs programs would they be? Would they be run by Wirtz in the Labor Department, an old-line agency administering a large-scale jobs program, or by a new administering agency, the Office of Economic Opportunity (OEO) under Sargent Shriver, directing the new Job Corps for youth employment? So, to some degree, the story of the War on Poverty was also a familiar story of bureaucratic rivalry, although not purely over who would get the bulk of new programs to administer but over how they would be defined as well. There were other possible bureaucratic competitors for direction of the War on Poverty. The obvious candidates were the departments of Health Education and Welfare under Secretary Anthony Celebrezze and Housing and Urban Development under Secretary Robert Weaver, who was the first black cabinet member. But these two agencies never seriously competed for a central role. Celebrezze struggled with the Labor Department over the administration of jobs programs and was interested in educational programs. But he never coordinated a concerted effort to lay claim to a more central role in the War on Poverty, possibly because the idea of community action programs was antithetical to HEW's service orientation of functional experts—doctors, nurses, social workers—delivering services or income payments directly to individuals.[20] Weaver was more sympathetic to the idea of community action, but HUD's mortgage banking and big finance connections "diverted it from wanting to become a center of a war on poverty."[21]

The issues in this discussion diminish the appeal of a state capacities thesis in a number of ways. In the first place, if the state's capacity was the ultimate determining factor, this still does not explain why jobs failed to be the dominant idea with potential programs being run under the administration of OEO, which was set up both to coordinate the programs of the Economic Opportunity Act and to operate a large program of its own—the Job Corps. In particular, since Sargent Shriver and Adam Yarmolinsky were initially clearly unreceptive to the idea of community action and early on saw that jobs represented the central idea of the War on Poverty, other factors are needed to explain better the failure of the idea of large-scale jobs programs.

Shriver and Yarmolinsky both liked jobs programs. Yarmolinsky, a pivotal figure in the planning of the War on Poverty, has described the Job Corps as a program that expressed "the central idea of preparing poor people to do the kind of work for which society would pay them a decent wage."[22] "The basic problem of poverty" in the period, according to Yarmolinsky, "was making it possible for people to find and hold decent jobs."[23] Shriver and Yarmolinsky were initially quite hostile to the idea of Community Action Programs. Shriver thought the idea would "never fly" and understood (correctly) that community action would be difficult to push in Congress. He was willing to accept Community Action Programs, because they were very heavily promoted and were already an established proposition by the time he became director, but he was not going to see the War on Poverty *as* Community Action Programs.[24] Coordinating agencies, interests, and organizations as chairman of the Chicago Board of Education, Shriver had previously confronted the obstacles in the way of such coordination. Furthermore, he was convinced of the importance of single-purpose programs, "both in terms of being clean and in terms of his ability to describe them, to articulate them," to sell them, in Congress.[25]

While beliefs in the lack of administrative ability in the Labor Department can explain why Wirtz and his vision of jobs programs failed to succeed, and this appears to bear out the state capacities thesis, there are other questions. How, for example, does the establishment of OEO fit into the state capacities thesis? If existing structures and arrangements, or the lack thereof, may explain why policy ideas do or do not take hold, why exactly would the erection of an entirely new and unique office bear out this argument? Existing state apparatuses that already implement policies may bring advantages to particular policy ideas, but the very fact of the acceptance of the untried and unconventional idea of community action and the establishment of the OEO itself are a challenge to this thesis. OEO was a newly created agency with the unconventional mandate of coordinating other full-line agencies of cabinet rank, as well of brokering, or avoiding, existing political channels at the local and municipal level. Not only did it play the central coordination role in the War on Poverty, but it operated the experimental, and soon to become controversial, Job Corps programs as well as other programs.

The evidence reveals misgivings—whether real or calculated—that planners had about the Employment Service and its ability to make the transition to administering effectively large-scale jobs programs on behalf of the poor. In Labor Secretary Wirtz's view (see chapter 3), Shriver and Yarmolinsky were using the secretary's problems with the Employment Service to weaken his considerable claim to the major bureaucratic stakes involved in the War on Poverty and to advance their own agenda for the War on Poverty with administration of the new Job Corps youth employment program coming out of the OEO.[26] They were successful. The story of high bureaucratic rivalry in the planning of the War on Poverty suggests giving attention to at least two attributes of the state capacity thesis: first, the definition of administrative capacity, since the Department of Labor and OEO were both agencies of the state; and, second, the theory's insight concerning the determination of policy ideas, since the story of bureaucratic rivalry does not bear out some presumptions of the thesis regarding state structure, ideas, and public policy.

Do such state capacity arguments, then, advance our understanding of bureaucratic politics, as in the War on Poverty, beyond bureaucratic theories of capture and cooperative federalism such as Lowi's, Grodzin's, and Elazar's work or James Q. Wilson's work on the bureaucratic state, clientelism and self-perpetuating agencies, and triadic power relationships and various theories of subgovernments?[27] In a sense, nearly every story of policy making fits an established description of bureaucratic politics. Particularly in the case of the Labor Department and its problems with the Employment Service, it is possible that the state capacities thesis is essentially another way of recounting existing theoretical perspectives on the problems of bureaucracies.

In the case of the War on Poverty, however, bureaucracies and institutions were less important than the prevailing of ideas themselves. Had his perspective prevailed and his vision of large-scale jobs programs been the central feature of the Economic Opportunity Act of 1964, Wirtz could have acquired the institutional backing he needed to gain control of the Employment Service, which was nearly autonomous and had exceedingly strong ties to Congress's appropriations committees. Wirtz would have welcomed any outside support he could have gotten to rein in his employment service. But, instead of helping Wirtz get control of USES, Shriver, Yarmolinsky, and others used the Labor Department's incapacity to defeat Wirtz and his idea of jobs policies, claiming that he could not effectively control the state agencies, thereby vitiating his idea of large-scale jobs policies. They were especially effective in undermining Wirtz's argument of the need for such programs because of the acceptance of Heller's and the council's analysis of poverty and the way it was related to unemployment. If, in contrast, they had been more open to Wirtz's analysis of structural unemployment, they would logically have had to take the idea of large-scale jobs programs seriously. Does it matter whether Shriver and Yarmolinsky were sincere or whether they were using Labor's incapacity to promote their own agenda? Yes, because a moment was lost and the practical consequences for public policy are immeasurable. This was another political moment—similar to the period in 1945 when the United States could have given form and force to the goal of a full employment economy—combining, in this case, the macro measures of Heller and the concentrated effort of antipoverty measures to pull everyone into the workforce.

THE THIRD POLITICAL ARENA

In the third arena (covered in chapters 4 and 5), the decisive influences on the idea of jobs policies were the lack of governmental will: the government's incomplete commitment to the goal of pursuing full economic citizenship for black Americans. Despite the broad social forces at work, particularly in 1963, the civil rights leadership and black citizens were unable to affect the political agenda by securing a strong and wholehearted response by the Kennedy administration to their demonstrated appeals for jobs. An effective government response would have been to heed the calls for jobs and training and to make jobs policies the central strategy in the War on Poverty, thereby enabling the idea of jobs for the poor to become part of the national purpose in the form of public policy. When the weight of government is placed behind public policy, it determines the alternatives available in society, shapes the policy options we can imagine, affects the national mood in terms of receptivity to new policy initiatives or policy change, and establishes national priorities. The federal government played such a role when it actively intervened and engineered social policies in response to the catastrophe of the Depression. At that time, poverty was tied to joblessness, and 25 percent of the workforce was out of work, the same rate the *New York Times* front page announced for black male youth on August 23, 1964, two days after President Johnson signed the Economic Opportunity Act.[28]

There was no single, right point of entry into the problem of poverty when planning began for the War on Poverty in 1963 but choices that were determined by many relevant factors. When policy makers ultimately conceptualized and defined poverty broadly, as a multifaceted cultural and social phenomena—reifying the idea of a culture of poverty—they were drawing on some of the available knowledge of that time.[29] The relationship they created among sets of ideas was intended to order and explain a connection among factors that seemed to reflect the real condition of the poor, as they saw it, as a "culture of poverty."[30] But this interdependence was a fiction that, instead of describing a condition, created one by ascribing a wholeness and unity—and causal relationships—to the situation of the poor. A focus on the psychology and attitudes of the poor was the result. Yet

> these were, after all, people who had for generations been doing the dirtiest work at the lowest wages under the most exploitative conditions, who are now suddenly defined as lacking incentives, or not having appropriate attitudes or family systems or other cultural patterns which facilitate mobility, so on and so forth, when in fact what they are really is just people who were dislodged from the occupational system because of the inexorable march of mechanization, who were cast into the cities where the urban economics could not absorb them for one reason or another and for whom the society simply had made no adequate provision for employment at wages that would permit families to form and maintain themselves.[31]

The emphasis on the interrelatedness of the factors associated with (not necessarily causing) poverty led to policies designed to address the total situation of the poor, so that the Economic Opportunity Act of 1964 emerged as a broad act with inchoate features such as Community Action Programs. CAPs, presumably, were going to coordinate programs to rectify the multifaceted dysfunction of poor people and families. While it was true that poverty was characterized by multiple interrelated causes and effects, not all the characteristics of poverty were equally important. At the same time, the opportunity was available to define poverty more narrowly as the lack of income-producing ability—the lack of a job—and to make the elimination of joblessness the policy goal. This had been the central idea in the New Deal when peak unemployment in the Depression was nearly 25 percent of the work force. In 1933 civilian unemployment in the United States was at the highest rate, 24.9 percent, it would reach in the Depression. In November of that year, President Roosevelt established the Civilian Works Administration (CWA) to cope with this unprecedented unemployment. The CWA provided jobs at the same minimum wage rates as did the Public Works Administration that had been negotiated in collective bargaining agreements; by January 1934 over "4 million Americans were on the payroll of the most massive work-relief experiment ever undertaken."[32] Similarly, the idea of providing a massive government program of jobs and job training was also prominent at the time of the War on Poverty among key participants in the policy-making process—Secretary of Labor Wirtz and his department, in particular—and jobs were prominent goals of the civil rights leadership who represented the dual agenda of the black poor and the black poor themselves.[33]

CONSENSUS ON KNOWLEDGE AND THE POLICY GOAL

The explicit policy goal of the War on Poverty was to eliminate poverty from American life. In the first State of the Union message in twenty-five years to assign priority to urgent domestic issues, President Johnson announced to Congress on January 8, 1964, his declaration of unconditional war on poverty and his intention "not only to relieve the symptoms of poverty, but to cure it, and above all prevent it."[34] While, as I have argued here, large-scale jobs policies were the right policy idea to eliminate poverty, the conclusions from the analysis of the three decisive political arenas demonstrate no consensus about what the causes of poverty were, no consensus on the means to achieve the policy goal, and no consensus on what the policy goal was to be.

Does this mean, then, that there could not have been jobs policies without consensus in all three arenas? Not necessarily. The idea of jobs policies could have prevailed despite the lack of consensus in the second and third arenas. Yet the lack of consensus in the arena of economic ideas—where the structuralist thesis about unemployment and poverty failed to be persuasive—would have been decisive in any case. Jobs policies were the clear answer to the structural argument, yet the dominance of Heller's and the council's interpretation of unemployment and the measures they chose to stimulate the economy and combat unemployment obstructed their appeal.

We can speculate about how jobs policies could have fared had the outcome in the political arenas been different and about whether jobs policies could not have made it to the center of the War on Poverty without consensus in the first political arena. If, however, consensus had formed in the arena of economic ideas, then the administrative incapacity of the Labor Department could have been overcome in three ways. First, a separate agency could have been set up—like the OEO was to run the Jobs Corps—to administer large-scale jobs programs (such agencies were created in the New Deal). Second, Heller and Wirtz's other detractors could have been brought on board to help Secretary Wirtz get the em-

ployment service (USES) into shape to administer large-scale jobs programs. Third, OEO could have run a large-scale jobs program itself.

Regarding the importance of political will—that is, had government
responded to the dual agenda of the civil rights movement—the definition
of the problem of poverty would still have remained a problem. It is
tempting to infer that the succession of Johnson to the presidency
brought into government the governmental will to act decisively on behalf of the black poor. And perhaps it did, but by the time Johnson became president and adopted the War on Poverty as his own it was too late
to act because the decisive planning elements had been in the hands of
Heller, of William Capron of the council, and of Kermit Gordon and
William Cannon of the Budget Bureau.[35] These planners were enamored
of the untried idea of comprehensive, locally initiated community action
programs as the "basic concept around which the program will be built,"
and the decisions in favor of CAPS were made by these men.[36] The fight
among the Labor Department, the Budget Bureau, and the council over
the shape of the poverty program was "terribly sharp during November
and December" of 1963 as they struggled to resolve their respective
"completely antithetical positions as to how to proceed, organizationally,
bureaucratically and in terms of focus."[37] Thus the die was cast in the fall
and winter of 1963 in the Kennedy administration. "What came to be
called the War on Poverty probably would not have got that name and
been launched the way it was, and certainly would have been different in
its outlines and focus, had it not been for the Council of Economic Advisors and the role that it played."[38]

Everything about President Johnson, who was instantly attracted to
the idea of a large domestic program attacking poverty, would have been
drawn to a War on Poverty organized around jobs. But such a program
never had a chance to be presented to him with the full consensual backing of the task force. Had it been, in spite of his campaign for "frugality
in government" to convince Congress and the business community that
his would not be a spendthrift Democratic administration, Johnson had
the political skills and nerve to find the greater revenues that jobs programs would have entailed.

For the sphere of economic ideas, however, there is no scenario imag-
inable (outside of luck) in which without consensual technical knowledge
on what the problem was the nation could have arrived at a large-scale
jobs initiative to address poverty as it appeared to Heller. Even with all

the political will in the world and a fully modernized Labor Department, with the primacy of Walter Heller in the planning process, and his council's view of the normal workings of the American economy, the particular set of macroeconomic measures they espoused would still have been seen as correct in formulating the main solution to poverty. It was the dominance of the CEA's definition and analysis of the problem of poverty that determined the outcome and eclipsed the more appropriate structural definition and analysis.

A PERIOD OF SOCIAL OPPORTUNITY

The chief task of this book has been to tell the story of the causes of the defeat of Willard Wirtz's idea of jobs programs. While the answer has been found to lie in how the problem of poverty was defined and analyzed, still another kind of answer is provided when we consider Wirtz's agenda in the larger context of the struggle for full-employment policy in the United States, a context that has been shaped by the limited scope and role of American government in social welfare policy. Captured in Katznelson's view of the exceptional limits to American social and economic policy, the political and economic biases and structural barriers imposed on large-scale active labor market policies by American capitalism have been a persistent obstruction to the realization of full-employment in the United States. This tale has been told authoritatively by Margaret Weir, who demonstrates how the requisites of American capitalism, the historical relationship between business and government, and the interaction of ideas, ideology, politics, and public policy have permitted a narrow range of particularistic responses and repeatedly thwarted broader, aggressive attempts to address unemployment and move full employment to the top of the nation's priorities.[39]

By the end of the 1960s a wide range of antipoverty policies had been offered to the American poor. What is obvious today about these policies is the absence of coordination and linkage among them. Looking back, one of the striking things about these fragmented programs was the superficial assessment of the causes of the poverty they were designed to allay. In no case was the persistence of poverty correctly tied to the regular functioning of the American economic system in growth or recession. Instead of focusing on the estrangement of poor people from ordinary economic life, policy makers frequently focused on their behavior and worldview.[40] Instead of fighting poverty by opening the doors to economic opportunity and providing a comprehensive employment program, policy makers provided a plethora of poorly—if at all—coordinated programs that did little to change the income-earning ability of most poor Americans. Conservatives such as Charles Murray and Lawrence Mead, among others writing in the 1980s, would hold these policies responsible for worsening the problem by diminishing initiative and creating welfare dependency.[41]

As we see clearly today, in the early 1960s what was happening to black unemployed and underemployed workers and to unskilled black youth seeking entry into the job market were the consequences of contraction in the sector of the American economy most widely available to them at that time, the manufacturing sector, and of additional transformations in that sector as industries relocated outside central cities and the nature of manufacturing activity shifted labor demand away from less educated and skilled workers. In other words, in this period lay the origins of the structural transformations in the economy that would be especially devastating to the black poor.

As William Julius Wilson has said, the poor need a "program that would lead to the sustained employment of ghetto men at respectable wages."[42] Dead-end jobs or job training without secure employment at the end will not enable the poor to break out of poverty. Jobs must provide enough income to "enable a man to maintain his self-respect as a provider, and stable enough to make it worthwhile to change the nature of his adaptation to his world."[43] Willard Wirtz said this forty years ago. While some jobs programs of the War on Poverty were intended to meet this need, they were too few and too disjointed to constitute an effective attack on the real causes of poverty. The manpower programs that went into the War on Poverty were developed under intense political pressure in a short period of time. They were implemented and directed under equally intense political pressure to produce results for congressional reauthorization. Since jobs programs were expensive to administer and constituted only one, albeit important, part of the War on Poverty, and since the overall appropriation for the Office of Economic Opportunity came to just $800 million, these programs never had a chance to operate effectively as antipoverty measures. Unemployment and underemployment were serious problems in the ghettos, and the programs the United States had scarcely scratched the surface. Part of the difficulty was in the multiplicity of programs, which led to administrative chaos. This, combined with inflexible funding arrangements, meant that the delivery of manpower training services was inefficient and ineffective. Another part of the problem was that, beginning in the midsixties, large amounts of money designated for job training began to be siphoned off into the ghettos for summer programs in concentrated poverty areas in response to, or in anticipation of, urban unrest.[44] This had the effect of eviscerating the programs. One reason "the jobs programs didn't work is that we drained off from it money that we probably, in hindsight, could have used much more effectively for real job training."[45]

Political institutions and politics clearly matter in the determination of public policies, as this book has tried to show in examining state capacity and governmental will. In the particular case of the War on Poverty, what mattered most was the lack of consensus among experts on economic ideas—on the nature of unemployment and the way it was related to poverty. The problem of poverty was misunderstood and misdiagnosed from the beginning by key antipoverty planners led initially by Walter Heller.[46] The importance of this was that the War on Poverty was directed away from jobs. The consequence in this case was that a period of social opportunity was missed.

In his retrospective assessment of community action programs in the War on Poverty, Daniel Patrick Moynihan warns of the "scarcity of social opportunity," cautioning those who would make public policy not to squander those rare political moments when the chance to make large and important change presents itself.[47] Certainly the window created in 1963 and 1964 was one such period. Everything seemed to be in place: the political mood of the country was soundly and progressively liberal for the first time since the Depression, the great ideological cold war battles within Congress had been stilled, the economy had begun to experience its longest recorded cyclical expansion ever (between 1961 and 1969), a Democrat was in the White House—with heavy Democratic majorities after 1964 in Congress—and likely to be there two terms, and there was tremendous confidence in the technical ability of government to solve social problems.[48] Moynihan believed that "the great failing of the Johnson Administration was that an immense opportunity to institute more or less permanent social changes—a fixed full employment program, a measure of income maintenance—was lost, while energies were expended in ways that very probably hastened the end of the brief period when such options were open."[49] Although he missed targeting the Kennedy administration—because it was then and there that the decisive economic ideas that would shape antipoverty policy came into play for the first time—Moynihan was right about the scarcity of social opportunity. And such a rare opportunity was missed by late 1963.

THE FUTURE OF JOBS AND ANTIPOVERTY POLICY

The case for jobs policies in 1963 was compelling, and a social opportunity was lost that has yet to recur. Jobs policies should have been the centerpiece of the War on Poverty: there were vigorous forces behind it; the logic supporting it as a solution to poverty was sound; and it was a clear argument given the structural understandings of poverty in the Kennedy administration that centered around the Department of Labor. Yet the decisive influence of Walter Heller and the Council of Economic Advisers had the impact of cutting off a critical opportunity for the structural argument. The essential economic consensus needed was not fully formed in government as of 1963 because of the prevalence of fiscal Keynesianism as the basis of economic policy making. Limited structural measures had been introduced in the Kennedy years with the MDTA, vocational education, and area redevelopment legislation to address structural economic problems, which were seen as regional or technological in nature. Yet when it came to antipoverty policy, the 1964 tax cut to stimulate growth coupled with specific measures of the Economic Opportunity Act appeared to be the chosen answer to poverty, in part because of the belief that the problems of unemployment in the black community were not government responsibilities.

Strong government sponsorship of the idea of jobs programs would have strengthened the claim to a right to employment as part of the public philosophy. The War on Poverty was an opening to renew such a claim because it was a chance to affect positively the ideological consensus in society on the right to employment, embracing millions of black Americans and affecting future generations who would otherwise be consigned to live in desperate poverty. In American history, government responsibility for employment had been most strongly exemplified by the New Deal. Samuel Beer has pointed to this period for its distinct public philosophy in domestic affairs. The New Deal was not merely a set of policies; it was also a state of mind and an outlook on politics and government having a general character. As Beer has remarked, we recognize this when we use the term "New Deal" more broadly as an adjective, as when a candidate is characterized as a New Deal liberal. Underwriting the policies of the New Deal were broad premises that represented the public interest.[50]

Government has a central role in the formation of public philosophy, and we derive our sense of the public interest from government action. Such a view of government is antithetical to the classic pluralist conception of American government as a mere arena through which competing interests pass.[51] The contrasting view here is that the power of the government role and the policy choices governments make are so important in ideological consensus that they also affect future policy choices, the electoral fortunes of future governments, and the life chances of future generations. The Kennedy and Johnson years were witness to the most liberal governments in American life since the New Deal and were the last in which the public interest was energetically shaped and defined by aggressive liberal public policies. The American presidency needs energy to work. To act forcefully in the public interest, the president must have energy, drive, initiative, a sense of history, and a point of view capable of transcending partisan political objectives. In spite of Lyndon Johnson's enormous complexity—or perhaps because of it—he was an immense president who molded public policy in the turbulent sixties when, as Bill Moyers said, "a . . . simpler man might have been crushed in the awful sweep of" those years.[52] President Johnson was committed to the idea that the government has to help the ordinary citizen.

In contrast, in contemporary American life the government share in representing the public interest is considerably circumscribed. We have nearly become accustomed to a public sphere bereft of public initiative. Few of the burdens that beset the poor in today's society are seen as problems for which government does, or should, bear responsibility. The United States has no concerted antipoverty policy at present, although the inventory of entitlements for the well-off, including a proposed tax cut in the trillions of dollars, is on the increase.

This book's analysis buttresses Daniel Patrick Moynihan's counsel that the point of entry into antipoverty policy in the early sixties was an opportune time to bring about large-scale social change. We had an economy that permitted it, unburdened by the policy-inhibiting budget deficit and slow growth of the 1980s and 1990s. We had a window of opportunity in terms of policy making, we had the right president with the largest majorities in both houses in Congress since 1937, and we had the right national mood. We have not had such an opportunity since then. The Nixon administration's proposed Family Assistance Plan to provide a guaranteed income failed over two Congresses to overcome both liberal and conservative efforts to kill it.[53] Moreover, neither the Nixon nor the Carter economy permitted attention to costly and potentially inflation-inducing wage measures, and the public mood in both administrations was decidedly antigovernment.

The "failure to include jobs programs in the War on Poverty led to another effort to do so and by one of the major players in the Kennedy and Johnson years": Senator Hubert Humphrey.[54] Introduced in the Carter administration, the Full Employment and Balanced Growth Act (the Humphrey-Hawkins Act) was a fainthearted reprise of the 1946 Full Employment Act. Introduced and signed by President Carter in 1978, it was a repeat of the earlier bill in that it required Congress to create public sector jobs as "reservoirs" of useful public service employment—which Congress failed to do—and made full employment an explicit goal, albeit qualified by numerous other policy goals including the reduction of the inflation rate and maintaining a balanced budget. In the end, the act was so eviscerated by compromised goals to ensure its passage it too fell far short of its original objectives.

In the Reagan years, opportunities for reform were driven out by concerted efforts to reduce the scale of social welfare policies coupled with the escalating federal deficit. In George Bush's administration, unemployment and the deficit soared and, outside of the Weed and Seed program and Jack Kemp, little interest was shown in antipoverty policy. When Democratic president Bill Clinton won the 1992 presidential election, there was speculation in his first term that an opportunity for more liberal social welfare initiatives was at hand. But Clinton's lack of success with his first Congress coupled with the budget deficit and the internal struggle in his party between old-line liberals and the new generation of centrist Democrats deterred such initiatives, if they had ever been a legitimate option. On September 11, 2001, the policy goals of President George W. Bush were refocused instantaneously on foreign policy and counterterrorism in the wake of the terrorist attacks on the United States.

Willard Wirtz and the structuralists in and around the Labor Depart-

ment provided a pertinent analysis of the kind of structural unemployment that was beginning to loom large in 1963. We could say they "discovered" structural unemployment and prescribed large-scale jobs polices
nearly four decades ago. What their analysis shows us today are the an-
tecedents of the structural problems that have confronted not only the
black community in devastating proportions but the broader workforce as
well beginning in the 1980s and 1990s.[55] Forty years ago, Wirtz foresaw
the critical need for employment for poor heads of households and predicted the social consequences of failing to provide them with substantive
employment. The concentration of poverty in the inner cities today and
the overrepresentation of young black female-headed families among the
poor are symptoms, not causes, of the lack of viable economic opportunities. The dimensions of inner-city poverty have changed enormously, as
have social attitudes toward the poor.[56] It would be considerably more
difficult today—if not impossible—to arrive at the social consensus necessary to produce programs specifically targeted at the black poor. If the
problem of unemployment among the poor had been addressed as Wirtz
saw it—and when Wirtz saw it—characteristics of entrenched poverty
such as female-headed families, welfare dependency, social isolation, and
near-permanent joblessness might never have evolved as they have.

The War on Poverty should have taught us practical lessons. One is
that such deeply embedded structural unemployment problems—and
ones that are characteristic of the normal workings of the American capitalist economy—may be impossible to affect in the absence of large-scale,
concerted government effort. Presidents Kennedy and Johnson's secretary
of labor, Willard Wirtz, was unsuccessful at calling attention to the problem as it began to emerge in 1961; President Clinton's secretary of labor,
Robert Reich, was no more successful. The post–September 11 policy environment under George W. Bush will be less hospitable.

The United States has continued to be plagued with structural unemployment and underemployment even in the boom economy of the 1990s
up to 2000. Not only did poor and lower-income workers struggle to find
respectable jobs in the fully employed U.S. economy, but they were virtually shut out of the new economy by their inability to meet the education
and skill requirements of the newly created jobs that began to emerge in
the 1980s, and neither were there adequate training and education programs to pull them in. Such evolutions in our economy should be expected as the natural functioning of a capitalist economy. Today, as it did

in the 1960s, government has a responsibility to ensure education, training, and reskilling of workers to compete in a global economy; schools and industry alone cannot meet these challenges without government help.[57] Such policy was one of President Clinton's promises to the nations' workers as he executed international trade agreements and policies such as the North Atlantic Free Trade Agreement NAFTA that were guaranteed to spin off low-skill jobs outside the United States. It was also one of the chief missions of his first secretary of labor, Robert Reich.

With the devolution of welfare responsibility to the states in 1996, numerous and diverse job-training programs for the poor took effect. In spite of their high cost, the evidence suggests that such programs are the best way to address unemployment-related poverty, with job-creation policies following close behind. The economic advantages of even marginally successful training programs over unemployment have demonstrated that paying for the development and utilization of more employment opportunities is better public policy than paying people for nonwork or makework.[58] A particularly American phenomenon that has confounded the successful widespread implementation of jobs programs and undermined the policy environment has been the near obsessiveness with which evaluation studies based on cost-benefit analysis have been used as political ammunition to thwart jobs proposals. Such programs have been so parsimoniously funded, and so short term in application, that it is nearly impossible to draw reasonable conclusions about their effectiveness.[59] Two caveats follow, however, about state training programs for welfare and former welfare recipients. First, there is a scarcity of systematic evidence tracking trainees' success at moving into regular employment. Second, in a robust economy, states have been able to manage the high costs of implementing such training programs because of the solidity of their fiscal revenues. In a sustained economic downturn, states trim considerably their outlays for job training for the poor, and nothing in the Personal Responsibility and Work Opportunity Reconciliation Act stops them.

Many retrospective assessments of the War on Poverty concede that jobs programs were the answer to poverty in the sixties and the route antipoverty policy should have taken.[60] Even conservative criticisms of the War on Poverty, and of government social welfare initiatives generally, assert that government must link support to work—in this case, as an obligation—for government programs to have a measure of success and to avoid dependency.[61]

The biggest obstacle in the way of a fully employed economy is the failure of the national government to back up this goal. Only under these circumstances do jobs programs have a shot at success. The first and foremost means to end poverty is a national-level commitment to genuine full employment, and the United States has always backed away from guaranteeing jobs for everyone who wants to work. Without a major political commitment from the White House, we cannot hope that the idea of jobs policies will come together into a major government initiative.[62] It may be that a government commitment to implement such proposals will only be made when they appear to be indispensable to the continued functioning of the nation, as they were in the Depression.

What the failure of the idea of jobs policies in the War on Poverty also signified was the importance of another kind of consensus, a consensus on the definitions and causes of social problems. In the case of poverty in the early 1960s, the lack of consensus on economic thinking in the earliest planning stages of antipoverty policy was decisive. But the centrality of expert consensus on the causes of social problems is applicable to other cases as well, especially where the causes of problems are not entirely understood or are at the center of serious disagreement. National and global environmental issues, for example, are potential applications of analysis centered on expert consensus or lack of consensus.[63] How has the failure of expert consensus on the causes, extent, and consequences of global warming (both the whole range of environmental issues and by issue area) affected policy change and perceptions of policy options, and what has the role of national politics been in preventing expert consensus and—consequently—agreement within the global environmental policy community?

At this book's beginning, I cited a range of opinion that seemed to illustrate aptly the lack of clarity on the U.S. governmental role in eliminating poverty. At its narrowest, Daniel Patrick Moynihan saw the origins of the War on Poverty in the search for a presidential campaign agenda. Charles Hamilton described poverty and inequality as inevitable characteristics of U.S. capitalism and, consistent with the American ethos, not the business of government. For Hugh Heclo, the political moments that permit social opportunity in politics have been rare, ephemeral—maybe unique—and may never return. Yet perhaps the most astute judge of the formidable forces arrayed against Wirtz in the War on Poverty was a political economist and philosopher who had been dead for eighty years

when the War on Poverty was undertaken: Karl Marx. Given the circumstances of the struggle, Marx would have said the outcome of the battle
for jobs policies was inevitable. Capitalism's requirements—especially
capitalism's need to advance to a new stage of increasing concentration
and rationalization—meant also that the subsequent costs to society would
be greater, in the form of higher and higher natural levels of unemployment as each successive wave of recession seemed to raise the level that
was compatible with the need to temper inflation. Thus Willard Wirtz's
battle for jobs policies in the War on Poverty—which was also the battle
for full employment—was framed.

Appendix: Joblessness, Poverty, and Public Policy in the United States

The general government response to joblessness in the United States began in earnest with the Depression. Before the Depression, however, a number of measures contained components of what we think of today as manpower policy. The Homestead Act of 1862, which opened the program of public land grants to independent farmers, included mobilization measures; the Northwest Ordinance of 1785, the Land Grant Colleges Act of 1862 (the Morrill Act), and the Smith-Hughes Act of 1917 provided educational programs; and the Smith-Hughes Act also provided for vocational education.[1] Before the 1930s unemployment was not thought of as a problem that government was supposed to solve.

The line of government responsibility for joblessness can be drawn from the Social Security Act of 1935, which acknowledged the responsibility of the federal government to the victims of market misfortunes; to the Employment Act of 1946, which located a federal government role in maximizing employment; to the 1964 tax cut, which embodied the dominant Keynesian thinking of the Kennedy years concerning the role of government in alleviating unemployment; and to the Economic Opportunity Act of 1964, which acknowledged that there was a government responsibility for persistent joblessness.

It was the magnitude and scope of the Depression as a national and international economic crisis that enabled Franklin Roosevelt, and a willing Congress, to bring massive government energies and monies to bear on the problem of unemployment. Two principal legacies of that era were the establishment of unemployment insurance and the "widespread impression with the public and government leaders that the federal government could successfully generate useful temporary jobs during periods of severe economic distress."[2] Both unemployment insurance and government job-creation programs, though, were directed to the middle and working classes and not directly to the poor, since unemployment insurance only benefited workers who already had an attachment to the labor market; and job-creation programs were responses to the catastrophic reality that one in four Americans was out of work, a sizable proportion that could not be ignored. Most of the employment measures of this period were intentionally temporary and were aimed at reducing suffering, not unemployment. The more permanent manpower efforts were the Wagner-Peyser Act of 1933, which established the United States Employment Service, a reintroduction and consolidation of the temporary job-matching programs of the federal government in World War I; the Social Security Act of 1935, including compensatory unemployment; the National Labor Relations Act of 1935; and the Fair Labor Standards Act of 1938.

Another series of programs—the Federal Emergency Relief Act of 1933, the Civil Works Administration of 1933, the Public Works Administration of 1933, the Works Progress Administration of 1935, the National Youth Administration of 1935, and the Civilian Conservation Corps of 1937—were job-creation measures that have been remembered, incorrectly, as "make work" programs. With the exception of the Fitzgerald Act, which was intended to encourage apprenticeship, there was no general interest in providing for job training and employment skills or preparing people for jobs that did not yet exist.[3] The experience of the Depression impressed on not just the United States but Western industrial democracies generally the instabilities attendant to capitalism and the need for responsive government to address industrial dislocations.

Issues concerning employment and manpower seemed to drift in the immediate postwar period through the Eisenhower administration, possibly because high unemployment between 1946 and 1960 was sporadic rather than sustained. While public attention was drawn to unemployment and jobs because of the recessions of the period, the Eisenhower administration was loath to acknowledge the recessionary economy and even more reluctant to act.

Most initiatives proposed in the period addressed structural employment problems. In 1949 legislation was proposed to supplement the Employment Act, and in 1954 and 1958 there were proposals for "tax reduction, public works, and 'depressed areas' legislation, . . . demands from organized labor for a 'conference on unemployment,' and . . . criticisms from liberals and academics of public inaction."[4] Growing interest in unemployment was demonstrated by the appointment of the Senate Special Committee on Unemployment Problems in 1959. Eugene McCarthy (D-Minnesota) chaired the committee, and it included Senators Joseph S. Clark, Jennings Randolph, and Winston L. Prouty, all of whom in later years would go on to important roles in antipoverty legislation. Area redevelopment, a youth conservation corps, changes in vocational education and retraining programs, and social insurance programs were among the recommendations of the committee. These concerns found form in depressed areas legislation for federal aid to areas with high unemployment rates. At the end of the decade, the Labor Department was also coming to recognize that the problems of structural unemployment confronting the nation required more active manpower policy. In the Kennedy administration, the Department of Labor became the center for proponents of interventionist manpower measures to address structural unemployment as a strategy to complement the macroeconomic management of the economy.

A number of initiatives emerged in the 1960s to address changes in the nature of unemployment. Both manpower and economic development approaches in the 1960s included measures to increase the number and quality of jobs for the poor and to promote local or national economic growth to make more jobs available. Linking the two approaches were convictions that unemployment is a major cause of poverty and that general economic development (growth and productivity) is a key factor in producing jobs. In the Kennedy years, the role of general economic growth as an antipoverty measure was central, and the tax cut of 1964 was considered a companion piece of legislation to the Economic Opportunity Act as a means to stimulate the economy and expand available jobs, thereby reducing the level of unemployment.

There were also a number of important new federal measures for the unemployed in these years. First, the Area Redevelopment Act of 1961 provided grants to attract industry and train or retrain workers between 1961 and 1965. It was targeted to unemployed residents of economically depressed regions. Second, the Public Works Acceleration Act of 1962 provided temporary jobs from 1962 to 1963 on federal public works projects. This program was aimed at employed and unemployed job applicants in areas of high unemployment. Third, the Manpower Development and Training Act of 1962 was the first of the major new programs aimed at the unemployed and poor. It was designed to provide participants with employment skills in the classroom. Its initial emphasis on vocational training for technologically displaced workers shifted in the sixties to training for low-income youth and adults. Fourth, the Economic Opportunity Act of 1964 was the omnibus bill for the War on Poverty and contained a number of job-training measures.

Notes

1. Introduction: The Other War on Poverty

1. New York City Partnership, *Working Together to Accelerate New York's Recovery: Economic Impact Analysis of the September 11th Attack on New York City* (New York: New York City Partnership and Chamber of Commerce, November 2001), 7. The Partnership's economic analysis found that the city's economy would sustain a gross loss of approximately $83 billion as a result of the attack; this includes $30 billion in capital losses, $14 billion in cleanup costs, and an economic output loss of $39 billion. In the fourth quarter of 2001 the city would lose some 125,000 jobs. Although some would return, 57,000—beyond recession-related losses—would not at the end of 2003.

2. New York City Partnership, *Working Together to Accelerate New York's Recovery*.

3. Neil Kleiman, "City Needs a System to Retrain the Jobless," *Daily News*, November 26, 2001, 1.

4. Ibid.

5. "Remarks By President Clinton at the Welfare Reform Bill Signing Thursday, August 22, 1996." acf.dhhs.gov/news/welfare/wr/8822potus.htm.

6. See appendix.

7. Daniel P. Moynihan, *Family and Nation* (New York: Harcourt, Brace, Jovanovich, 1986), 82–83.

8. Charles V. Hamilton, "Social Policy and the Welfare of Black Americans: From Rights to Resources," *Political Science Quarterly* 101, no. 2 (1986): 250.

9. Hugh Heclo, "The Political Foundations of Antipoverty Policy," in *Fighting Poverty: What Works and What Doesn't*, ed. Sheldon H. Danziger and Daniel H. Weinberg (Cambridge: Harvard University Press, 1986), 313.

10. Margaret Weir's *Politics and Jobs: The Boundaries of Employment Policy in the United States* (Princeton: Princeton University Press, 1992) and Gary Mucciaroni's *The Political Failure of Employment Policy, 1945–1982* (Pittsburgh: University of Pittsburgh Press, 1990) are two such analyses.

11. Administrative History of the Office of Economic Opportunity, vol. 1, part 1, chaps. 1–2, Lyndon B. Johnson Library, Austin.

12. Alan Wolfe has made such analyses, as have Samuel Bowles and Herbert Gintis. For example, see Wolfe's "Presidential Power and the Crisis of Modernization," *Democracy* (April 1981): 19–32; and Bowles and Gintis, "The Crisis of Liberal Capitalism: The Case of the United States," *Politics and Society* 11, no. 1 (1982): 51–94.

13. Ira Katznelson, "Rethinking the Silences of Social and Economic Policy," *Political Science Quarterly* 101, no. 2 (1986): 307–325.

14. Heclo, "The Political Foundations of Antipoverty Policy," 336.

15. Such arguments have been made by Thomas Byrne Edsall and Mary D. Edsall, *Chain Reaction: The Impact of Race, Riots, and Taxes on American Politics* (New York: Norton, 1991); Weir *Politics and Jobs*; and Jill Quadagno, *The Color of Welfare: How Racism Undermined the War on Poverty* (New York: Oxford University Press, 1994). Arguing a variant of this argument are analyses of the anxieties shared by the middle and working class over their falling economic status beginning in the 1970s even as they, unlike racial minorities, could not turn to government affirmative action and welfare programs (paid for by their taxes) for special assistance. For examples, see Kevin Phillips, *Boiling Point: Democrats, Republicans, and the Decline of Middle-Class Prosperity* (New York: Random House, 1993); Katherine Newman, *Falling from Grace: The Experience of Downward Mobility in the American Middle Class* (New York: Free, 1988).

16. Memorandum, Willard Wirtz to Theodore Sorensen, January 23, 1964, "A Declaration of Unconditional War on Poverty," White House General File, Record Group 174, Records of the Department of Labor, National Archives, 2. Of course, if poverty is a description of income, it can also be addressed by types of antipoverty policies in which income is distributed to the poor directly through welfare programs such as Aid to Families with Dependent Children (AFDC) or indirectly through negative income tax proposals or family assistance plans. But because such policies are politically unpopular and perceived to create dependency, they are not the most feasible or effective means to eliminate poverty in the United States. While such programs are also necessary, the most important means to eliminate poverty is to provide decent jobs and job training so that individuals and families can find employment and support themselves.

17. David Remnick, "Profiles: Dr. Wilson's Neighborhood," *New Yorker*, April 29 and May 6, 1996, 96–107.

18. William Julius Wilson, *The Truly Disadvantaged: The Inner City, the Un-*

derclass, and Public Policy (Chicago: University of Chicago Press, 1987); and *The Declining Significance of Race: Blacks and Changing American Institutions* (Chicago: University of Chicago Press, 1978). See also idem, *When Work Disappears* (New York: Knopf, 1996).

19. My analysis of the front pages, editorial pages, and "Week in Review" sections of the *New York Times* for 1963 demonstrated the high salience of issues of employment and civil rights (see chap. 4). In 1944 a *Fortune* magazine poll reported that 68 percent of those asked supported the proposal that the federal government should guarantee a job for everyone seeking work if necessary (cited in Stephen K. Bailey, *Congress Makes a Law: The Story Behind the Employment Act of 1946* (New York: Columbia University Press, 1950), 179. Governor Thomas Dewey of New York, the Republican candidate for president that year, held that "government can and must create job opportunities, because there must be jobs for all in this country of ours" (42). Again and again in the 1950s, 1960s, 1970s, and 1980s, public opinion polls show high support for a positive government role in providing productive work or training. See Robert Y. Shapiro, Kelly D. Patterson, Judith Russell, and John T. Young "The Polls—A Report: Employment and Social Welfare," *Public Opinion Quarterly* 51 (summer 1987): 268–281.

20. Unemployment in the black community was catastrophic; at 13.5 percent in March 1964, the adjusted rate of black employment was nearly three times the white rate. The War on Poverty was critical to blacks because aggregate demand economic policies would do little to eliminate disastrous unemployment rates among unskilled blacks. See John C. Donovan, *The Politics of Poverty*, 3d ed. (Washington, D.C.: University of America Press, 1980), 100. See also chap. 5 of this book, which provides specific data on unemployment in the black community.

21. The statistics in this paragraph are taken from Philip Harvey, *Securing the Right to Unemployment: Social Welfare Policy and the Unemployed in the United States* (Princeton: Princeton University Press, 1989), 51–52, and are largely drawn from the U.S. Bureau of the Census, *Statistical Abstract of the United States: 1987*, 107th ed. (Washington, D.C.: U.S. Government Printing Office, 1987), and numerous other U.S. government sources.

22. Harvey points out that most of what we give up in the costs of lost production we spend in the costs of income maintenance.

23. Alexander Keyssar, "History and the Problem of Unemployment," *Socialist Review* 19, no. 4 (October–December 1989): 15–34.

24. There are plenty of secondary sources on the origins of the War on Poverty; this description is based on the Administrative History of the Office of Economic Opportunity, vol. 1, part 1, chap. 1, Lyndon B. Johnson Library, Austin. Kennedy had been impressed with the poverty conditions he saw di-

rectly in the hills of West Virginia when he was campaigning during the 1960 primaries. In 1962 his interest was further developed by Dwight MacDonald's "Our Invisible Poor," a review of Michael Harrington's *The Other America* that appeared in the *New Yorker* on January 19, 1963, and by other books that were apparently brought to his attention by Special Assistant to the President Theodore Sorensen. There is additional speculation from William Capron, Walter Heller's assistant, that an article by Homer Bigart on Appalachian problems that appeared in the *New York Times* on October 20, 1963, was also a catalyst to the Kennedy poverty program; see "Poverty and Urban Policy, Conference Transcript of 1973 Group Discussion of the Kennedy Administration Urban Poverty Programs and Policies," John F. Kennedy Library, Boston, 92–94a. This transcript reproduces the proceedings of the conference "The Federal Government and Urban Poverty," cosponsored by the Florence Heller School for Advanced Studies in Social Welfare at Brandeis University and the John F. Kennedy Library at Brandeis University and held on June 16 and 17, 1973, The purpose of this conference was to bring together a number of participants, scholars, and commentators who had roles in the planning, formulation, and/or execution of the federal poverty initiatives that focused on urban poverty in the Kennedy and Johnson administrations. Hereafter, references to this conference will list the speaker's name and "Brandeis conference."

25. Capron was staff director of the Council of Economic Advisers. He had, under Heller's name, asked for ideas from the cabinet heads on a poverty program and pulled together a small planning group on an antipoverty initiative in the fall of 1963. The response was a disappointment, resulting in "the reincarnation of all the obsolete programs and stale ideas of the past" (Administrative History of the Office of Economic Opportunity, vol. 1, part 1, 16, Lyndon B. Johnson Library, Austin).

26. Christopher Weeks, interview by Michael L. Gillette, December 10, 1980, tape recording, Lyndon B. Johnson Library, Washington, D.C., 4.

27. See Weir, *Politics and Jobs*; and Mucciaroni, *Political Failure of Employment Policy*.

28. Stephen Steinberg, *Turning Back: The Retreat From Racial Justice in American Thought and Policy* (Boston: Beacon, 1995); and Robert C. Lieberman, *Shifting the Color Line: Race and the American Welfare State* (Cambridge: Harvard University Press, 1998) are exceptions.

29. E. P. Thompson, *The Making of the English Working Class* (New York: Vintage, 1966), 10.

2. ECONOMIC IDEAS AND THE WAR ON POVERTY

1. Memorandum, Walter Heller to Lyndon B. Johnson, May 1, 1963, "Progress and Poverty," Legislative Background EOA 1964 WoP, CEA Draft History of WoP, box 1, Lyndon B. Johnson Library, Austin; memorandum, Robert Lampman to Walter Heller, 10 June 1963, "An Offensive Against Poverty," Legislative Background EOA 1964 WoP, CEA Draft History of WoP, box 1, Lyndon B. Johnson Library, Austin.

2. These positions were not necessarily mutually exclusive since the Department of Labor position was that structural and aggregate strategies were both indicated. Secretary of Labor Wirtz advocated the tax cut as a first step toward the reduction of unemployment. See Willard Wirtz, press conference, October 10, 1963, President's Office Files, Departments and Agencies/Labor (3–62 to 4–62) File, John F. Kennedy Library, Boston.

3. See Leon Keyserling, interview by Stephen Goodell, January 9, 1969, tape recording, Lyndon B. Johnson Library, Washington, D.C., for his interpretation of why the economic response after the 1964 tax cut was two years in coming. This response was ambiguously related to fiscal stimulation; by 1966 the nation was in a war economy, which accounted for the increased economic growth that occurred.

4. Erwin C. Hargrove and Samuel A. Morley, eds., *The President and the Council of Economic Advisors* (Boulder: Westview, 1984), 38.

5. Walter Heller, Kermit Gordon, James Tobin, Gardner Ackley, and Paul Samuelson, interview by Joseph Pechman, August 1, 1964, tape recording, John F. Kennedy Library, Boston. Citations of this Oral History interview henceforth will be abbreviated as CEA OH.

6. Seymour E. Harris, *The Economics of the Kennedy Years* (New York: Harper and Row, 1964), 122.

7. Ibid.

8. M. Stephen Weatherford and Lorraine M. McDonnell, "Macroeconomic Policymaking Beyond the Electoral Constraint," in *The Presidency and Public Policy Making*, ed. George C. Edwards, Stephen A. Schull, and Norman C. Thomas (Pittsburgh: University of Pittsburgh Press, 1985), 106.

9. The council preferred fiscal and monetary policies to increase demand; these, they felt, would significantly reduce unemployment. They eschewed the use of public spending as a Keynesian measure, which would have consequences for any jobs policy. Early in the Kennedy administration, the council underestimated structuralist arguments coming from the Labor Department, Chairman Martin of the Federal Reserve, the Republican party generally, and economist Arthur Burns, among others, who stressed that rising unemployment was related to structural changes in the economy.

10. Richard E. Neustadt, *Presidential Power: The Politics of Leadership From FDR to Carter* (New York: Wiley, 1980), 44. This community cuts across geography and includes members of Congress and the president's administration, governors of states, military commanders in the field, leading politicians in both parties, representatives of private organizations, journalists, diplomats, and principals abroad.

11. The secretary of the treasury spoke to Congress and to the nation for the president on matters of economic policy making; he had statutory obligations and served as the president's chief financial officer in congressional accountability (see Hargrove and Morley, *The President and the Council of Economic Advisors*, 7). These functions, and the treasury secretary's position in the president's "inner cabinet," made him the most appropriate spokesperson for the president on economic policy (ibid.). The Federal Reserve System's independence assured its control over monetary policy. Because it was the only agency with comprehensive knowledge of overall government operations—through its budget preparation and legislative clearance functions—and had its own operations reaching down into the departmental and subdepartmental levels, the Budget Bureau had the most authoritative advisory impact in the executive branch. The economists at the head of the BOB at this time were Kermit Gordon, Charles Schultze, and William Capron. President Kennedy also created several new committees to handle particular economic issues in his administration.

12. See CEA OH. The Quadriad came to be formalized and named by Heller during his tenure as chairman. It was originally called the "Financial Summit Meeting" or the "Fiscal and Financial Group." Heller refers to the former in the CEA OH, 326, and the latter in Hargrove and Morley, *The President and the Council of Economic Advisors*, 190. See Heller's November 29, 1963, memorandum for the president, "Interest Rates and the Quadriad," for details on the Quadriad's role (Walter Heller Papers, John F. Kennedy Library, Boston). It met with President Kennedy every four to ten weeks, usually at Heller's call, after consultation with the president. See also Heller's memoranda to Johnson and CEA OH for Heller's description and definition of the council role in Johnson's administration.

13. See memorandum, Walter Heller to Lyndon B. Johnson, December 1, 1963, Gen FG. 11–2/A 11/22/63, FG 11–3 Council of Economic Advisers 11/22/63–1/31/64, box 56, Lyndon B. Johnson Library, Austin, for an elaboration of the personal services the council provided to the president. During Heller's tenure, the Troika had three operating levels: a technical/staff level; a member level, with James Tobin of the CEA, Bob Turner (and Charles Schultze) of the BOB, and Bob Wallace of the Treasury Department; and a chairman level, with Dillon, Bell, and Heller (later Kermit Gordon) putting

"the final imprint on what went to the president in writing" (CEA OH page 327).

14. During Kennedy's administration, the CEA chaired the following groups either by presidential order or by interagency agreement: the Cabinet Committee on Economic Growth, the Committee on Housing Credit Policy, and the Committee on the Economic Impact of Defense and Disarmament. The council was a member of the Cabinet Committee on the Balance of Payments, the Long-Run International Payments Committee, the Steering Committee to Coordinate U.S. Views on Reforms of the World's Monetary System, the Interdepartmental Energy Study, the Interagency Committee on Transportation Mergers, advisory committees on natural resources, and the Trade Executive Committee. It participated in the following international committees and meetings: U.S.-Japan Cabinet Committee on Trade and Economic Affairs, U.S.-Canada Cabinet Committee on Trade and Economic Affairs, U.S. Delegation to the IMF-IBRD (adviser on annual meetings), and U.S. Delegation to the Economic Policy Committee of the OECD. It met periodically with the Conference of Business Economists (top fifty U.S. business economists), the Business Council Liaison Group, select individuals in the business and financial community, top trade union economists, the AFL-CIO Economic Policy Committee, and the Consumer Advisory Council. See memo from Heller to Johnson, December 1, 1963, for elaboration on these roles.

15. CEA OH, 32b.

16. See memo from Heller to Johnson, December 1, 1963, for elaboration on these roles.

17. Heller and Tobin remember at least two occasions when there were dissenting footnotes in the Troika report and parallel sets of figures in which one agency adhered to one set and the other two agencies to the other set. See CEA OH, 328.

18. CEA OH, 329.

19. Heller in ibid.

20. The principals of the Heller Council were Walter Heller, from the University of Minnesota, who was chairman of the council from January 1961 to November 1964; Kermit Gordon, from Williams College and the Ford Foundation, who was a member from January 1961 to December 1962, when he became director of the Budget Bureau and was replaced by John P. Lewis—formerly on the staff of the Keyserling Council—in May 1963; James Tobin, from Yale University, who was a member from January 1961 to August 1962, when he was succeeded by Gardner Ackley, on leave from the University of Michigan, who went on to succeed Heller as sixth chairman of the council in November 1964. The Heller Council staff members by the end of the first year were Catherine H. Furlong, Frances James, David Lusher, Walter F. Stettner,

and fourteen new economists: Richard E. Attiyeh (graduate student at Yale), Sidney G. Winter, Jr. (the RAND Corporation), Barbara Berman (Harvard), Rashi Fein (University of North Carolina), Richard Nelson (Carnegie Institute of Technology), Arthur M. Okun (Yale), Lee E. Preston and Lloyd Ulman (Berkeley), Vernon W. Ruttan (Purdue), Robert M. Solow (MIT), and three recent graduates, Charles A. Cooper from MIT, Richard N. Cooper from Harvard, and George L. Perry from the University of Minnesota. Part-time economists retained as consultants by the CEA were Paul Samuelson (who also advised the president), Joseph Pechman, Charles Schultze (who joined the Budget Bureau as assistant secretary in the administration), Henry Briefs, Burton Klein, Charles Taff, Robert Triffin, Kenneth Arrow, Martin Brofenbrenner, James Dusenberry, and Otto Eckstein.

21. Heller, in CEA OH, 81–82.

22. Samuelson and Heller, in CEA OH, 81.

23. CEA OH, 80.

24. Tobin, in CEA OH, appendix A, 456.

25. Samuelson, in CEA OH, 82.

26. See Margaret Weir's *Politics and Jobs: The Boundaries of Employment Policy in the United States* (Princeton: Princeton University Press, 1992) on the development of American Keynesianism.

27. See Keyserling interview for his analysis of how the New Economics was "the opposite of everything Keynes stood for" (22) and the consequences of this for the public sector.

28. Herbert Stein, *The Fiscal Revolution in America* (Chicago: University of Chicago Press, 1969), 381–382.

29. Charles Schultze, interview by David McComb, March 28, 1969, tape recording, Lyndon B. Johnson Library, Austin.

30. Ibid.

31. Ibid.

32. Also with President Johnson. Walter Heller's memoranda were legendary.

33. Samuelson, in CEA OH, 45. Kennedy received a C from manpower economist Russell Nixon in the sole economics course he took at Harvard.

34. Speculation on how his ambivalence was related to the influence of his wealthy and economically conservative father can be found in CEA OH, 47.

35. Samuelson, in CEA OH, 46.

36. Hargrove and Morley, *The President and the Council of Economic Advisors*, 170.

37. Edwin G. Nourse, the first chairman of the Council of Economic Advisers under President Truman, served from 1946 to 1949. Dissension on the council led him to resign, and he was succeeded by Leon Keyserling.

38. Walter S. Salant, "The Spread of Keynesian Doctrines and Practices in the United States," in *The Political Power of Economic Ideas: Keynesianism Across Nations*, ed. Peter A. Hall (Princeton: Princeton University Press, 1989), 48. For Leon Keyserling's views on his, and his council's, role in promoting the idea of maximum employment and the misapplication of Keynesian precepts in the Kennedy and Johnson administrations, see Keyserling interview. See also Weir's *Politics and Jobs* and Gary Mucciaroni's *The Political Failure of Employment Policy, 1945–1982* (Pittsburgh: University of Pittsburgh Press, 1990).

39. Although the following section is based primarily on the August 1, 1964, joint oral history interview of Walter Heller, Kermit Gordon, James Tobin, Gardner Ackley, and Paul Samuelson by Joseph Pechman, other oral history interviews, and primary documents, there are additional relevant sources on economic influences in the Kennedy and Johnson administrations. Particularly useful are Edward S. Flash, Jr., *Economic Advice and Presidential Leadership* (New York: Columbia University Press, 1965); Hargrove and Morley, *The President and the Council of Economic Advisors*; James D. Savage, *Balanced Budgets and American Politics* (Ithaca: Cornell University Press, 1988); Hall, *The Political Power of Economic Ideas*; Margaret Weir and Theda Skocpol, "State Structures and the Possibilities for 'Keynesian' Responses to the Great Depression in Sweden, Britain, and the United States," in *Bringing the State Back In*, ed. Peter B. Evans, Dietrich Rueschemeyer, and Theda Skocpol (Cambridge: Cambridge University Press, 1985), 107–163; and Weir, *Politics and Jobs*.

40. See Margaret Weir, "Ideas and Politics: The Acceptance of Keynesianism in Britain and the United States," in *The Political Power of Economic Ideas*, 53–86, for her analysis of the causes of the particular pattern of Keynesian ideas that came to be practiced in the United States.

41. These are selected ideas; others, like the balance of payments or defending the dollar, for example, are not dealt with here. What sets this study apart from other studies of economics in the Kennedy administration is that evidence concerning the ideas that will be examined here has been drawn primarily from Oral History interviews, internal administration documents, and other materials from the John F. Kennedy and Lyndon B. Johnson presidential archives.

42. Weir, *Politics and Jobs*.

43. Tobin, Gordon, Ackley, and Pechman, in CEA OH, 83–91.

44. Tobin and Heller, in CEA OH, 84–85.

45. See CEA OH, 34–38 and 46–49.

46. Samuelson and Tobin, in CEA OH, 46 and 49. Also see 32–49 for extended discussion of influences on Kennedy's economic attitudes.

47. Tobin believes that Keyserling's bitterness toward the council may have originated in this episode. See CEA OH, 34. Leon Keyserling says that it was a

pronounced characteristic of the Kennedy administration deliberately to ex-
clude advice from those whose ideas "they felt they couldn't afford exposure to."
See Keyserling interview, 15.

48. CEA OH, 34.

49. Heller, in CEA OH, 368.

50. Samuelson, in CEA OH, 84.

51. Ibid., 121.

52. Heller, in CEA OH, 142.

53. Samuelson, in CEA OH, 170–171. Kennedy recommended that the
council look at specific articles by Galbraith and Rostow on wage-price relationships. He said he was "inclined to make hard requests of both business and
labor as part of his philosophy of asking some sacrifices of the American people
in the interests of growth, stability, and a strong defense posture" (CEA OH,
181).

54. Samuelson, quoting Ted Sorensen, in CEA OH, 174. Walter Heller
said "there were several times during the spring when Kennedy said to me,
'God, look at what Nixon is doing to me on this whole question of fiscal responsibility,' or 'Look what I have to face here by way of the banker mentality,'
and so on. So he kept coming back to it" (CEO OH, 217).

55. Tobin, in CEA OH, appendix 7. Sorensen's economic sophistication
improved over time as he too learned economics from Kennedy's council tutors.

56. Samuelson, in CEA OH, 61.

57. Pechman and Samuelson, in CEA OH, 171.

58. Samuelson and Tobin, in CEA OH, 172–173.

59. Tobin, in CEA OH, 173.

60. Heller, in CEA OH, 178–179.

61. Samuelson, in CEA OH, 296.

62. Tobin, in CEA OH, 175.

63. Samuelson, in CEA OH, 175.

64. Tobin, in CEA OH, appendix 7.

65. Ibid.

66. Ibid.

67. Heller, in CEA OH, 216.

68. The Kennedy administration rarely missed an opportunity to point out
that this budget was Eisenhower's, as was the deficit.

69. See Eileen Shanahan, "Kennedy and Economy: Administration Moves
into the Third Phase in Its Policy for Solving Nation's Economic Problems,"
New York Times, July 28, 1963, sec. E, 5.

70. Heller, in CEA OH, 231.

71. Pechman, in CEA OH, 219. One of the reasons Kennedy reappointed
Republican appointee William McChesney Martin as chairman of the Federal

Reserve Bank was his need "to maintain a strong front as far as the financial community" was concerned. See also Heller, in CEA OH, 195.

72. Pechman, in CEA OH, 407.

73. See Samuelson, in CEA OH, 405.

74. See CEA OH, 425.

75. Heller, in CEA OH, 429.

76. Heller, in CEA OH, 294–295.

77. Tobin, in CEA OH, 292.

78. Heller, in CEA OH, 316.

79. Samuelson, in CEA OH, 319.

80. Heller, in CEA OH, 322.

81. Tobin, in CEA OH, 320.

82. Tobin, in CEA OH, appendix 7.

83. Pechman, in CEA OH, 405.

84. Weatherford and McDonnell, "Macroeconomic Policymaking," 107.

85. CEA OH, 252.

86. Samuelson, in CEA OH, 252.

87. Samuelson, in CEA OH, 255.

88. James L. Sundquist, *Politics and Policy: The Eisenhower, Kennedy, and Johnson Years* (Washington, D.C.: Brookings Institution, 1968), 57–58.

89. See chap. 4 for further discussion of Wirtz and his role in the War on Poverty.

90. Wirtz, press conference, 25.

91. Ibid., 26.

92. Ibid., 27.

93. Memorandum, Willard Wirtz to Theodore Sorensen, "A Declaration of Unconditional War on Poverty," January 23, 1964, White House General File, Record Group 174, Records of the Department of Labor, National Archives, Washington, D.C.

94. Willard Wirtz, author interview, Washington, D.C., November 26, 2001, tape recording.

95. Willard Wirtz, interview by author, Washington, D.C., July 23, 1991, tape recording. Also see Walter Heller's letter to the *New York Times*, dated November 11, 1963, defending the council's record against a news story in the financial pages of the October 31 *Times* charging the council with having "previously belittled the issue of structural unemployment" (*New York Times*, November 18, 1963, sec. A, 32).

96. Russell A. Nixon, "The Historical Development of the Conception and Implementation of Full Employment as Economic Policy," in *Public Service Employment: An Analysis of Its History, Problems, and Prospects*, ed. Alan Gartner, Russell A. Nixon, and Frank Riessman (New York: Praeger, 1973), 9.

97. William H. Beveridge, *Full Employment in a Free Society* (New York: Norton, 1945).

98. Cited in Philip Harvey, *Securing the Right to Employment: Social Welfare Policy and the Unemployed in the United States* (Princeton: Princeton University Press, 1989), 3–4.

99. Tobin, in CEA OH, 272.

100. For extended discussion of this, see CEA OH, 266–274.

101. Tobin, in CEA OH, 276.

102. Ibid., 283.

103. Ibid.

104. Wirtz interview, July 23, 1991.

105. Furthermore, based on the reliability of the record of economists to gauge and forecast macroeconomic behavior, the prospects for the future are not bright. No reliable trend in unemployment has ever been demonstrated by economists. See George Jaszi, "An Economic Accountant's Audit," *American Economic Review* 76, no. 2 (May 1986): 411–18; and Arthur Burns, cited in Hargrove and Morley, *The President and the Council of Economic Advisors*, 37; Harvey, *Securing the Right to Employment*, chap. 1; Alexander Keyssar, "History and the Problem of Unemployment," *Socialist Review* 19, no. 4 (October–December 1989): 15–34.

107. Defined in Harvey, *Securing the Right to Employment*, 14, as 2 percent.

3. CHANGE AND INCAPACITY IN THE DEPARTMENT OF LABOR

1. The service has 2,200 local offices nationwide according to Stanley H. Ruttenberg and Jocelyn Gutchess, *The Federal-State Employment Service: A Critique* (Baltimore: Johns Hopkins University Press, 1970), 1.

2. National Research Council, Committee on Department of Labor Manpower Research and Development, Assembly of Behavioral and Social Sciences, *Knowledge and Policy in Manpower: A Study of the Manpower Research and Development Program in the Department of Labor* (Washington, D.C.: National Academy of Sciences, 1975), 51.

3. Willard Wirtz, interview by author, Washington, D.C., July 23, 1991, tape recording.

4. This was Senator Gaylord Nelson's proposal.

5. William Cannon, interview by Michael L. Gillette, May 21, 1982, tape recording, Lyndon B. Johnson Library, Austin.

6. Margaret Weir and Theda Skocpol, "State Structures and the Possibilities for 'Keynesian' Responses to the Great Depression in Sweden, Britain, and the United States," in *Bringing the State Back In*, ed. Peter B. Evans, Dietrich

Rueschemeyer, and Theda Skocpol, 107–163. See also Margaret Weir, "The Federal Government and Unemployment: The Frustration of Policy Innovation from the New Deal to the Great Society," in *The Politics of Social Policy in the United States*, ed. Margaret Weir, Ana Shola Orloff, and Theda Skocpol, 149–197; Theda Skocpol and Kenneth Finegold, "Economic Intervention and the Early New Deal," *Political Science Quarterly* 97, no. 2 (1982): 255–278; Stephen Skowronek, *Building a New American State: The Expansion of National Administrative Capacities, 1877–1920* (Cambridge: Cambridge University Press, 1982); Hugh Heclo, *Modern Social Policies in Britain and Sweden* (New Haven: Yale University Press, 1974). See also Margaret Weir, *Politics and Jobs: The Boundaries of Employment Policy in the United States* (Princeton: Princeton University Press, 1992).

7. Weir and Skocpol, "State Structures," 118. The novel policy aspects of the Economic Opportunity Act of 1964—the establishment of a new agency within the executive branch (the Office of Economic Opportunity) to administer it—contradict this theory. Demetrios Caraley believes that the development of the New Deal also rebuts the theory in part since new bureaus were set up to administer new federal programs during that period (Demetrios Caraley, personal communication, October 19, 1991), though some states had applicable bureaucratic and administrative experiences and histories, as Theda Skocpol and others have shown.

8. Memorandum, Willard Wirtz to Theodore Sorenson, "A Declaration of Unconditional War on Poverty," January 23, 1964, White House General File, Record Group 174, Records of the Department of Labor, National Archives.

9. Some of the following discussion draws from "The Administrative History of the Department of Labor During the Administration of President Lyndon B. Johnson," vol. 1 and 2 (part 2), Lyndon B. Johnson Library, Austin. Henceforth this will be cited as "Labor Administrative History."

10. This office is referred to as the Office of Automation and Training in "Labor Administrative History."

11. "Labor Administrative History," 3.

12. Stanley Ruttenberg, interview by David G. McComb, February 25, 1969, tape recording, Lyndon B. Johnson Library, Austin.

13. Garth Mangum, *MDTA: Foundation of Federal Manpower Policy* (Baltimore: Johns Hopkins University Press, 1968), 1. The discussion of the MDTA in the rest of the paragraph is drawn from Mangum's *MDTA* and also owes much to "Labor Administrative History."

14. Ibid.

15. "Labor Administrative History," 5.

16. The chairman of the Labor Department–HEW appropriations subcommittee was also a former building tradesman. See Mangum, *MDTA*, 45.

17. Mangum, *MDTA*, 46.

18. See Ruttenberg interview.

19. Ruttenberg and Gutchess, *The Federal-State Employment Service*, 3.

20. Arnold L. Nemore and Garth L. Mangum, *Reorienting the Federal-State Employment Service*, Policy Papers in Human Resources and Industrial Relations, No. 8 (Ann Arbor: Institute of Labor and Industrial Relations; Washington, D.C.: National Manpower Policy Task Force, 1968), 2.

21. Wight Bakke, in U.S. Congress, House, Committee on Education and Labor, Select Committee on Labor, *Hearings, Public Employment Service*, 88th Cong., 2d sess., 1964, 6, cited in Nemore and Mangum, *Reorienting the Federal-State Employment Service*, 8.

22. Ruttenberg and Gutchess, *The Federal-State Employment Service*, 7.

23. Ibid., 12.

24. Nemore and Mangum, *Reorienting the Federal-State Employment Service*, 28.

25. The Vocational Educational Act of 1963, the Youth Employment Act, administration of the MDTA, and the developing antipoverty policy agenda in the White House and throughout the executive branch were measures that would involve USES. The passage of the Economic Opportunity Act of 1964 added the Neighborhood Youth Corps (NYC) to the Manpower Administration's inventory of jobs policies. Administration of the program was delegated to the Labor Department by the Office of Economic Opportunity in the beginning.

26. "Labor Administrative History," 4.

27. Ibid.

28. Included in these efforts to strengthen its advocacy role for the unemployment policies it wanted, the department created a community of academic manpower experts. For the findings of the early stages of their research, see National Research Council, *Knowledge and Policy in Manpower*.

29. See Ruttenberg interview, Wirtz interview, and Willard Wirtz, author interview, Washington, D.C., November 26, 2001, tape recording.

30. For extended discussion of the misunderstanding between Wirtz and President Johnson, see Ruttenberg interview; James Reynolds, interview by Joe B. Frantz, February 1, 1971, tape recording, Lyndon B. Johnson Library, Austin; Clifford Clark, interview by Joe B. Frantz, June 16, 1970, tape recording, Lyndon B. Johnson Library, Austin.

31. Richard Blumenthal, "The Bureaucracy: Antipoverty and the Community Action program," in *American Political Institutions and Public Policy*, ed. Allan P. Sindler (Boston: Little, Brown, 1969), 146.

32. Cannon interview.

33. Cannon interview. Willard Wirtz denies that friction existed between

him and Moynihan on this subject, saying that the lack of accord that did develop between them was concerned with the release of Moynihan's report "The Negro Family" (Wirtz interview).

34. Stephen Pollack, interview by Thomas H. Baker, January 29, 1969, tape recording, Lyndon B. Johnson Library, Austin.

35. Christopher Weeks, interview by Michael L. Gillette, December 10, 1980, tape recording, Lyndon B. Johnson Library, Austin.

36. Jack Conway, interview by Michael L. Gillette, August 13, 1980, tape recording, Lyndon B. Johnson, Austin.

37. Ruttenberg interview.

38. Ibid.

39. Ibid.

40. Ibid.

41. All the information and quotations in this paragraph thus far are from the Wirtz interview.

42. The quotations in the remainder of this paragraph are from memorandum, Wirtz to Sorensen. See this document for Wirtz's proposals for specific measures related to organizing a jobs-related antipoverty program.

43. See William Julius Wilson, *The Truly Disadvantaged: The Inner City, the Underclass, and Public Policy* (Chicago: University of Chicago Press, 1987), for a contemporary analysis that posits the centrality of male head of household employment.

44. As would be the effects of unemployment.

45. Willard Wirtz to journalist Hobart Rowen in 1962. Cited in Hobart Rowen, "Poor People in Rich America," *Washington Post*, July 4, 1991.

46. Kermit Gordon, in Walter Heller, Kermit Gordon, James Tobin, Gardner Ackley, and Paul Samuelson, interview by Joseph Pechman, August 1, 1964, tape recording, John F. Kennedy Library, Boston, 287. Citations of this Oral History Interview henceforth will be abbreviated as CEA OH.

47. Walter Heller, in CEA OH, 287.

48. Ibid.

49. Ibid., 288.

50. Wirtz interview.

51. Ibid. Perhaps Wirtz was right. The CEA's James Tobin believed that "all non-professional economists, all laymen in economic matters are instinctively attracted by the idea of structural unemployment; by the idea that people are just displaced from work by machines and then they don't move and are permanently out of work" (Tobin, in CEA OH, 285).

52. Wirtz interview.

53. Ibid.

54. James Tobin of the council expressed his unhappiness with the council's

role, feeling that at times it was not used as the president's staff proper in economic matters but rather as another contending party. See appendix, CEA OH, n. 5.

55. Wirtz concedes only a "conversational 10 percent" of his goals were territorial ambition (Wirtz interview). The information and quotations in the balance of the chapter are from this interview.

4. Social Forces, Civil Rights, and the Struggle for Jobs

1. See Dona Cooper Hamilton and Charles V. Hamilton, *The Dual Agenda: Social Policies of Civil Rights Organizations, New Deal to the Present* (New York: Columbia University Press, 1997), for a thorough analysis of the "dual agenda" of the civil rights movement and its concern with employment-related social policy issues. See August Meier's "Civil Rights Strategies for Negro Employment," in *Employment, Race, and Poverty*, ed. Arthur M. Ross and Herbert Hill (New York: Harcourt, Brace, and World, 1967), 175–204, for a review of the approaches civil rights groups took to bring the issue of black employment to the attention of government, employers, and the public.

2. William Capron, in "Poverty and Urban Policy, Conference Transcript of 1973 Group Discussion of the Kennedy Administration Urban Poverty Programs and Policies," John F. Kennedy Library, Boston, 182. The oral history records from this conference suggest there was little direct link between the civil rights leadership and the War on Poverty, which is interesting in itself.

3. Citations of the *New York Times* articles and editorials follow in an appendix at the end of this chapter.

4. The research for this section included a page-by-page analysis of 365 days of *New York Times* coverage for the year 1963, examining the front pages, editorial pages, and "Week in Review" pages for evidence of the relationship between employment and the needs of the black community. Items fell into four categories: there were 53 on poverty, 110 on employment, 214 on the economy, and 495 on civil rights.

5. This was followed by a June 14 item on the impending release of a union hiring study.

6. A June 23 "Week in Review" story reported on the Philadelphia and NYC confrontations and the NAACP's charge that New York City colluded with the unions to bar blacks from skilled work because "it did not use its authority to prevent such practices."

7. On June 28 "Governor Speeds Projects to Open Jobs to Negroes" said that Rockefeller agreed to accelerate $4 billion of state construction contracts to

create more jobs for blacks and mentioned again Mayor Wagner's efforts to seek more jobs for blacks.

8. The two other stories were June 8th's editorial linking the situation to problems of race and, on the same day, a letter to the editor questioning the efficacy of the tax cut in pulling the young unemployed into the economy.

9. He went on to mention the president's initiation of a campaign of national education with his June 12 television address and to clarify that "what is now being discussed here is legislation that would not only finance a much larger job-training program for those on relief, but would make welfare payments dependent in many cases on participating in job-training programs."

10. Charts illustrating the widely divergent life chances of a black child and a white child born in the United States appeared on the same page, a metaphor President Kennedy used in his June 12 national television address. Half of the six charts illustrated the economic status of blacks as against whites.

11. The job-training expansion would require a separate bill with new authorization and additional appropriations that were described as "huge."

12. A few miscellaneous articles were outside of these categories.

13. These items appeared on August 1–12, 14, 15, 17, 19, and 28.

14. Among these stories were "Near-Riot Flares in Race Protest at Project Here," on August 1, about Brooklyn demonstrations at the Downstate Medical facility, pressing for more jobs for blacks and Puerto Ricans in the construction industry; "Wagner's Panel on Hiring Negroes Notes Progress," on August 3, on the first meeting of Mayor Wagner's committee to ease the racial tension that had produced more than 800 arrests and sporadic violence in recent weeks; "Jim Crow on the Job," in the "Week in Review" on August 4, which pointed out the increasing focus in the North on "economic opportunity for the Negro" and the growing intensity of the demonstrations in New York; and, on August 19, "CORE Expects Agreements on Jobs Here in 2 Weeks," on James Farmer's announcement of a pending settlement between the city and civil rights organizations to end discrimination in the construction industry.

15. One other story, "Kennedy Opposes Quotas for Jobs on Basis of Race" (August 21), and three letters in August (August 7, 8, 25, and 26) dealt with job issues.

16. The *Times* noted that it was the "greatest assembly for a redress of grievances that this capital has ever seen." On the same day, the lead editorial said the marchers' demand for equality in all aspects of American life was, in concept and execution, in the noblest tradition of American democracy. The marchers made it clear, the *Times* continued, that "they regarded the Administration package as a minimum legal underpinning for equal treatment and equal opportunity."

17. Claude Sitton, "In the South: Main Emphasis Is Shifted from Demonstrations to Political Activity," *New York Times*, October 20, 1963, sec. E, 3.

18. It described the direct action struggle in recent months in the North in housing and hiring. The gains were small, it said, resulting from the difficulty of eliminating de facto segregation, "because it rests in part on economic factors." It noted the concentration in the North of protest aimed at hiring practices, particularly in the construction industry, the role of organized labor, and the establishment of committees in certain northern cities, including New York, to try to provide more job opportunities for minorities. The story described the great battle to come over the president's civil rights bill and noted that it included an attack on job discrimination.

19. The story also included an analysis of the dimensions of black unemployment.

20. Among other stories, one on the same front page announced "City Aide Confident Unions Will Accept 600 Negroes Soon." A September 8 story, "Rights Groups Plan March on City Hall for Jobs Sept. 29," told of a planned mass demonstration, similar to the march on Washington, to protest discrimination in the construction industry. Another story, on September 14, "Non-Bias Job Plan Here Draws 2,600," told of the disappointing turnout in applications for jobs and union apprenticeship training during the city's drive to get more blacks and Puerto Ricans into the construction trades. "Negro Job Quotas Urged in Jersey," on September 25, announced a New Jersey Advisory Committee's findings in a report to the U.S. Commission on Civil Rights, rebuking county, state, and federal governments for their unwillingness or inability to enforce existing civil rights laws on employment bias.

21. A story on October 16, "Robert Kennedy Tries to Prevent Rights Deadlock," with a subheading "Attorney General Calls for Bipartisanship—Supports Fair Employment Plan," concerned Attorney General Robert Kennedy's appearance before the House Judiciary Committee to rescue the legislation from "a developing impasse" partly resulting from the objections of some moderate Republicans to certain provisions of the bill. Robert Kennedy supported the FEPC, but weakly. The October 20 item "Moves on Rights" reiterated the problems the administration faced with passage of its civil rights bill and noted the FEPC provision's endorsement by Robert Kennedy. It concluded with criticism from civil rights leaders of the administration's attempted "sell-out." Two stories—"Halleck Pressed for Commitment on a Rights Bill," on October 25, and "House Unit Votes Bipartisan Plan for Civil Rights," on October 30—continued to tell of the legislation's progress in Congress, both mentioning the provisions for prohibiting job discrimination. The FEPC remained in the revised bill.

22. Two final miscellaneous items were the October 9 story "Job Training Bill Passed by Senate," which told of the Senate's overwhelming approval of a five-year program of expanded vocational education for a long-range attack on

unemployment that went beyond the measure voted by the House, and a letter to the editor on October 21 upholding the use of ethnic surveys to improve minority job opportunities.

23. They appear on November 4, 11, 14, 21, 24, and 30.

24. The occasion for this message was the release of a special Labor Department study disclosing that the federal retraining program was shutting out many of those in need of skills to qualify for work. This was the creaming process of the United State Employment Service (USES). The *Times* said this was part of the unemployment situation that demanded national attention and action. Two stories, on December 5, "Johnson Appeals for Aid of Labor and Businessmen," and December 8's "Week in Review" piece, "Situation on Rights," dealt with President Johnson's meeting with business and labor groups to enlist their help in "destroying the numbing attrition of discrimination in employment."

25. An editorial on December 26, "Civic On-Job Training," commended the city's acting labor commissioner, James McFadden, for initiating an experiment in job training in municipal agencies as a useful addition to the "limited range of instruments the community has for reducing the waste of large-scale unemployment."

26. "Legislative Background of Economic Opportunity Act of 1964: War on Poverty," "History: Part of Social Problems Chapter," President's Papers, 1963–69, Legislative Background EOA 1964 WoP, box 1, Lyndon B. Johnson Library, Austin, 1.

27. MDTA was also an exceptionally popular bill.

28. Paul Burstein, *Discrimination, Jobs, and Politics: The Struggle for Equal Employment Opportunity in the United States Since the New Deal* (Chicago: University of Chicago Press, 1985), 46. Public opinion, according to Burstein's own work and other studies, seems to have been the primary reason Congress acted on EEO (70).

29. Chap. 2 of *Economic Report of the President* (Washington, D.C.: U.S. Government Printing Office, 1964), cited in John C. Donovan, *The Politics of Poverty*, 3d ed. (Washington, D.C.: University of America Press, 1980), 94–95. William Capron has said that the significance of this chapter was ignored by antipoverty planners in the period. See "Poverty and Urban Policy, Conference Transcript of 1973 Group Discussion of the Kennedy Administration Urban Poverty Programs and Policies, " John F. Kennedy Library, Boston.

30. Charles C. Killingsworth, "Negroes in a Changing Labor Market," in *Employment, Race, and Poverty*, ed. Arthur M. Ross and Herbert Hill (New York: Harcourt, Brace, and World, 1967), 49–75. The following two paragraphs draw on Killingsworth's analysis. Contemporary analyses of the dimensions of black unemployment have been done by William Julius Wilson, for example. See his

Declining Significance of Race: Blacks and Changing American Institutions (Chicago: University of Chicago Press, 1978) and *The Truly Disadvantaged: The Inner City, the Underclass, and Public Policy* (Chicago: University of Chicago Press, 1987). Killingsworth's work on the labor market is used here because it was available in the period under study, as was that of Arthur Ross and Herman P. Miller, an expert on income distribution. See Miller's *Poverty: American Style* (Belmont, Calif.: Wadsworth, 1966) and *Rich Man, Poor Man* (New York: Crowell, 1964).

31. A pattern we see repeated today with the continued displacement of low- and unskilled workers by the new technological changes in products and production techniques.

32. Moreover, the traditional center-city vertical factory was being replaced by the new spread-out single-level factories employing assembly-line modes of production, which could be built on the broad and comparatively inexpensive tracts of land available outside central cities. See chap. 5 of Wilson's *Declining Significance of Race* for an analysis of how the factors of industrialization affected central-city employment.

33. A pattern in evidence today, although it is now called "spatial mismatch." For a review of the empirical literature on the spatial mismatch hypothesis, see Harry J. Holzer, "The Spatial Mismatch Hypothesis: What Has The Evidence Shown?" *Urban Studies* 28, no. 1 (1991): 105–122.

34. Killingsworth, "Negroes in a Changing Labor Market," 57. Killingsworth does not offer adjusted white rates, although hidden unemployment would presumably increase among whites as well when white unemployment rates are up.

35. Donovan, *The Politics of Poverty*, 101.

36. Arthur M. Ross, "The Negro in the American Economy," in *Employment, Race, and Poverty*, ed. Arthur M. Ross and Herbert Hill (New York: Harcourt, Brace, and World, 1967), 33.

37. Donovan, *The Politics of Poverty*, 102.

38. This information is from Killingsworth, "Negroes in a Changing Labor Market," 27.

39. Michael K. Brown and Stephen P. Erie, "Blacks and the Legacy of the Great Society: The Economic and Social Impact of Federal Social Policy," *Public Policy* 29, no. 3 (summer 1981): 314.

40. Ibid. This assessment was confirmed by Secretary of Labor Willard Wirtz. See Willard Wirtz, interview by author, Washington, D.C., July 23, 1991, tape recording.

41. The information in this paragraph is from Whitney M. Young, Jr., *To Be Equal* (New York: McGraw-Hill, 1964), 54–55.

42. Hamilton and Hamilton, *The Dual Agenda*.

43. Ibid. See Walter White correspondence, Correspondence of Walter White and Congressman Dow H. Harter, October 25 and 26, 1937, NAACP Papers, Group 1, C-256, Library of Congress, Manuscript Division, Washington, D.C.

44. Ibid., 290. The motto of the Urban League in the 1930s was "Jobs Not Alms." In 1953 the Tuskegee Institute raised the jobs issue when it announced a new annual report on Negro jobs and income figures to replace its annual Lynching Letter. With the demise of lynching (two in the previous two years and six since 1949) as the most serious problem facing the black community, the issue of jobs came to the fore.

45. Meier, "Civil Rights Strategies for Negro Employment," 176. Since sources on black approaches to employment issues are scarce, the following discussion draws heavily on Meier. Hamilton and Hamilton and Meier have been the principal sources for discussion of the role of national black organizations in pressing for government action on economic issues.

46. Robert Dallek, *Lone Star Rising: Lyndon Johnson and His Times, 1908–1960* (New York: Oxford University Press, 1991), 135–136. "The Negro was born in depression," Dallek quotes one commentator, "it only became official when it hit the white man" (ibid.).

47. Among blacks, the NRA was known as "Negro Run Around" and "Negroes Ruined Again." See ibid., 136.

48. Hamilton and Hamilton, *The Dual Agenda*, 297.

49. Ibid., 291.

50. NAACP Annual Report of 1934, cited in ibid., 291.

51. Hamilton and Hamilton, *The Dual Agenda*, 293. The Social Security Act created the federal/state unemployment compensation system, which was to serve as a national insurance program to protect against involuntary joblessness. Although it is subject to federal guidelines, the system consists of separate programs in each state.

52. Ibid.

53. Taylor Branch, *Parting the Waters: America in the King Years, 1954–1964* (New York: Simon and Schuster, 1988), 121.

54. Meier, "Civil Rights Strategies for Negro Employment," 180.

55. Hamilton and Hamilton, *The Dual Agenda*, 296.

56. James Farmer, interview by Harri Baker, October 1969, July 20, 1971, tape recording, Lyndon B. Johnson Library, Austin.

57. Benjamin Quarles, "A. Phillip Randolph: Labor Leader at Large," in *Black Leaders of the Twentieth Century*, ed. John Hope Franklin and August Meier (Urbana: University of Illinois Press, 1982), 161.

58. Branch, *Parting the Waters*, 849–850.

59. Bayard Rustin, interview by Thomas H. Baker, June 17, 1969, tape recording, Lyndon B. Johnson Library, Austin.

60. Wirtz interview. The second part of the program was job training. King's interest may have been a function of his need to be of relevance to ghetto youth as he tried to bridge the gap between his centrist stance and the impatience of activists in the movement. This stance became especially pronounced after his humiliating failure to affect the power structure in Albany, Georgia, in 1962, a failure that was followed by increasingly harsh criticism of King.

61. Young, *To Be Equal*, 29.

62. Nancy J. Weiss, "Whitney M. Young, Jr.: Committing the Power Structure to the Cause of Civil Rights," in *Black Leaders of the Twentieth Century*. ed. John Hope Franklin and August Meier (Urbana: University of Illinois Press, 1982), 338.

63. Rustin interview.

64. Hamilton and Hamilton, *The Dual Agenda*, 298.

65. The Freedom Budget was not taken seriously in Washington policy circles. See Hamilton and Hamilton, *The Dual Agenda*, 299–300, especially Arthur C. Logan's May 8, 1967, testimony before the Senate Subcommittee on Employment, Manpower and Poverty of the Committee of Labor and Public Welfare.

66. David Levering Lewis, "Martin Luther King, Jr., and the Promise of Nonviolent Populism," in *Black Leaders of the Twentieth Century*, ed. John Hope Franklin and August Meier (Urbana: University of Illinois Press, 1982), 292.

67. Ibid.

68. Ibid., 293.

69. Martin Luther King, Jr., cited in Lewis, "Martin Luther King, Jr.," 297.

70. Martin Luther King, Jr., "Remaining Awake Through a Great Revolution," speech at the Washington National Cathedral, March 31, 1968.

71. Lewis, "Martin Luther King, Jr.," 299.

72. Jack M. Bloom, *Class, Race, and the Civil Rights Movement* (Bloomington: Indiana University Press, 1987), 212–213.

73. Lewis, "Martin Luther King, Jr.," 302.

74. See chap. 17, "Recommendations for National Action," and chap. 7, "Unemployment, Family Structure, and Social Disorganization," in *The Report of the National Advisory Commission on Civil Disorders*, advance ed. (New York: Bantam, 1968). See Fred R. Harris and Roger W. Wilkins, eds., *Quiet Riots: Race and Poverty in the United States* (New York: Pantheon, 1988), for a retrospective assessment twenty years after the Kerner Commission report of conditions of race and poverty in the United States.

75. See chap. 4, "The Basic Causes," in *The Report of the National Advisory Commission*.

76. The argument for government intervention in the form of public works jobs programs or job provision had also been steadily delegitimized in the United States by politically right-wing opponents of Roosevelt during and following his administrations. Such critiques of the old approach of FDR and his public works jobs, especially from F. Hayek, are considered influences on the new Keynesian policy leaders as they shifted their emphasis from public works jobs to macroeconomic measures. See Haynes Walton, personal communication, November 15, 2001. Also Sumner Rosen, personal communication.

5. GOVERNMENTAL WILL: THE LIMITS OF NOBLESSE OBLIGE

1. Adam Yarmolinsky, in "Poverty and Urban Policy, Conference Transcript of 1973 Group Discussion of the Kennedy Administration Urban Poverty Programs and Policies," John F. Kennedy Library, Boston, 183.

2. Stephen Steinberg, *Turning Back: The Retreat from Racial Justice in American Thought and Policy* (Boston: Beacon, 1995).

3. Robert C. Lieberman, *Shifting the Color Line: Race and the American Welfare State* (Cambridge: Harvard University Press, 1998).

4. "Slow Start on Ending Bias," *New York Times*, April 28, 1963, sec. E, 10.

5. James Farmer, interview by Paige Mulhollan, July 20, 1971, tape recording, Lyndon B. Johnson Library, Austin.

6. Taylor Branch, *Parting the Waters: America in the King Years, 1954–1964* (New York: Simon and Schuster, 1988), 699–700.

7. Jack M. Bloom, *Class, Race, and the Civil Rights Movement* (Bloomington: Indiana University Press), 167–168.

8. SNCC worker John Lewis (Senator Lewis today) on August 28, 1963, cited in Branch, *Parting the Waters*, 870.

9. Branch, *Parting the Waters*, 866. A symbol of movement frustration, Albany had been a disaster for King in 1962 when he failed to secure concessions from the city in the campaign to desegregate public facilities there. To some movement activists, Albany represented the failure of nonviolence as a tactic.

10. James Reston, "No Longer a 'Problem,' but a Revolution," *New York Times*, June 16, 1963, sec. E, 10.

11. Branch, *Parting the Waters*, 863.

12. Roy Wilkins, interview by Thomas H. Baker, April 1, 1969, tape recording, Lyndon B. Johnson Library, Austin, 5.

13. Bayard Rustin, interview by by Thomas H. Baker, June 17, 1969, tape recording, Lyndon B. Johnson Library, Austin, pp. 3, 5.

14. Whitney M. Young, Jr., interview by Thomas H. Baker, June 18, 1969, tape recording, Lyndon B. Johnson Library, Austin, 3.

15. Ibid., pp. 6–7.

16. Bayard Rustin, interview by Thomas H. Baker, June 30, 1969, tape recording, Lyndon B. Johnson Library, Austin, 16.

17. James Farmer, interview by Harri Baker, October 1969, tape recording, Lyndon B. Johnson Library, Austin, 7.

18. James Farmer interview, July 20, 1971, Lyndon B. Johnson Library, Austin, 25.

19. Ibid.

20. Wilkins interview.

21. My analysis of the *Times* revealed 495 items on civil rights, twice the number in the next largest category, the economy.

22. The *Times* also regularly pressed Kennedy on the need for jobs and job training, as demonstrated in the previous chapter.

23. "New Showdown In Race Struggle," *New York Times*, May 26, 1963, sec. E, 2.

24. James Reston, "How to Make Things Worse Than They Really Are," *New York Times*, May 31, 1963, sec. A, 24.

25. Anthony Lewis, "Kennedy Weighs New Rights Law: Strong Action Could Jeopardize His Programs in Congress," *New York Times*, June 2, 1963, sec. E, 8.

26. "Civil Rights Program," *New York Times*, June 5, 1963, sec. A, 20.

27. "A Presidential Gesture," *New York Times*, June 2, 1963, sec. E, 10. Such a gesture seems almost inconceivable today after the assassination of the Kennedys, King, and others in the decade.

28. James Reston, "Who Is Going to Dominate the Racial Debate?" *New York Times*, June 2, 1963, sec. E, 10.

29. Layhmond Robinson, "Robert Kennedy Consults Negros Here About North," *New York Times*, May 25, 1963, 1; James Reston, "The Nation and the Parties on the Racial Issue," *New York Times*, June 7, 1963, sec. A, 30.

30. James Reston, "Kennedy's Uncertain Approach to the Racial Crisis," *New York Times*, June 9, 1963, sec. E, 12.

31. Anthony Lewis, "Washington: Kennedy Commits Administration to Determined Effort to Improve Conditions," *New York Times*, June 16, 1963, sec. E, 3.

32. Wilkins interview.

33. Tom Wicker, "Johnson Acts to Build a Broad Base of National Support, His Procedure: President Has Adopted the Program and Approach of His Predecessor," *New York Times*, December 8, 1963, sec. E, 3.

34. Tom Wicker, "Johnson Bids Congress Enact Civil Rights Bill with Speed: Asks End of Hate and Violence," *New York Times*, November 28, 1963, sec. A, 1.

35. See "Quicker Pace On Rights," *New York Times*, December 5, 1963,

sec. E, 44; Anthony Lewis, "President Spurs Drive for House to Act on Rights," *New York Times*, December 4, 1963, sec. A, 1; Anthony Lewis, "Civil Rights Issue: Administration Will Be Judged to a Large Degree by the Fate of This Bill," *New York Times*, December 8, 1963, sec. E, 4.

36. *New York Times*, December 5, 1963, sec. E, 44.

37. "What's on Rights," *New York Times*, June 9, 1963, sec. E, 12.

38. James Reston, "On Exploring the Moon and Attacking the Slums," *New York Times*, December 20, 1963, sec. A, 28.

39. Robert Dallek. *Lone Star Rising: Lyndon Johnson and His Times, 1908–1960* (New York: Oxford University Press, 1991), 126.

40. The National Youth Administration was a Roosevelt program to get young people back to work.

41. Dallek, *Lone Star Rising*, 131.

42. Walter Heller, quoted cited in Nicholas Lemann, *The Promised Land* (New York: Knopf, 1991), 142.

43. For LBJ's enthusiastic descriptions of the program, see Michael R. Beschloss, *Taking Charge: The Johnson White House Tapes, 1963–1964* (New York: Simon and Schuster, 1997), 209, 211.

44. Yarmolinsky, Brandeis conference, 249–250.

45. Nicholas Lemann, *The Promised Land*, 143.

46. Ibid., 144.

47. Frances Fox Piven and Richard A. Cloward have made such arguments. See their *Regulating the Poor: The Functions of Public Welfare* (New York: Vintage, 1971) and *Poor Peoples' Movements: Why They Succeed, How They Fail* (New York: Vintage, 1979).

48. Memo from Robert Lampman to Walter Heller, June 10, 1963, 4, President's Papers, 1963–69, Legislative Background EOA 1964 WoP, box 1, Lyndon B. Johnson Library, Austin.

49. David Zarefsky, *President Johnson's War on Poverty: Rhetoric and History* (University: University of Alabama Press, 1986), 27.

50. Doris Kearns, *Lyndon Johnson and the American Dream* (New York: Harper and Row, 1976), 85.

51. For some sources on task forces, see David M. Welborn and Jesse Burkhead, *Intergovernmental Relations in the American Administrative State: The Johnson Presidency* (Austin: University of Texas Press, 1989); Hugh Davis Graham, *The Uncertain Triumph: Federal Education Policy in the Kennedy and Johnson Years* (Chapel Hill: University of North Carolina Press, 1984); Nancy Kegan Smith, "Presidential Task Force Operation During the Johnson Administration," *Presidential Studies Quarterly* 15 (spring 1985): 320–329; Emmette S. Redford and Richard T. McCulley, *White House Operations: The Johnson Presidency* (Austin: University of Texas Press, 1986); and Norman C. Thomas and Harold L. Wol-

man, "The Presidency and Policy Formulation: The Task Force Device," *Public Administration Review* 29 (September/October 1969): 459–491.

52. Heller's interagency poverty committee itself stemmed from the dearth of imaginative responses from existing agencies when polled for ideas for dealing with poverty.

53. James Gaither, interview by Dorothy Pierce, January 17, 1969, tape recording, Lyndon B. Johnson Library, Austin.

54. Ann Oppenheimer Hamilton, interview by Michael L. Gillette, October 22, 1980, tape recording, Lyndon B. Johnson Library, Austin, 10.

55. Harold W. Horowitz, interview by Michael L. Gillette, February 23, 1983, tape recording, Lyndon B. Johnson Library, Austin, 27; Norbert A. Schlei, interview by Michael L. Gillette, May 15, 1980, tape recording, Lyndon B. Johnson Library, 2. Other Oral History interviews at the Lyndon B. Johnson Library that I consulted for information on the task force operations include William Cannon, interview by Michael L. Gillette, May 21, 1982; Douglas Cater, interview by David G. McComb, April 29, 1969; Jack T. Conway, interview by Michael L. Gillette, August 13, 1980; James Gaither, interview by Dorothy Pierce, January 15 and 17, 1969; Hamilton interview; Robert Lampman, interview by Michael L. Gillette, May 24, 1983; C. Robert Perrin, interview by Stephen Goodell, March 10, 1969; James J. Reynolds, interview by Joe B. Frantz, February 1, 1971; James L. Sundquist, interview by Charles T. Morrissey and Ronald J. Grele, September 13, 1965, for the John F. Kennedy Library, Boston, and interview by Steven Goodell, April 7, 1969, tape recording, Lyndon B. Johnson Library, Austin; and Christopher Weeks, interview by Michael L. Gillette, December 10, 1980, and September 28, 1981.

56. Schlei interview. Also see interviews of Weeks, Oppenheimer, Lampman.

57. See interviews of Weeks, Oppenheimer, Gaither, Cannon, Schlei, Conway, and others.

58. Schlei interview.

59. Sundquist interview, April 7, 1969.

60. Schlei interview.

61. Ibid. See also interviews of Weeks, Oppenheimer, Lampman, Horowitz, Conway, Cannon, Gaither, and others.

62. Weeks interview, September 28, 1981.

63. Presumably Yarmolinsky borrowed this phrase from contemporary Ivory soap ads and commercials claiming the soap was "99 & 44/100 percent pure."

64. Brandeis conference, 189.

65. Ibid., 166.

66. For example, two important radical voices on institutional racism have

been those of Adolph Reed, Jr., and Stephen Steinberg. "Neither Reed nor Steinberg is a serious scholar," according to William Julius Wilson (cited in David Remnick, "Profiles: Dr. Wilson's Neighborhood," *New Yorker*, April 29 and May 6, 1996, 104).

67. Moynihan's "Report on the Negro Family" is found in Lee Rainwater and William L. Yancy, eds., *The Moynihan Report and the Politics of Controversy* (Cambridge, Mass.: MIT Press, 1967); William Julius Wilson, *The Truly Disadvantaged: The Inner City, the Underclass, and Public Policy* (Chicago: University of Chicago Press, 1987).

68. Stokely Carmichael and Charles V. Hamilton, *Black Power: The Politics of Liberation in America* (New York: Vintage, 1967). Some subsequent theoretical works dealing with the concept are L. K. Knowles and K. Prewitt, *Institutional Racism in America* (Englewood Cliffs, N.J.: Prentice-Hall, 1969); W. K. Tabb, *The Political Economy of the Black Ghetto* (New York: Norton, 1970); J. M. Jones, *Prejudice and Racism* (New York: Addison-Wesley, 1972); R. Blauner, *Racial Oppression in America* (New York: Harper and Row, 1972); and D. Wellman, *Portraits of White Racism* (Cambridge: Cambridge University Press, 1977).

69. Carmichael and Hamilton, *Black Power*, 4.

70. Steinberg, *Turning Back*, 56.

71. Ibid., 179. See William E. Forbath, "Caste, Class, and Equal Citizenship," *Michigan Law Review* 98, no. 1 (1999), for an unusual essay on the social citizenship tradition of constitutional interpretation, which posits that economic transformations in industrial society mandated that new duties of government include decent work, broad social provision, and a measure of economic democracy.

72. Ibid., 179–180.

73. Ibid., 183, 184.

74. Ibid., 184.

75. Robert C. Lieberman, "Structure and Choice in Race and American Political Development" (paper prepared for the conference "Race in the Development of American Politics and Society," University of Rochester, Rochester, N.Y., May 1–2, 1998), 8–9. Lieberman cites V. O. Key, Jr., with the assistance of Alexander Heard, *Southern Politics in State and Nation* (New York: Random House, Vintage, Caravelle, 1949); Richard Franklin Bensel, *Sectionalism and American Political Development, 1880-1980* (Madison: University of Wisconsin Press, 1984).

76. Carmichael and Hamilton, *Black Power*, 4. See Robert C. Lieberman, "The Political Construction of Race and the Development of American Institutions" (photocopy).

77. Lieberman does analyze the War on Poverty period, but his efforts are to explain the War on Poverty's failure to incorporate blacks successfully into

full social citizenship following their successes in the realms of civil and political rights. He views the War on Poverty as a failed attempt to establish social citizenship for U.S. blacks on national grounds, which would have mitigated against their parochial disadvantage in the South. See Lieberman, "Structure and Choice."

78. Between 1930 and 1970, the percentage of blacks living outside of the South grew from .3 percent in 1930 to nearly 50 percent in 1970. See U.S. Bureau of the Census, *Historical Statistics of the United States, Colonial Times to 1970* (Washington, D.C.: U.S. Government Printing Office, 1975), part 1, 22.

79. Mike N. Manatos, interview by Joe B. Frantz, August 25, 1969, tape recording, Lyndon B. Johnson Library, Austin.

80. Weeks interview, September 28, 1981, 18.

81. Yarmolinsky, Brandeis conference, 239–240.

82. Weeks interview, September 28, 1981, 41.

83. Ibid., 40.

84. Zarefsky, *President Johnson's War on Poverty*, 43.

85. Ibid., 27.

86. Cannon, Brandeis conference, 235.

87. Yarmolinsky, Brandeis conference, 235.

88. Yarmolinsky, Cannon, and Fenn (attributing the comment to Shriver), Brandeis conference, 234–240.

89. Yarmolinsky, Brandeis conference, 235.

90. Ibid., 236.

91. Capron, Brandeis conference, 168.

92. Cannon, Brandeis conference, 176.

93. Capron, Brandeis conference, 176.

94. Hayes, Brandeis conference, 191–192.

95. Ibid., 192.

96. Yarmolinsky, Brandeis conference, 194–195.

97. Ibid., 195.

98. Richard N. Goodwin, *Remembering America: A Voice from the Sixties* (New York: Harper and Row, 1988), 262, see also 257.

99. Steinberg, *Turning Back*, 135–136.

100. Fenn, Brandeis conference, 189. Fenn was on the White House staff in the Kennedy administration.

101. Charles Hamilton, personal communication, July 2, 1998.

102. Cohen, Brandeis conference, 320.

103. See Goodwin, *Remembering America*, 257, and Beschloss, *Taking Charge*, 209, 211, for Johnson comments to his aides on the importance and pacing of the poverty program.

104. Sundquist interview, April 7, 1969, 52.

105. Richard M. Pious, the Willen Seminar, Barnard College, November 9, 1995.

106. Lampman interview, May 24, 1983, 21.

107. Robert C. Smith and Richard Seltzer, *Race, Class and Culture: A Study in Afro-American Mass Opinion* (Albany: State University of New York Press, 1992), 124.

108. Capron, Brandeis conference, 168. Pages 158 to 168 deal with the issue of what social forces such as the civil rights movement and the social unrest of the period played in the planning of the War on Poverty. A clear-cut assessment of this role is elusive, however, since discussion among conference participants is muddled and contradictory. Lieberman discusses parochial politics in *Shifting the Color Line*, 217, 218–219, 228–229.

109. Paul Burstein, *Discrimination, Jobs, and Politics: The Struggle for Equal Employment Opportunity in the United States Since the New Deal* (Chicago: University of Chicago Press, 1985). 61.

110. See chap. 3 of Benjamin I. Page and Robert Y. Shapiro, *The Rational Public: Fifty Years of Trends in Americans' Policy Preferences* (Chicago: University of Chicago Press, 1992) for discussion of white Americans' attitudes on civil rights and racial equality.

6. IDEAS AND GOVERNMENT POLICY MAKING

1. The epigraph is cited in Lionel Trilling, *The Liberal Imagination* (Garden City, N.Y.: Doubleday, Anchor, 1957), ix. It translates as "Everything begins in sentiment and assumption and finds its issue in political action and institutions."

2. See Peter Hall, "Conclusion: The Politics of Keynesian Ideas," in *The Political Power of Economic Ideas*, ed. Peter Hall (Princeton: Princeton University Press, 1989), 361–391.

3. Indeed, some analysts have proposed that ideas may rival interests and organized groups as a catalyst in the development of new public policies. To John Kingdon, the content of ideas is as important as concepts such as power, influence, pressure, and strategy. Such an approach to policy ideas is compatible with the evolution in policy relationships that Hugh Heclo has described as issue networks. Heclo's issue networks are fluid policy communities of experienced and expert policy watchers who pursue intellectual and professional interests through cerebral, flexible, and at times ideological channels rather than the material interests at the center of the classic iron triangle. See John W. Kingdon, *Agendas, Alternatives, and Public Policies* (Boston: Little, Brown, 1984); and Hugh Heclo, "Issue Networks and the Executive Establishment," in *The*

New American Political System, ed. Anthony King (Washington, D.C.: American Enterprise Institute, 1980), 87–124.

4. See Judith Russell, "Ideas, Elites, and Antipoverty Policy" (paper prepared for delivery at the Annual Meeting of the Political Science Association, Chicago, September 3–6, 1987); Kingdon, *Agendas, Alternatives, and Public Policies*; and Peter Hall, ed., *The Political Power of Economic Ideas* (Princeton: Princeton University Press, 1989).

5. See Hall, "Conclusion," 362.

6. Ernst Haas has suggested that technological lack of consensus can be bridged. He defines knowledge as "the sum of technical information and of theories about that information which commands sufficient consensus at any given time among interested actors to serve as a guide to public policy designed to achieve some social goal." His approach to knowledge neutralizes ideology and permits a degree of autonomy for ideas since knowledge transcends ideology as a "professionally mediated body of theory and information." See Ernst B. Haas, "Why Collaborate? Issue-Linkage and International Regimes," *World Politics* 32, no. 3 (April 1980): 367–368.

7. The Phillips curve, for example, the council's Keynesians believed, illustrated a causal relationship between wage rates and inflation. Although it was later challenged, the Phillips curve posited that low unemployment rates automatically led to high inflation. See Walter Heller, Kermit Gordon, James Tobin, Gardner Ackley, and Paul Samuelson, interview by Joseph Pechman, August 1, 1964, tape recording, John F. Kennedy Library, Boston, 282, for Tobin's remarks on how structural changes in the economy were exemplified in increasingly higher unemployment rates.

8. The idea of full employment is discussed in chap. 3 of this book. Stephen K. Bailey's *Congress Makes a Law: The Story Behind the Employment Act of 1946* (New York: Columbia University Press, 1950), is the best book on the Employment Act of 1946.

9. Employment Act of 1946, Pub. L. No. 79-304, sec 2, 60 Stat. 23, 23 (1946), cited in Harvey, *Congress Makes a Law*, 228. See National Research Council, Committee on Department of Labor Manpower Research and Development, Assembly of Behavioral and Social Sciences, *Knowledge and Policy in Manpower: A Study of the Manpower Research and Development Program in the Department of Labor* (Washington, D.C.: National Academy of Sciences, 1975).

10. See the full employment studies in Margaret Weir, *Politics and Jobs: The Boundaries of Employment Policy in the United States* (Princeton: Princeton University Press, 1992), and Gary Mucciaroni, *The Political Failure of Employment Policy, 1945–1982* (Pittsburgh: University of Pittsburgh Press, 1990).

11. Garth L. Mangum, "The Emergence of Manpower Policy," in *Toward a Manpower Policy*, ed. Robert Aaron Gordon (New York: Wiley, 1967), 22.

12. The Conference Committee produced a bill that established the Council of Economic Advisers (CEA), the Annual Economic Report of the President, and the Joint Economic Committee of Congress (JEC).

13. Keyserling played a key role later on in the redrafting of this bill and was an unofficial adviser to Senator Wagner and the Banking and Currency Committee staff (Bailey, *Congress Makes a Law*, 46). He was vice chairman of the Council of Economic Advisers under Edwin Nourse in the Truman administration and later chairman. As a former chairman of the council, a shaper of the Employment Act of 1946, and an interpreter of economic policy, the brilliant and crusty Keyserling was an important voice in the outer ranges of the idea of full employment. Quotations from Keyserling and the discussion of full employment and the ideas behind employment and economic policy in this chapter are drawn from Leon Keyserling, interview by Stephen Goodell, January 9, 1969, tape recording, Lyndon B. Johnson Library, Austin.

14. For an interesting essay on FDR's postwar problems, see John W. Jeffries, "The 'New' New Deal: FDR and American Liberalism, 1937–1945," *Political Science Quarterly* 105, no. 3 (1990): 397–418.

15. Ira Katznelson, "Rethinking the Silences of Social and Economic Policy," *Political Science Quarterly* 101, no. 2 (1986): 305.

16. We have commercial instead of social Keynesianism, according to Margaret Weir and Theda Skocpol. See Weir and Skocpol, "State Structures and the Possibilities for 'Keynesian' Responses to the Great Depression in Sweden, Britain, and the United States," in *Bringing the State Back In*, ed. Peter B. Evans, Dietrich Rueschemeyer, and Theda Skocpol (New York: Cambridge University Press, 1985), 107–163; and Hall, *The Political Power of Economic Ideas*, especially the chapters by Weir and Salant on the acceptance of Keynesian ideas in the United States. Chapter 2 of Margaret Weir's *Politics and Jobs* is a first-rate discussion of how political patterns affected the kinds of Keynesian measures adopted in the United States. For an article on the cycles of Kennedy's fiscal policy, see Eileen Shanahan, "Kennedy and Economy: Administration Moves into the Third Phase in Its Policy for Solving Nation's Economic Problems," *New York Times*, July 28, 1963, sec. E, 5.

17. "It makes an economic difference," Keyserling said, because spending "would have provided better economic balance by getting more of the income where it was needed instead of getting it in the wrong places." General tax reduction tends to be regressive because the rich receive the biggest proportional benefits, whereas public spending can be directed to have the greatest societal effect.

18. William Capron, in "Poverty and Urban Policy, Conference Transcript of 1973 Group Discussion of the Kennedy Administration Urban Poverty Programs and Policies," John F. Kennedy Library, Boston, 140.

19. Quoted in Richard N. Goodwin, *Remembering America: A Voice from the Sixties* (New York: Harper and Row, 1988), 257.

20. William Cannon, interview by Michael L. Gillette, May 21, 1982, tape recording, Lyndon B. Johnson Library, Austin, 25.

21. Ibid., 26.

22. Adam Yarmolinsky, "The Beginnings of OEO," in *On Fighting Poverty: Perspectives from Experience*, ed. James L. Sundquist (New York: Basic, 1969), 39.

23. Yarmolinsky, Brandeis conference, 286. Yarmolinsky goes on to illustrate a key tactical mistake of the War on Poverty: their decision to concentrate on preparing people for jobs first rather than finding jobs for people.

24. Yarmolinsky and Richard Boone, Brandeis conference, 283–284.

25. Boone, Brandeis conference, 239.

26. Willard Wirtz, interview by author, Washington, D.C., July 23, 1991, tape recording.

27. See James Q. Wilson, "The Rise of the Bureaucratic State," in *American Government: Readings and Cases*, 10th ed., ed. Peter Woll (New York: Harper-Collins, 1990), 432–454; idem, *The Politics of Regulation* (New York: Basic, 1980); Theodore Lowi, *The End of Liberalism: The Second Republic of the United States*, 2d ed. (New York: Norton, 1979); Morton Grodzins, *The American System* (Chicago: Rand McNally, 1966); and Daniel J. Elazar, *American Federalism: The View from the States* (New York: Crowell, 1966). See Andrew McFarland, "Interest Groups and Theories of Power in America," *British Journal of Political Science*, no. 17 (1987): 129–147, for some interesting insights into existing theories of power and interest and propositions about such theories and their potential as a "school."

28. Edwin L. Dale, Jr., "Joblessness Rate of Negro Youths Increases to 25%: U.S. Statistics Show Figure Is Twice as High as That of White Teenagers," *New York Times*, August 23, 1964, sec. A, 1.

29. Historian James Patterson says, "It was impossible to know how many Americans believed these ideas about a culture of poverty. It was also impossible to know exactly what the term meant" (*America's Struggle Against Poverty, 1900–1985* [Cambridge: Harvard University Press, 1981], 120). We do know, though, that this set of ideas about poverty and its consequences was believed, if not clearly understood, by key policy participants who drafted the Economic Opportunity Act of 1964. The term "culture of poverty" gained prominence because of the influential—and frequently misrepresented—work of anthropologist Oscar Lewis. See Oscar Lewis, *La Vida: A Puerto Rican Family in the Culture of Poverty—San Juan and New York* (New York: Random House, 1965), and idem, "The Culture of Poverty," *Scientific American*, no. 215 (October 1966): 19–25.

30. See Gareth Stedman-Jones, *Outcast London* (London: Oxford University Press, 1971), for a fascinating account of how antipoverty experts in nineteenth-

century London, peering through an ideological frame of reference shaped by professional and class-related assumptions of their own, also saw a "residuum" of the poor.

31. David Austin, Brandeis conference, 365–366. These were, in fact, the people Nicholas Lemann studied in *The Promised Land* (New York: Knopf, 1991), his book on the disruption experienced by southern black sharecroppers who came north in the post—World War II period.

32. See Bonnie Fox Schwartz, *The Civil Works Administration, 1933–1934* (Princeton: Princeton University Press, 1984), vii.

33. See chap. 4 on Hamilton and Hamilton's work on the politics of the dual agenda.

34. Lyndon Johnson, "Annual Message to Congress on the State of the Union," in *Public Papers of the President of the United States, 1963–1964* (Washington, D.C.: U.S. Government Printing Office, 1965), 1:112. The rhetorical excesses of Johnson in framing the goals of the War on Poverty are studied in David Zarefsky, *President Johnson's War on Poverty: Rhetoric and History* (University: University of Alabama Press, 1986); and Jeffrey K. Tulis, *The Rhetorical Presidency* (Princeton: Princeton University Press, 1987).

35. There is a genuine irony to Heller's role in directing the War on Poverty away from jobs programs. His father had worked in the WPA after losing his job in the Depression, and Heller himself was aided in his research on his Ph.D. thesis, on the state income tax, by a National Youth Administration (NYA) grant. See Lemann, *The Promised Land*, 129 and 142.

36. Memorandum, Kermit Gordon and Walter Heller to the secretaries of agriculture, commerce, labor, health education, and welfare, and interior and the administrator of the Housing and Home Finance Agency, "Outline of a Proposed Poverty Program," January 6, 1964, Legislative Background EOA 1964 WoP, box 1, Bureau of the Budget Papers on Poverty, Lyndon B. Johnson Library, Austin. Community action programs were also much less expensive to implement than were large-scale jobs programs.

37. Capron, Brandeis conference, 39.

38. Ibid., 139.

39. See Weir's *Politics and Jobs*.

40. Bernard R. Gifford, "War on Poverty: Assumptions, History, and Results, a Flawed but Important Effort," in *The Great Society and Its Legacy*, ed. Marshall Kaplan and Peggy Cuciti (Durham: Duke University Press, 1986), 66.

41. Charles A. Murray, *Losing Ground: American Social Policy, 1950–1980* (New York: Basic, 1984); Lawrence M. Mead, *Beyond Entitlement* (New York: Free, 1986).

42. William Julius Wilson, *The Declining Significance of Race* (Chicago: University of Chicago Press, 1978), 160.

43. Lee Rainwater, "Crucible of Identity: The Negro Lower-Class Family," *Daedalus* 95 (winter 1966): 179–180, cited in ibid., 160. Rainwater was writing before the problem of black female-headed households had assumed its current dimensions.

44. Wirtz interview.

45. Ibid.

46. See Capron, Brandeis conference, for an account of economist Robert Lampman's considerable influence on Heller's thinking about poverty.

47. Daniel Patrick Moynihan, *Maximum Feasible Misunderstanding: Community Action in the War on Poverty* (New York: Free, 1970), 193.

48. Lemann, *The Promised Land*, 148.

49. Moynihan, *Maximum Feasible Misunderstanding*, 193.

50. Samuel H. Beer, "In Search of a New Public Philosophy," in *The New American Political System*, ed. Anthony King (Washington, D.C.: American Enterprise Institute, 1978), 5.

51. For pluralist views on American government in their purest form, see Arthur F. Bentley, *The Process of Government* (Chicago: University of Chicago Press, 1908; reprint, Bloomington, Ind.: Principia, 1935, 1949); and David Truman, *The Governmental Process* (New York: Knopf, 1951).

52. Moyers cited in Harry McPherson, interview by Thomas H. Baker, January 16, 1969, tape recording, Lyndon B. Johnson Library, Austin, 11. The full quotation reads "How do you judge a President's performance when you cannot begin to understand the currents of change and upheaval that engulfed his era? He tried to act as he thought the crises demanded, at a time when no one really knew what the crises were. Perhaps in time it will be said that a lesser, simpler man might have been crushed in the awful sweep of things we have experienced in the last five years."

53. See Daniel Patrick Moynihan, *The Politics of a Guaranteed Income: The Nixon Administration and the Family Assistance Plan* (New York: Random House, 1973).

54. Haynes Walton, personal communication, November 15, 2001.

55. Wilson, *The Truly Disadvantaged*; John Kasarda, "Urban Industrial Transition and the Underclass," *Annals of the American Academy of Political and Social Sciences* 501 (January 1989): 27–47; D. T. Ellwood "The Spatial Mismatch Hypothesis: Are There Jobs Missing in the Ghetto?" in *The Black Youth Employment Crisis*, ed. R. Freeman and Harry Holzer (Chicago: University of Chicago Press, 1986).

56. See Christopher Jencks and Paul E. Peterson, eds., *The Urban Underclass* (Washington, D.C.: Brookings Institution, 1991), for essays on inner-city poverty and theories that explain it.

57. Harold L. Wilensky, "Nothing Fails Like Success: The Evaluation-

Research Industry and Labor Market Policy," *Industrial Relations* 24, no. 1 (winter 1985): 1.

58. See Herbert S. Parnes, *Unemployment Experience of Individuals Over a Decade: Variations by Sex, Race and Age* (Kalamazoo, Mich.: Upjohn Institute for Employment Research, 1982); and Gosta Rehn, "Swedish Active Labor Market Policy: Retrospect and Prospect," *Industrial Relations*, 24, no. 1 (winter 1985): 62–89.

59. Wilensky, "Nothing Fails Like Success," 13.

60. Michael Harrington, "The Will to Abolish Poverty," *Saturday Review*, July 27, 1968, 12 and 40; Peter B. Edelman, "Creating Jobs for Americans: From MDTA to Industrial Policy," in *The Great Society and Its Legacy*, ed. Marshall Kaplan and Peggy Cuciti (Durham: Duke University Press, 1986), 91–105; Gifford, "War on Poverty"; and Brandeis conference.

61. See conservative critiques of the War on Poverty in Mead, *Beyond Entitlement*, and Murray, *Losing Ground*.

62. Frances Fox Piven, Brandeis conference, 157.

63. This has been an area of particular interest to Ernst Haas, in particular, in the area of Law of the Sea negotiations. It was also relevant in the economic negotiations among nations in the Bretton Woods Agreement on monetary management and the New International Economic Order. See Haas, "Why Collaborate?"

APPENDIX: JOBLESSNESS, POVERTY, AND PUBLIC POLICY IN THE UNITED STATES

1. The discussion of government policy toward joblessness is drawn in large part from the following literature: Donald C. Baumer and Carl E. Van Horn, *The Politics of Unemployment* (Washington, D.C.: Congressional Quarterly Press, 1985); Garth L. Mangum, "The Emergence of Manpower Policy," in *Toward a Manpower Policy*, ed. Robert Aaron Gordon (New York: Wiley, 1967), 11–34; Seymour E. Harris, *The Economics of the Kennedy Years* (New York: Harper and Row, 1964); Bonnie Fox Schwartz, *The Civil Works Administration, 1933–1934* (Princeton: Princeton University Press, 1984); National Research Council, Committee on Department of Labor Manpower Research and Development, Assembly of Behavioral and Social Sciences, *Knowledge and Policy in Manpower: A Study of the Manpower Research and Development Program in the Department of Labor* (Washington, D.C.: National Academy of Sciences, 1975); Philip Harvey, *Securing the Right to Employment: Social Welfare Policy and the Unemployed in the United States* (Princeton: Princeton University Press, 1989); and Stephen K. Bailey, *Congress Makes a Law: The Story Behind the Employment Act of 1946* (New

York: Columbia University Press, 1950). The effects of the postwar GI Bill on employment seem not to have been conclusively demonstrated. Such a study would be important since this legislation had great social consequences in bringing education and other benefits to people who otherwise might not have attained them.

2. Baumer and Van Horn, *The Politics of Unemployment*, 9.

3. Mangum, "The Emergence of Manpower Policy," 16.

4. Ibid., 14.

Bibliography

Aaron, Henry J. *Politics and the Professors: The Great Society in Perspective.* Washington, D.C.: Brookings Institution, 1978.

Auletta, Ken. *The Underclass.* New York: Vintage, 1983.

Bachrach, Peter and Morton S. Baratz. "Decisions and Nondecisions: An Analytical Framework." *American Political Science Review* 57 (1950): 632–642.

Bailey, Stephen K. *Congress Makes a Law: The Story Behind the Employment Act of 1946.* New York: Columbia University Press, 1950.

Bakke, E. Wight. *A Positive Labor Market Policy.* Columbus: Charles E. Merrill, 1963.

Barton, Allen H. "Background, Attitudes, and Activities of American Elites." *Politics and Society* 1 (1985): 173–218.

———. "Determinants of Economic Attitudes in the American Business Elite." *American Journal of Sociology* 91, no. 1 (1985): 54–87.

———. "Diffusion of Economic Ideas Among Elites." Unpublished draft. November 1985.

Baumer, Donald C. and Carl E. Van Horn. *The Politics of Unemployment.* Washington, D.C.: Congressional Quarterly Press, 1985.

Beck, Kent M. "What Was Liberalism in the 1950's?" *Political Science Quarterly* 102, no. 2 (1987): 233–258.

Beer, Samuel H. "In Search of a New Public Philosophy." In *The New American Political System*, ed. Anthony King, 5–44. Washington, D.C.: American Enterprise Institute, 1978.

Bell, Daniel. *The Coming of a Post-Industrial Society.* New York: Basic, 1973.

Bensel, Richard Franklin. *Sectionalism and American Political Development, 1880–1980.* Madison: University of Wisconsin Press, 1984.

Bentley, Arthur F. *The Process of Government*. Chicago: University of Chicago Press, 1908. Reprint, Bloomington, Ind.: Principia, 1935, 1949.

Bernstein, Irving. *Promises Kept: John F. Kennedy's New Frontier*. New York: Oxford University Press, 1991.

Beschloss, Michael R. *Taking Charge: The Johnson White House Tapes, 1963–1964*. New York: Simon and Schuster, 1997.

Best, James J. "Who Talked to the President When? A Study of Lyndon B. Johnson." *Political Science Quarterly* 103, no. 3 (1988): 531–545.

Beveridge, William H. *Full Employment in a Free Society*. New York: Norton, 1945.

Blauner, R. *Racial Oppression in America*. New York: Harper and Row, 1972.

Bloom, Jack M. *Class, Race, and the Civil Rights Movement*. Bloomington: Indiana University Press, 1987.

Blumenthal, Richard. "The Bureaucracy: Antipoverty and the Community Action Program." In *American Political Institutions and Public Policy*, ed. Allen P. Sindler, 129–179. Boston: Little, Brown, 1969.

Bottomore, T. B. *Elites and Society*. New York: Basic, 1964.

Bowles, Samuel and Herbert Gintis. "The Crisis of Liberal Capitalism: The Case of the United States." *Politics and Society* 11, no. 1 (1982): 51–94.

Brager, George A. and Francis P. Purcell. *Community Action Against Poverty: Readings from the Mobilization Experience*. New Haven, Conn: College and University Press, 1967.

Branch, Taylor, *Parting the Waters: America in the King Years, 1954–1964*. New York: Simon and Schuster, 1988.

Brecher, Charles. *The Impact of Federal Antipoverty Policies*. New York: Praeger, 1973.

Brimmer, Andrew F. "Economic Developments in the Black Community." *Public Interest* 34 (winter 1974): 146–163.

Brown, Michael K. and Stephen P. Erie. "Blacks and the Legacy of the Great Society: The Economic and Social Impact of Federal Social Policy." *Public Policy* 29, no. 3 (summer 1981): 314–328.

Bunce, Valerie. *Do New Leaders Make A Difference: Public Policy Under Capitalism and Socialism*. Princeton: Princeton University Press, 1981.

Burstein, Paul. *Discrimination, Jobs, and Politics: The Struggle for Equal Employment Opportunity in the United States Since the New Deal*. Chicago: University of Chicago Press, 1985.

Burtless, Gary, ed. *A Future of Lousy Jobs?* Washington, D.C.: Brookings Institution, 1990.

Califano, Joseph A., Jr. *The Triumph and Tragedy of Lyndon Johnson: The White House Years*. New York: Simon and Schuster, 1991.

Caplan, Nathan, Andrea Morrison, and Russell J. Stambaugh. *The Use of Social Science Knowledge in Policy Decisions at the National Level: A Report to Respondents.* Ann Arbor: University of Michigan Press, 1975.

Caraley, Demetrios. *The Politics of Military Unification.* New York: Columbia University Press, 1966.

Carmichael, Stokely and Charles V. Hamilton. *Black Power: The Politics of Liberation in America.* New York: Vintage, 1967.

Carmines, Edward G. and James A. Stimson. *Issue Evolution: Race and the Transformation of American Politics.* Princeton: Princeton University Press, 1989.

Clague, Ewan and Leo Kramer. *Manpower Policies and Programs: A Review, 1935–1975.* Kalamazoo, Mich: Upjohn Institute for Employment Research, 1976.

Clark, Kenneth B. *Dark Ghetto: Dilemmas of Social Power.* 2d ed. Middletown, Conn.: Wesleyan University Press, 1989.

Clark, Kenneth B. and Jeanette Hopkins. *A Relevant War Against Poverty.* New York: Harper and Row, 1968.

Cobb, Roger and Charles D. Elder. *Participation in American Politics: The Dynamics of Agenda-Building.* 2d ed. Baltimore: Johns Hopkins University Press, 1983.

Coughlin, Richard M. *Ideology, Public Opinion, and Welfare Policy: Attitudes Toward Taxes and Spending in Industrialized Societies.* Berkeley: Institute of International Studies of the University of California, 1980.

Cross, Theodore. *Black Capitalism.* New York: Atheneum, 1969.

Dahl, Robert. *Who Governs?* New Haven: Yale University Press, 1961.

Dale, Edwin L., Jr. "Joblessness Rate of Negro Youths Increases to 25%: U.S. Statistics Show Figure Is Twice as High as That of White Teenagers." *New York Times*, August 23, 1964, sec. A, 1.

Dallek, Robert. *Lone Star Rising: Lyndon Johnson and His Times, 1908–1960.* New York: Oxford University Press, 1991.

Danziger, Sheldon H. and Daniel H. Weinberg, eds. *Fighting Poverty: What Works and What Doesn't.* Cambridge: Harvard University Press, 1986.

Davidson, Roger H. *The Politics of Comprehensive Manpower Legislation.* Baltimore: The Johns Hopkins University Press, 1972.

Delli Carpini, Michael X. *Stability and Change in American Politics: The Coming of Age of the Generation of the 1960's.* New York: New York University Press, 1986.

Dempsey, John J. *The Family and Public Policy: The Issue of the 1980's.* Baltimore: Paul H. Brookes, 1981.

Donovan, John C. *The Politics of Poverty.* 3d ed. Washington, D.C.: University of America Press, 1980.

Durbin, Elizabeth F. *Welfare Income and Employment.* New York: Praeger, 1969.

Economic Report of the President. Washington, D.C.: U.S. Government Printing Office, 1964.

Edelman, Peter B. "Creating Jobs for Americans: From MDTA to Industrial Policy." In *The Great Society and Its Legacy,* ed. Marshall Kaplan and Peggy Cuciti, 91–105. Durham: Duke University Press, 1986.

Edsall, Thomas Byrne and Mary D. Edsall. *Chain Reaction: The Impact of Race, Riots, and Taxes on American Politics.* New York: Norton, 1991.

Edwards, George C., III, Steven A. Shull, and Norman C. Thomas, eds. *The Presidency and Public Policy Making.* Pittsburgh: University of Pittsburgh Press, 1985.

Elazar, Daniel J. *American Federalism: The View from the States.* New York: Crowell, 1966.

Ellwood, D. T. "The Spatial Mismatch Hypothesis: Are There Teenage Jobs Missing in the Ghetto?" In *The Black Youth Employment Crisis,* ed. Richard B. Freeman and Harry Holzer, 147–185. Chicago: University of Chicago Press, 1986.

Ellwood, D. T. and D. A. Wise. "Youth Employment in the Seventies: The Changing Circumstances of Young Adults." *American Families and the Economy: The High Costs of Living,* ed. Richard Nelson and Felicity Skidmore, 59–108. Washington, D.C.: National Academy Press, 1983.

Evans, Peter B., Dietrich Rueschemeyer, and Theda Skocpol, eds. *Bringing the State Back In.* Cambridge: Cambridge University Press, 1985.

Everett, Robinson O., ed. *Antipoverty Programs: Urban Problems and Prospects.* Dobbs Ferry, N.Y.: Oceana, 1966.

Flash, Edward S., Jr. *Economic Advice and Presidential Leadership.* New York: Columbia University Press, 1965.

Forbath, William E. "Caste, Class, and Equal Citizenship." *Michigan Law Review* 98, no. 1 (1999).

Freeman, Richard, "Changes in the Labor Market for Black Americans, 1948–72." *Brookings Papers on Economic Activity* 1 (1973): 67–132.

Friedman, Milton. *Capitalism and Freedom.* Chicago: University of Chicago Press, 1962.

Gartner, Alan, Russell A. Nixon, and Frank Riessman, eds. *Public Service Employment: An Analysis of Its History, Problems, and Prospects.* New York: Praeger, 1973.

Garraty, John A. *Unemployment in History: Economic Thought and Public Policy.* New York: Harper and Row, 1978.

Gellner, Ernest. *Relativism and the Social Sciences.* Cambridge: Cambridge University Press, 1985.

Geertz, Clifford. "Ideology as a Cultural System." *Ideology and Discontent*, ed. David E. Apter, 47–76. New York: Free, 1964.

Gifford, Bernard R. "War on Poverty: Assumptions, History, and Results, a Flawed but Important Effort." In *The Great Society and Its Legacy*, ed. Marshall Kaplan and Peggy Cuciti, 60–72. Durham: Duke University Press, 1986.

Gilpatrick, Eleanor G. *Structural Unemployment and Aggregate Demand: A Study of Employment and Unemployment in the United States, 1948–1964*. Baltimore: Johns Hopkins University Press, 1964.

Ginzberg, Eli, Terry Williams, and Anna Dutka. *Does Job Training Work? The Clients Speak Out*. Boulder: Westview, 1989.

Giraldo, Z. I. *Public Policy and the Family*. Lexington, Mass.: Heath, Lexington Books, 1980.

Goldstein, Judith. "Ideas, Institutions, and American Trade Policy." *International Organization* 41, no. 1 (winter 1988): 179–217.

Goodwin, Leonard. *Do the Poor Want to Work? A Social Psychological Study of Work Orientation*. Washington, D.C.: Brookings Institution, 1972.

Goodwin, Richard N. *Remembering America: A Voice from the Sixties*. New York: Harper and Row, 1988.

Gordon, Kermit, ed. *Agenda for the Nation*. Washington, D.C.: Brookings Institution, 1968.

Gordon, Robert Aaron, ed. *Toward a Manpower Policy*. New York: Wiley, 1967.

Graham, Hugh Davis. *The Uncertain Triumph: Federal Education Policy in the Kennedy and Johnson Years*. Chapel Hill: University of North Carolina Press, 1984.

Grodzins, Morton. *The American System*. Chicago: Rand McNally, 1966.

Grossman, Jonathan. *The Department of Labor*. New York: Praeger, 1973.

Grubb, W. Norton and Marvin Lazerson. *Broken Promises: How Americans Fail Their Children*. New York: Basic, 1982.

Geuss, Raymond. *The Idea of a Critical Theory*. Cambridge: Cambridge University Press, 1981.

Haas, Ernst B. "Is There a Hole in the Whole? Knowledge, Technology, Interdependence, and the Construction of International Regimes." *International Organization* 29, no. 3 (summer 1975): 827–876.

———. "On Systems and International Regimes." *World Politics* 27, no. 2 (January 1975): 147–174.

———. "Why Collaborate? Issue-Linkage and International Regimes." *World Politics* 32, no. 3 (April 1980): 357–405.

Hall, Peter. "Conclusion: The Politics of Keynesian Ideas." In *The Political Power of Economic Ideas*, ed. Peter Hall, 361–391. Princeton: Princeton University Press, 1989.

Hall, Peter, ed. *The Political Power of Economic Ideas*. Princeton: Princeton University Press, 1989.

Hamilton, Charles V. "The Patron-Recipient Relationship and Minority Politics." *Political Science Quarterly* 94, no. 2 (1979): 211–227.

———. "Social Policy and the Welfare of Black Americans: From Rights to Resources." *Political Science Quarterly* 101, no. 2 (1986): 239–256.

———. "Social Policies, Civil Rights, and Poverty." *Fighting Poverty: What Works and What Doesn't*, ed. Sheldon H. Danziger and Daniel H. Weinberg, 287–311. Cambridge: Harvard University Press, 1986.

Hamilton, Dona Cooper and Charles V. Hamilton. *The Dual Agenda: Social Policies of Civil Rights Organizations, New Deal to the Present*. New York: Columbia University Press, 1997.

Hargrove, Erwin C. and Samuel A. Morley. eds. *The President and the Council of Economic Advisors*. Boulder: Westview, 1984.

Harrington, Michael. *The New American Poverty*. New York: Penguin, 1984.

———. *The Other America*. Baltimore: Penguin, 1962.

———. "The Will to Abolish Poverty." *Saturday Review*, July 27, 1968, 12 and 40.

Harris, Fred R. and Roger W. Wilkins, eds. *Quiet Riots: Race and Poverty in the United States*. New York: Pantheon, 1988.

Harris, Seymour E. *The Economics of the Kennedy Years*. New York: Harper and Row, 1964.

Harrison, Bennet, Harold L. Sheppard, and William J. Spring. "Public Jobs, Public Needs." *New Republic* 164, no. 4 (1972).

Harvey, Philip. "Combating Joblessness: An Analysis of the Principal Strategies That Have Influenced the Development of American Employment and Social Welfare Law During the 20the Century." *Berkeley Journal of Employment and Labor Law* 21, no. 2 (2000).

———. *Securing the Right to Employment: Social Welfare Policy and the Unemployed in the United States*. Princeton: Princeton University Press, 1989.

Haveman, Robert, ed. *A Decade of Federal Antipoverty Programs: Achievements, Failures, and Lessons*. New York: Academic, 1977.

Heclo, Hugh. "General Welfare and Two American Political Traditions." *Political Science Quarterly* 101, no. 2 (1986): 179–296.

———. "Issue Networks and the Executive Establishment." In *The New American Political System*, ed. Anthony King, 87–124. Washington, D.C.: American Enterprise Institute, 1980.

———. *Modern Social Policies in Britain and Sweden*. New Haven: Yale University Press, 1974.

———. "The Political Foundations of Antipoverty Policy." In *Fighting Poverty:*

What Works and What Doesn't, ed. Sheldon H. Danziger and Daniel H. Weinberg, 312–340. Cambridge: Harvard University Press, 1986.

Heller, Walter. "Interest Rates and the Quadriad." Memorandum, November 29, 1963. Walter Heller Papers, John F. Kennedy Library, Boston.

Heymann, Philip B. "How Government Expresses Public Ideas." *The Power of Public Ideas*, ed. Robert B. Reisch. Cambridge, Mass.: Ballinger, 1988.

Hill, Kim Quaile. *Democracies in Crisis: Public Policy Responses to the Great Depression*. Boulder: Westview, 1988.

Hirschman, Albert O. *The Passion and the Interests: Political Arguments for Capitalism Before Its Triumph*. Princeton: Princeton University Press, 1977.

———. "Reactionary Rhetoric." *Atlantic Monthly* 263, no. 5 (May 1989): 63–70.

Hochschilds, Jennifer L. *What's Fair*. Cambridge: Harvard University Press, 1981.

Hofstadter, Richard. *Anti-intellectualism in American Life*. New York: Vintage, 1963.

Holland, Susan S. "Long-Term Unemployment in the 1960's." *Monthly Labor Market Review* 88 (September 1965): 1069–1076.

Holzer, Harry J. "The Spatial Mismatch Hypothesis: What Has The Evidence Shown?" *Urban Studies* 28, no. 1 (1991): 105–122.

Huntington, Samuel. *American Politics: The Promise of Disharmony*. Cambridge: Harvard University Press, 1981.

Ikenberry, G. John and Theda Skocpol. "Expanding Social Benefits: The Roll of Social Security." *Political Science Quarterly* 102, no. 3 (1987): 389–416.

Jacobs, Paul, Arthur McCormack, Bayard Rustin, Leon Keyserling, Robert Theobald, Nat Hentoff, and Don Benson. *Dialogue on Poverty*. Indianapolis: Bobbs-Merrill, 1967.

Jaszi, George. "An Economic Accountant's Audit." *American Economic Review* 76, no. 2 (May 1986): 411–18.

Jaynes, Gerald David and Robin M. Williams, Jr., eds. *A Common Destiny: Blacks and American Society*. Washington, D.C.: National Academy Press, 1989.

Jeffries, John W. "The 'New' New Deal: FDR and American Liberalism, 1937–1945." *Political Science Quarterly* 105, no. 3 (1990): 397–418.

Jencks, Christopher and Paul E. Peterson, eds. *The Urban Underclass*. Washington, D.C.: Brookings Institution, 1991.

Johnson, Lyndon. "Annual Message to Congress on the State of the Union." In *Public Papers of the President of the United States, 1963–1964*, 1:112–118. Washington, D.C.: U.S. Government Printing Office, 1965.

Johnston, Janet Wegner. *An Overview of U.S. Federal Employment and Training Programs*. Sage Modern Politics Series, ed. Jeremy Richardson and Richard Henning, no. 8. Beverly Hills: Sage, 1984.

Jones, J. M. *Prejudice and Racism*. New York: Addison-Wesley, 1972.

Kadushin, Charles. *The American Intellectual Elite*. Boston: Little, Brown, 1974.

Kaplan, Marshall and Peggy Cuciti, eds. *The Great Society and Its Legacy*. Durham: Duke University Press, 1986.

Kasarda, John. "Urban Industrial Transition and the Underclass." *Annals of the American Academy of Political and Social Sciences* 501 (January 1989): 27–47.

Katz, Michael B. *The Undeserving Poor: From the War on Poverty to the War on Welfare*. New York: Pantheon, 1989.

Katznelson, Ira. "Rethinking the Silences of Social and Economic Policy." *Political Science Quarterly* 101, no. 2 (1986): 307–325.

Kearns, Doris. *Lyndon Johnson and the American Dream*. New York: Harper and Row, 1976.

Kelley, Robert. "Ideology and Political Culture from Jefferson to Nixon." *American Historical Review* 82 (1977): 531–582.

Kershaw, Joseph A. *Government Against Poverty*. Chicago: Markham, 1976.

Kettl, Donald F. *Deficit Politics: Public Budgeting in Its Institutional and Historical Context*. New York: Macmillan, 1992.

Keynes, John Maynard. *The General Theory of Employment, Interest, and Money*. New York: Harcourt, Brace, and Jovanovich, 1985.

Key, V. O., Jr., with the assistance of Alexander Heard. *Southern Politics in State and Nation*. New York: Random House, Vintage, Caravelle, 1949.

Keyssar, Alexander. "History and the Problem of Unemployment." *Socialist Review* 19, no. 4 (October–December 1989): 15–34.

Killingsworth, Charles C. *Jobs and Income for Negroes*. Policy Paper in Human Resources and Industrial Relations, no. 6. Ann Arbor, Mich.: Institute of Labor and Industrial Relations, 1968.

———. "Negroes in a Changing Labor Market." *Employment, Race, and Poverty*, ed. Arthur M. Ross and Herbert Hill, 49–75. New York: Harcourt, Brace, and World, 1967.

Kingdon, John W. *Agendas, Alternatives, and Public Policies*. Boston: Little, Brown, 1984.

———. "Ideas, Politics, and Public Policies." Paper prepared for delivery at the Annual Meeting of the American Political Science Association, Chicago, September 1988.

King, Martin Luther, Jr. "Remaining Awake Through a Great Revolution." Speech at Washington National Cathedral, March 31, 1968.

Knapp, Daniel and Kenneth Polk. *Scouting the War on Poverty: Social Reform Politics in the Kennedy Administration*. Lexington, Mass.: Heath, Lexington Books, 1971.

Knowles, L. K. and K. Prewitt. *Institutional Racism in America*. Englewood Cliffs, N.J.: Prentice-Hall, 1969.

Kuhn, Thomas S. *The Structure of Scientific Revolutions*. Chicago: University of Chicago Press, 1962.

Larner, Jeremy and Irving Howe, eds. *Poverty: Views from the Left*. New York: Morrow, 1968.

Lawyers Committee for Civil Rights Under Law. *Falling Down on the Job: The United States Employment Service and the Disadvantaged*. Washington, D.C.: National Urban Coalition and the Lawyers Committee for Civil Rights Under Law, 1971.

Leiter, Robert. "Alms and Attitudes." *Pennsylvania Gazette*, October 1982.

Lemann, Nicholas. "Out of Sympathy." *Atlantic Monthly* 264, no. 1 (July 1989): 91–94.

———. *The Promised Land*. New York: Knopf, 1991.

Levitan, Sar A. *Great Society's Poor Law*. Baltimore: Johns Hopkins University Press, 1969.

———. *Programs in Aid of the Poor for the 1970s*. Baltimore: Johns Hopkins University Press, 1985.

———, ed. *The Federal Social Dollar in Its Own Back Yard*. Washington, D.C.: Bureau of National Affairs, 1973.

Levitan, Sar A. and Frank Gallo. *A Second Chance: Training for Jobs*. Kalamazoo, Mich.: Upjohn Institute for Employment Research, 1988.

Levitan, Sar A. and Garth Mangum. *Federal Training and Work Programs in the Sixties*. Ann Arbor: Institute of Labor and Industrial Relations, 1969.

Lewis, Anthony. "Civil Rights Issue: Administration Will Be Judged to a Large Degree by the Fate of This Bill." *New York Times*, December 8, 1963, sec. E, 4.

———. "Kennedy Weighs New Rights Law: Strong Action Could Jeopardize His Programs in Congress," *New York Times*, June 2, 1963.

———. "President Spurs Drive for House to Act on Rights." *New York Times*, December 4, 1963, sec. A, 1.

———. "Washington: Kennedy Commits Administration to Determined Effort to Improve Conditions." *New York Times*, June 16, 1963, sec. E, 3.

Lewis, David Levering. "Martin Luther King, Jr., and the Promise of Nonviolent Populism." In *Black Leaders of the Twentieth Century*, ed. John Hope Franklin and August Meier, 277–304. Urbana: University of Illinois Press, 1982.

Lewis, Oscar. "The Culture of Poverty." *Scientific American*, no. 215 (October 1966): 19–25.

———. *La Vida: A Puerto Rican Family in the Culture of Poverty—San Juan and New York*. New York: Random House, 1965.

Lieberman, Robert C. "The Political Construction of Race and the Development of American Institutions." Department of Political Science, Columbia University, New York. Photocopy.

———. *Shifting the Color Line: Race and the American Welfare State*. Cambridge: Harvard University Press, 1998.

———. "Structure and Choice in Race and American Political Development." Paper prepared for the conference "Race in the Development of American Politics and Society," University of Rochester, Rochester, N.Y., May 1–2, 1998.

Lippmann, Walter. *The Public Philosophy*. New York: Mentor, 1955.

Lowi, Theodore. *The End of Liberalism: The Second Republic of the United States*. 2d ed. New York: Norton, 1979.

McClosky, Herbert and John Zaller. *The American Ethos: Public Attitudes Toward Capitalism and Democracy*. Cambridge: Harvard University Press, 1984.

MacDonald, Dwight. "Our Invisible Poor." Review of Michael Harrington's *The Other America*. *New Yorker*, January 19, 1963, 82–132.

McFarland, Andrew. "Interest Groups and Theories of Power in America." *British Journal of Political Science*, no. 17 (1987): 129–147.

Mangum, Garth L. "The Emergence of Manpower Policy." In *Toward a Manpower Policy*, ed. Robert Aaron Gordon, 11–34. New York: Wiley, 1967.

———. *The Emergence of Manpower Policy*. New York: Holt, Rinehart, and Winston, 1969.

———. *MDTA: Foundation of Federal Manpower Policy*. Baltimore: Johns Hopkins University Press, 1968.

Manpower Report of the President. Washington, D.C.: U.S. Government Printing Office, 1969.

Margolis, Michael and Gary A. Mauser. *Manipulating Public Opinion*. Pacific Grove, Calif.: Brooks/Cole, 1989.

Marmor, Theodore R., ed. *Poverty Policy*. Chicago: Aldine Atherton, 1971.

Marris, Peter and Martin Rein. *Dilemmas of Social Reform: Poverty and Community Action in the United States*. New York: Atherton, 1967.

Marx, Karl, and Frederick Engels. *Manifesto of the Communist Party*. Moscow: Progress, 1971.

Mead, Lawrence M. *Beyond Entitlement*. New York: Free, 1986.

Meier, August. "Civil Rights Strategies for Negro Employment." *Employment, Race, and Poverty*, ed. Arthur M. Ross and Herbert Hill, 175–204. New York: Harcourt, Brace, and World, 1967.

Miller, Herman P. *Poverty: American Style*. Belmont, Calif.: Wadsworth, 1966.

———. *Rich Man, Poor Man*. New York: Crowell, 1964.

Moynihan, Daniel Patrick. *Family and Nation*. New York: Harcourt, Brace, Jovanovich, 1986.

———. *Maximum Feasible Misunderstanding: Community Action in the War on Poverty*. New York: Free, 1970.

————. *The Politics of a Guaranteed Income: The Nixon Administration and the Family Assistance Plan.* New York: Random House, 1973.

————, ed. *On Understanding Poverty: Perspectives From the Social Sciences.* New York: Basic, 1969.

Mucciaroni, Gary. *The Political Failure of Employment Policy, 1945–1982.* Pittsburgh: University of Pittsburgh Press, 1990.

Murray, Charles A. *Losing Ground: American Social Policy, 1950–1980.* New York: Basic, 1984.

Nathan, Richard P. *Jobs and Civil Rights: The Role of the Federal Government in Promoting Equal Opportunity in Employment and Training.* Washington, D.C.: U.S. Government Printing Office, 1969.

National Association of Social Workers. Encyclopedia of Social Work. Washington, D.C.: National Association of Social Workers, 1974.

National Research Council, Committee on Department of Labor Manpower Research and Development, Assembly of Behavioral and Social Sciences. *Knowledge and Policy in Manpower: A Study of the Manpower Research and Development Program in the Department of Labor.* Washington, D.C.: National Academy of Sciences, 1975.

National Science Foundation. *Knowledge Into Action: Improving the Nation's Use of the Social Sciences.* Report of the Special Commission on the Social Sciences of the National Science Board. Washington, D.C.: National Science Foundation, 1969.

Nelson, Barbara. *Making an Issue of Child Abuse.* Chicago: University of Chicago Press, 1984.

Nemore, Arnold L. and Garth L. Mangum. *Reorienting the Federal-State Employment Service.* Policy Papers in Human Resources and Industrial Relations, no. 8. Ann Arbor: Institute of Labor and Industrial Relations; Washington, D.C.: National Manpower Policy Task Force, 1968.

Neustadt, Richard E. *Presidential Power: The Politics of Leadership From FDR to Carter.* New York: Wiley, 1980.

Newman, Katherine. *Falling from Grace: The Experience of Downward Mobility in the American Middle Class.* New York: Free, 1988.

New York City Partnership. *Working Together to Accelerate New York's Recovery: Economic Impact Analysis of the September 11th Attack on New York City.* New York: New York City Partnership and Chamber of Commerce, November 2001.

Nixon, Russell A. "The Historical Development of the Conception and Implementation of Full Employment as Economic Policy." In *Public Service Employment: An Analysis of Its History, Problems, and Prospects,* ed. Alan Gartner, Russell A. Nixon, and Frank Riessman, 9–27. New York: Praeger, 1973.

North, Douglass C. "Ideology and Political/Economic Institutions." *Cato Journal* 8, no. 1 (spring/summer 1988): 15–28.

———. *Institutions, Institutional Change and Economic Performance*. Cambridge: Cambridge University Press, 1990.

Page, Benjamin I. and Robert Y. Shapiro. *The Rational Public: Fifty Years of Trends in Americans' Policy Preferences*. Chicago: University of Chicago Press, 1992.

Parnes, Herbert S. *Unemployment Experience of Individuals Over a Decade: Variations by Sex, Race and Age*. Kalamazoo, Mich.: Upjohn Institute for Employment Research, 1982.

Patterson, James T. *America's Struggle Against Poverty, 1900–1985*. Cambridge: Harvard University Press, 1981.

Phillips, Cabell. "How About Another WPA?" *New Republic* 164, no. 6 (February 1971).

Phillips, Kevin. *Boiling Point: Democrats, Republicans, and the Decline of Middle-Class Prosperity*. New York: Random House, 1993.

Pierson, Frank C. *The Minimum Level of Unemployment and Public Policy*. Kalamazoo, Mich.: Upjohn Institute for Employment Research, 1980.

Piore, Michael J., ed. *Unemployment and Inflation*. White Plains, N.Y.: Sharpe, 1979.

Pious, Richard M. "Policy and Administration." *Politics and Society* 1, no. 3 (May 1971): 365–391.

Piven, Frances Fox and Richard A. Cloward. *The Politics of Turmoil: Poverty, Race, and the Urban Crisis*. New York: Vintage, 1975.

———. *Poor People's Movements: Why They Succeed, How They Fail*. New York: Vintage, 1979.

———. *Regulating the Poor: The Functions of Public Welfare*. New York: Vintage, 1971.

Plotnick, Robert D. and Felicity Skidmore. *Progress Against Poverty: A Review of the 1964–1974 Decade*. New York: Academic, 1975.

Polsby, Nelson. *Political Innovation in America: The Politics of Policy Innovation*. New Haven: Yale University Press, 1984.

Porter, Roger B. "Economic Advice to the Presidents: From Eisenhower to Reagan." *Political Science Quarterly* 98, no. 3 (1983): 403–426.

Putnam, Robert D. *The Beliefs of Politicians: Ideology, Conflict, and Democracy in Britain and Italy*. New Haven: Yale University Press, 1973.

Quadagno, Jill. *The Color of Welfare: How Racism Undermined the War on Poverty*. New York: Oxford University Press, 1994.

Quarles, Benjamin. "A. Phillip Randolph: Labor Leader at Large." *Black Leaders of the Twentieth*, ed. John Hope Franklin and August Meier, 139–166. Urbana: University of Illinois Press, 1982.

Rainwater, Lee and William L. Yancy, eds. *The Moynihan Report and the Politics of Controversy*. Cambridge, Mass.: MIT Press, 1967.

Redford, Emmette S. and Marlon Blissett. *Organizing the Executive Branch: The Johnson Presidency*. Chicago: University of Chicago Press, 1981.

Redford, Emmette S. and Richard T. McCulley. *White House Operations: The Johnson Presidency*. Austin: University of Texas Press, 1986.

Rehn, Gosta. "Swedish Active Labor Market Policy: Retrospect and Prospect." *Industrial Relations* 24, no. 1 (winter 1985): 62–89.

Remnick, David. "Profiles: Dr. Wilson's Neighborhood." *New Yorker*, April 29 and May 6, 1996, 96–107.

The Report of the National Advisory Commission on Civil Disorders. New York: Bantam, 1968.

Reston, James. "How to Make Things Worse Than They Really Are." *New York Times*, May 31, 1963, sec. L, 24.

———. "Kennedy's Uncertain Approach to the Racial Crisis." *New York Times*, June 9, 1963, sec. E, 12.

———. "The Nation and the Parties on the Racial Issue." *New York Times*, June 7, 1963, sec. L, 30.

———. "No Longer a 'Problem,' but a Revolution." *New York Times*, June 16, 1963, sec. E, 10.

———. "On Exploring the Moon and Attacking the Slums." *New York Times*, December 20, 1963, sec. L, 28.

———. "Who Is Going to Dominate the Racial Debate?" *New York Times*, June 2, 1963, sec. E, 10.

Robson, R. Thayne, ed. *Employment and Training R & D*. Kalamazoo, Mich.: Upjohn Institute for Employment Research, 1984.

Rosen, Sumner. "Social Policy and Manpower Development." In *Encyclopedia of Social Work*, 2:1395–1414. 16th ed. Washington, D.C.: National Association of Social Workers, 1971.

Ross, Arthur. "The Negro in the American Economy." In *Employment, Race, and Poverty*, ed. Arthur M. Ross and Herbert Hill, 3–48. New York: Harcourt, Brace, and World, 1967.

Rossi, Peter. "No Good Idea Goes Unpunished: Moynihan's Misunderstandings and the Proper Role of Social Science in Policy Making." *Social Science Quarterly* 50 (December 1969): 469–479.

Rossi, Peter H. and Katharine C. Lyall. *Reforming Public Welfare: A Critique of the Negative Income Tax Experiment*. New York: Russell Sage, 1976.

Rowen, Hobart. "Poor People in Rich America." *Washington Post*, July 4, 1991.

Russell, Judith. "Ideas, Elites, and Antipoverty Policy." Paper prepared for delivery at the Annual Meeting of the Political Science Association, Chicago, September 3–6, 1987.

Ruttenberg, Stanley H. and Jocelyn Gutchess. *The Federal-State Employment Service: A Critique*. Baltimore: Johns Hopkins University Press, 1970.

Salant, Walter S. "The Spread of Keynesian Doctrines and Practices in the United States." In *The Political Power of Economic Ideas: Keynesianism Across Nations*, ed. Peter A. Hall, 27–52. Princeton: Princeton University Press, 1989.

Savage, James D. *Balanced Budgets and American Politics*. Ithaca: Cornell University Press, 1988.

Sayre, Wallace S. and Bruch L. R. Smith. "Government, Technology, and Social Problems." Paper for the Institute for the Study of Science in Human Affairs. New York: Trustees of Columbia University, 1969.

Schick, Allan, ed. *Making Economic Policy in Congress*. Washington, D.C.: American Enterprise Institute for Public Policy Research, 1983.

Schott, Richard L. and Dagmar S. Hamilton. *People, Positions, and Power: The Political Appointments of Lyndon Johnson*. Chicago: University of Chicago Press, 1983.

Schuman, Howard, Charlotte Steeh, and Lawrence Bobo. *Racial Attitudes in America*. Cambridge: Harvard University Press, 1985.

Schwartz, Bonnie Fox. *The Civil Works Administration, 1933–1934*. Princeton: Princeton University Press, 1984.

Schwarz, John E. *America's Hidden Success: A Reassessment of Twenty Years of Public Policy*. New York: Norton, 1983.

Shanahan, Eileen. "Kennedy and Economy: Administration Moves into the Third Phase in Its Policy for Solving Nation's Economic Problems." *New York Times*, July 28, 1963, sec. E, 5.

Shapiro, Robert Y., Kelly D. Patterson, Judith Russell, and John T. Young. "A Report: Employment and Social Welfare." *Public Opinion Quarterly* 51 (summer 1987): 268–281.

Shulman, Paul R. and Brian J. Cook. "Political Science and the Analysis of Policy Ideas." Paper prepared for delivery at the Annual Meeting of the American Political Science Association, Chicago, September 3–6, 1987.

Sindler, Allen P. *American Political Institutions and Public Policy*. Boston: Little, Brown, 1969.

Singal, Daniel Joseph. "Beyond Consensus: Richard Hofstadter and American Historiography." *American Historical Review* 89, no. 4 (1984): 976–1004.

Skidmore, Felicity. *Progress Against Poverty: A Review of the 1964–1974 Decade*. New York: Academic, 1975.

Skocpol, Theda. "Targeting Within Universalism: Politically Viable Policies to Combat Poverty in the United States." Unpublished paper commissioned for the Conference on the Truly Disadvantaged, Social Science Research Council. Evanston, Ill., October 1989.

————, ed. *Vision and Method in Historical Sociology*. Cambridge: Cambridge University Press, 1984.

Skocpol, Theda and Kenneth Finegold. "Economic Intervention and the Early New Deal." *Political Science Quarterly* 97, no. 2 (1982): 255–278.

Skowronek, Stephen. *Building a New American State: The Expansion of National Administrative Capacities, 1877–1920*. Cambridge: Cambridge University Press, 1982.

Sloan, John W. "Economic Policymaking in the Johnson and Ford Administrations." *Presidential Studies Quarterly* 20 (winter 1990): 89–98.

Smith, James A. *The Idea Brokers: Think Tanks and the Rise of the New Policy Elite*. New York: Free, 1991.

Smith, Nancy Kegan. "Presidential Task Force Operation During the Johnson Administration." *Presidential Studies Quarterly* 15 (spring 1985): 320–29.

Smith, Robert C. and Richard Seltzer. *Race, Class and Culture: A Study in Afro-American Mass Opinion*. Albany: State University of New York Press, 1992.

Snyder, David Pearce, ed. *The Family in Post-Industrial America: Some Fundamental Perceptions for Public Policy Development*. Boulder: Westview, 1979.

Sorensen, Theodore C. *Decision-Making in the White House*. New York: Columbia University Press, 1963.

Stedman-Jones, Gareth. *Outcast London*. London: Oxford University Press, 1971.

Stein, Herbert. *The Fiscal Revolution in America*. Chicago: University of Chicago Press, 1969.

Steinberg, Stephen. *Turning Back: The Retreat from Racial Justice in American Thought and Policy*. Boston: Beacon Press, 1995.

Stigler, George. "The Economics of Minimum Wage Legislation." *American Economic Review* 36, no. 3 (June 1946): 358–365.

Stone, Deborah A. *Policy Paradox and Political Reason*. Boston: Scott, Foresman, 1988.

Suleiman, Ezra. *Politics, Power, and Bureaucracy in France: The Administrative Elite*. Princeton: Princeton University Press, 1974.

Sundquist, James L. "Has America Lost Its Social Conscience and How Will It Get It Back?" *Political Science Quarterly* 101, no. 4 (1986): 513–533.

————. "Jobs, Training, and Welfare for the Underclass." In *Agenda for the Nation*, ed. Kermit Gordon, 49–76. Washington, D.C.: Brookings Institution, 1968.

————. *Politics and Policy: The Eisenhower, Kennedy, and Johnson Years*. Washington, D.C.: Brookings Institution, 1968.

————, ed. *On Fighting Poverty: Perspectives from Experience*. New York: Basic, 1969.

Tabb, W. K. *The Political Economy of the Black Ghetto*. New York: Norton, 1970.

Taggart, Robert. *Hardship: The Welfare Consequences of Labor Market Problems.* Kalamazoo, Mich.: Upjohn Institute for Employment Research, 1982.

Theobald, Robert. *Free Men and Free Markets.* New York: Clarkson and Tatten, 1953.

Thomas, Norman C. and Harold L. Wolman. "The Presidency and Policy Formulation: The Task Force Device." *Public Administration Review* 29 (September/October 1969): 459–491.

Thompson, E. P. *The Making of the English Working Class.* New York: Vintage, 1966.

Thompson, Kenneth W., ed. *The Johnson Presidency: Twenty Intimate Perspectives of Lyndon B. Johnson.* Lanham, Md.: University Press of America, 1986.

———. *The Kennedy Presidency: Seventeen Intimate Perspectives of John F. Kennedy.* Lanham, Md.: United Press of America, 1985.

Thurow, Lester C. *Dangerous Currents: The State of Economics.* New York: Random House, 1983.

Tobin, James. "Growth Through Taxation." *New Republic* 143, no. 4 (July 1960): 15–18.

Tobin, James and Murray Weidenbaum, eds. *Two Revolutions of Economic Policy: The First Economic Reports of Presidents Kennedy and Reagan.* Cambridge, Mass.: MIT Press, 1988.

Tomlinson, Jim. *Employment Policy: The Crucial Years, 1939–1955.* Oxford: Oxford University Press, Clarendon, 1987.

Trilling, Lionel. *The Liberal Imagination.* Garden City, N.Y.: Doubleday, Anchor, 1957.

Tulis, Jeffrey K. *The Rhetorical Presidency.* Princeton: Princeton University Press, 1987.

Truman, David. *The Governmental Process.* New York: Knopf, 1951.

U.S. Bureau of the Census. *Statistical Abstract of the United States: 1987.* 107th ed. Washington, D.C.: U.S. Government Printing Office, 1987.

U.S. Congress. House. Subcommittee on Research and Technical Programs. *The Use of Social Research in Federal Domestic Programs: Part II, The Adequacy and Usefulness of Federally Financed Research on Major National Social Problems.* 90th Cong., 1st sess., 1967. Committee Print.

———. *The Use of Social Research in Federal Domestic Programs: Part III, The Relation of Private Social Scientists to Federal Programs on National Social Problems.* 90th Cong., 1st sess., 1967. Committee Print.

U.S. Congress. House. Subcommittee on the War on Poverty Program. *Antipoverty Programs in New York City and Los Angeles.* 89th Cong., 1st sess., 1965. Committee Print.

———. *The Economic Opportunity Act of 1964.* 88th Cong., 2d sess., 1964. Committee Print.

U.S. Congress. Senate. Select Committee on Poverty. *Economic Opportunity Act of 1964*. 88th Cong., 2d sess., 1964. Committee Print.

U.S. Congress. Senate. Select Subcommittee on Poverty. *Report of the Select Subcommittee on Poverty*. Senate Report 2642. 88th Cong., 2d sess., 1964.

U.S. Congress. Senate. Special Committee on Unemployment Problems. *Report of the Special Committee on Unemployment Problems*. Senate Report 1206. 86th Cong., 2d sess., March 30, 1960.

U.S. Congress. Senate. Subcommittee on Employment and Manpower. *Toward Full Employment: Proposals for a Comprehensive Employment and Manpower Policy in the United States*. 88th Cong., 2d sess., 1964. Committee Print.

U.S. Congress. Senate. Subcommittee on Employment and Manpower of the Committee on Labor and Public Welfare. *Nation's Manpower Revolution*. 88th Cong., 1st sess., 1963. Committee Print.

U.S. Department of Labor. *A Report on Manpower Requirements, Resources, Utilization, and Training*. Washington, D.C., March 1964.

———. *The Department of Labor During the Administration of President Lyndon B. Johnson, November 1963–January 1969*. Vols. 1 and 2. Washington, D.C., 1969.

Van Horn, Carl and Donald Baumer. "Policy Learning and Reauthorization Politics: A Decade of Employment and Training Programs." Paper presented to the convention of the American Political Science Association, Washington D.C., August 30–September 2, 1984.

Walker, Jack L., Jr. "Setting the Agenda in the U.S. Senate: A Theory of Problem Selection." *British Journal of Political Science* 7 (1977): 423–445.

Weatherford, M. Stephen and Lorraine M. McDonnell. "Macroeconomic Policymaking Beyond the Electoral Constraint." In *The Presidency and Public Policy Making*, ed. George C. Edwards, Stephen A. Schull, and Norman C. Thomas, 95–113. Pittsburgh: University of Pittsburgh Press, 1985.

Weir, Margaret. "The Federal Government and Unemployment: The Frustration of Policy Innovation from the New Deal to the Great Society." In *The Politics of Social Policy in the United States*, ed. Margaret Weir, Ana Shola Orloff, and Theda Skocpol, 149–197. Princeton: Princeton University Press, 1988.

———. "Ideas and Politics: The Acceptance of Keynesianism in Britain and the United States." In *The Political Power of Economic Ideas: Keynesianism Across Nations*, ed. Peter A. Hall, 53–86. Princeton: Princeton University Press, 1989.

———. *Politics and Jobs: The Boundaries of Employment Policy in the United States*. Princeton: Princeton University Press, 1992.

Weir, Margaret, Ann Shola Orloff, and Theda Skocpol, eds. *The Politics of Social Policy in the United States*. Princeton: Princeton University Press, 1988.

Weir, Margaret and Theda Skocpol. "State Structures and the Possibilities for 'Keynesian' Responses to the Great Depression in Sweden, Britain, and the United States." In *Bringing the State Back In*, ed. Peter B. Evans, Dietrich Rueschemeyer, and Theda Skocpol, 107–163. New York: Cambridge University Press, 1985.

Weiss, Carol H. "Evaluation for Decisions: Is Anybody There?" *Evaluation Practice* 9, no. 1 (February 1988): 5–20.

Weiss, Nancy J. "Whitney M. Young, Jr.: Committing the Power Structure to the Cause of Civil Rights." In *Black Leaders of the Twentieth Century*. ed. John Hope Franklin and August Meier, 331–358. Urbana: University of Illinois Press, 1982.

Welborn, David M. and Jesse Burkhead. *Intergovernmental Relations in the American System: The Johnson Presidency*. Austin: University of Texas Press, 1989.

Wellman, D. *Portraits of White Racism*. Cambridge: Cambridge University Press, 1977.

Wicker, Tom. *JFK and LBJ: The Influence of Personality Upon Politics*. Chicago: Ivan R. Dee, 1991.

———. "Johnson Acts to Build a Broad Base of National Support, His Procedure: President Has Adopted the Program and Approach of His Predecessor." *New York Times*, December 8, 1963, sec. E, 3.

———. "Johnson Bids Congress Enact Civil Rights Bill with Speed: Asks End of Hate and Violence." *New York Times*, November 28, 1963, sec. L, 1.

Wilensky, Harold L. "Nothing Fails Like Success: The Evaluation-Research Industry and Labor Market Policy." *Industrial Relations* 24, no. 1 (winter 1985): 1–19.

———. *The Welfare State and Equality: Structural and Ideological Roots of Public Expenditures*. Berkeley: University of California Press, 1975.

Wilking, Roger W. and Fred R. Harris, eds. *Quiet Riots: Race and Poverty in the United States*. New York: Pantheon, 1988.

Williams, Leonard. "Articulations of Ideological Change: Dewey and Neoliberalism." Paper prepared for delivery at the Annual Meeting of the American Political Science Association, Chicago, September 3–6, 1987.

Williamson, John B., Jerry F. Boren, Frank J. Mifflen, Nancy A. Cooney, Linda Evans, Michael F. Foley, Richard Steiman, Jody Garber, Nancy Theberge, and Donna J. B. Turek. *Strategies Against Poverty in America*. New York: Wiley, 1975.

Wilson, James Q. *The Politics of Regulation*. New York: Basic, 1980.

———. "The Rise of the Bureaucratic State." In *American Government: Readings and Cases*, 10th ed., ed. Peter Woll, 432–454. New York: HarperCollins, 1990.

Wilson, William Julius. *The Declining Significance of Race: Blacks and Changing American Institutions.* Chicago: University of Chicago Press, 1978.

———. *The Truly Disadvantaged: The Inner City, the Underclass, and Public Policy.* Chicago: University of Chicago Press, 1987.

———. *When Work Disappears.* New York: Knopf, 1996.

Wirtz, Willard. Press conference, October 10, 1963. President's Office Files, Departments and Agencies/Labor (3–62 to 4–62) File, John F. Kennedy Library, Boston.

Wolfe, Alan. "Presidential Power and the Crisis of Modernization." *Democracy* 1, no. 2 (April 1981): 19–32.

Yarmolinsky, Adam. "The Beginnings of OEO." In *On Fighting Poverty*, ed. James L. Sundquist, 34–51. New York: Basic, 1969.

Young, Whitney M., Jr. *To Be Equal.* New York: McGraw-Hill, 1964.

Zarefsky, David. *President Johnson's War on Poverty: Rhetoric and History.* University: University of Alabama Press, 1986.

Znaniecki, Florian. *The Social Role of the Man of Knowledge.* New Brunswick: Transaction, 1986.

Oral History Interviews

Except where otherwise noted, these interviews are available as tape recordings in the Oral History Collection at the Lyndon Baines Johnson Presidential Library, Austin, Texas.

Alden, Vernon. Interview by Michael L. Gillette. October 7, 1981.

Beebe, Leo C. Interview by Joe B. Frantz. February 4, 1971.

Cannon, William B. Interview by Michael L. Gillette. May 21, 1982.

Cater, Douglas. Interview by David G. McComb. April 29, 1969.

———. Interview by David G. McComb. May 8, 1969.

Celebrezze, Anthony J. Interview by Paige Mulhollan. January 26, 1971.

Clark, Clifford. Interview by Joe B. Frantz. June 16, 1970.

Cohen, Wilbur J. Interview by David G. McComb. December 8, 1968.

———. Interview by David G. McComb. March 2, 1969.

———. Interview by David G. McComb. May 10, 1969.

Conway, Jack T. Interview by Michael L. Gillette. August 13, 1980.

Farmer, James. Interview by Harri Baker. October 1969.

———. interview by Paige Mulhollan. July 20, 1971.

Gaither, James. Interview by Dorothy Pierce. November 19, 1968.

———. Interview by Dorothy Pierce. January 15, 1969.

———. Interview by Dorothy Pierce. January 17, 1969.

———. Interview by Dorothy Pierce. March 24, 1970.

Gordon, Kermit. Interview by David McComb. December 16, 1968.

———. Interview by David McComb. January 9, 1969.

———. Interview by David McComb. March 21, 1969.

Hamilton, Ann Oppenheimer. Interview by Michael L. Gillette. October 22, 1980.

Harding, Bertrand M. Interview by Steven Goodell. November 20, 1968.

———. Interview by Steven Goodell. November 25, 1968.

Heller, Walter, Kermit Gordon, James Tobin, Gardner Ackley, and Paul Samuelson. Interview by Joseph Pechman. August 1, 1964. John F. Kennedy Library, Boston.

Horowitz, Harold W. Interview by Michael L. Gillette. February 23, 1983.

Keyserling, Leon H. Interview by Stephen Goodell. January 9, 1969.

Lampman, Robert. Interview by Michael L. Gillette. May 24, 1983.

Levine, Robert A. Interview by Stephen Goodell. February 26, 1969.

McPherson, Harry. Interview by Thomas H. Baker. December 5, 1968.

———. Interview by Thomas H. Baker. December 19, 1968.

———. Interview by Thomas H. Baker. January 16, 1969.

———. Interview by Thomas H. Baker. March 24, 1969.

———. Interview by Thomas H. Baker. April 9, 1969.

Manatos, Mike N. Interview by Joe B. Frantz. August 25, 1969.

Mankiewicz, Frank. Interview by Stephen Goodell. April 18, 1969.

———. Interview by Stephen Goodell. May 1, 1969.

———. Interview by Stephen Goodell. May 5, 1969.

Perrin, C. Robert. Interview by Stephen Goodell. March 10, 1969.

———. Interview by Stephen Goodell. March 17, 1969.

Pollack, Stephen. Interview by Thomas H. Baker. January 27, 1969.

———. Interview by Thomas H. Baker. January 29, 1969.

———. Interview by Thomas H. Baker. January 30, 1969.

———. Interview by Thomas H. Baker. January 31, 1969.

Reynolds, James J. Interview by Joe B. Frantz. February 1, 1971.

Rustin, Bayard. Interview by Thomas H. Baker. June 17, 1969.

———. Interview by Thomas H. Baker. June 30, 1969.

Ruttenberg, Stanley H. Interview by David G. McComb. February 25, 1969.

Schlei, Norbert A. Interview by Michael L. Gillette. May 15, 1980.

Schultze, Charles L. Interview by Thomas H. Baker. December 19, 1968.

———. Interview by Thomas H. Baker. January 16, 1969.

———. Interview by Thomas H. Baker. March 24, 1969.

———. Interview by David McComb. March 28, 1969.

———. Interview by Thomas H. Baker. April 9, 1969.

———. Interview by David McComb. April 10, 1969.

Sundquist, James L. Interview by Charles T. Morrissey and Ronald J. Grele. September 13, 1965. For the John F. Kennedy Library, Boston.

———. Interview by Stephen Goodell. April 7, 1969.

Weeks, Christopher. Interview by Michael L. Gillette. December 10, 1980.

———. Interview by Michael L. Gillette. September 28, 1981.

Wilkins, Roy. Interview by Thomas H. Baker. April 1, 1969.

Wood, Robert C. Interview by David G. McComb. October 19, 1968.

Young, Whitney, Jr. Interview by Thomas H. Baker. June 18, 1969.

OTHER INTERVIEWS

Wirtz, Willard. Interview by author. Tape recording. Washington, D.C. July 23, 1991.

———. Interview by author. Tape recording. Washington, D.C. November 26, 2001.

Index

definition of, 145; enforcement of nondiscrimination in hiring, 65; entrenched joblessness, 10; federal programs addressing, 2–3; in Great Depression, 152; hidden, 81, 188*n*34; inflation and, 198*n*7; in Kennedy administration, 17, 18, 30–31, 33–39; lack of economic trends in, 180*n*105; legislation addressing, 165–167; natural rate of, 143; New Economy and, 161–162; *New York Times* coverage of civil rights issues, 92–101; plant decentralization in, 81, 188*n*32; poverty and, 8, 79, 137, 170*n*16; price stability and, 37; in recession of 2001, 9–10; social costs of, 9–10; structural (*see* structural unemployment); tax cut as solution for, 36; technological displacement of workers, 80, 188*n*31; unskilled and low-skilled workers, 8, 73; *see also* full employment
unemployment insurance, 165–166, 189*n*51
Unemployment Insurance Service, 46, 48
unions, *see* labor organizations
University of Alabama: desegregation of, 109
Urban League, *see* National Urban League (NUL)

Vocational Educational Act (1963), 182*n*25
voter registration, 104–105

Wagner, Robert, 68, 77, 184*n*7
Wagner Act, *see* National Labor Relations Act (1935)

Wagner-Peyser Act (1933), 47, 48, 165–166
Wallace, Bob, 174*n*13
Wallace, George, 78, 109
War on Poverty: appropriations for, 129; backlash against, 92; as "black" program, 7, 135–140, 171*n*20; bureaucratic rivalry over administration of, 52, 58–60, 147–150; economic ideas and, 14, 17–39; failure of, 5, 6, 138–139, 153–155, 195*n*77; fallacies regarding causes of poverty, 38; as generational event, 12; as high-impact program, 129; jobs programs, 5, 8, 58–60, 152–153, 156–157; Johnson administration cutbacks in, 90; Johnson announcement of, 3–4, 81; Johnson's goals for, 201*n*34; Kennedy administration and, 4, 10–11; lability in formulation of, 5; lack of black input into, 64; lack of focus on jobs, 8, 9, 38–39, 141; legislative viability of bill, 124; lessons of, 161; manpower programs, 156; as misapplied Keynesian theory, 146; motives for, 133–135; noblesse oblige and, 123, 133–135; policy goals, 153; as political necessity, 4, 112, 123, 133–135, 163; racism and public policy, 7, 15, 103, 112; services vs. redistribution, 113–114, 137, 170*n*16; Shriver as head of, 114, 116–118; social factors in, 197*n*108; state capacities and, 150; Task Force (*see* Task Force on Poverty); tax reductions and, 36, 147
Weaver, Robert, 148

Power, Conflict, and Democracy: American
Politics Into the Twenty-first Century

John G. Geer, *From Tea Leaves to Opinion Polls: A Theory of Democratic Leadership*
Kim Fridkin Kahn, *The Political Consequences of Being a Woman: How Stereotypes
    Influence the Conduct and Consequences of Political Campaigns*
Kelly D. Patterson, *Political Parties and the Maintenance of Liberal Democracy*
Dona Cooper Hamilton and Charles V. Hamilton, *The Dual Agenda: Race and
    Social Welfare Policies of Civil Rights Organizations*
Hanes Walton Jr., *African-American Power and Politics: The Political Context Vari-
    able*
Amy Fried, *Muffled Echoes: Oliver North and the Politics of Public Opinion*
Russell D. Riley, *The Presidency and the Politics of Racial Inequality: Nation-Keeping
    from 1831 to 1965*
Robert W. Bailey, *Gay Politics, Urban Politics: Identity and Economics in the Urban
    Setting*
Ronald T. Libby, *ECO-WARS: Political Campaigns and Social Movements*
Donald Grier Stephenson Jr., *Campaigns and the Court: The U.S. Supreme Court
    in Presidential Elections*
Kenneth Dautrich and Thomas H. Hartley, *How the News Media Fail American
    Voters: Causes, Consequences, and Remedies*
Douglas C. Foyle, *Counting the Public In: Presidents, Public Opinion, and Foreign
    Policy*
Ronald G. Shaiko, *Voices and Echoes for the Environment: Public Interest Represen-
    tation in the 1990s and Beyond*
Hanes Walton Jr., *Reelection: William Jefferson Clinton as a Native-Son Presidential
    Candidate*
Demetrios James Caraley, editor, *The New American Interventionism: Lessons from
    Successes and Failures—Essays from* Political Science Quarterly

Ellen D. B. Riggle and Barry L. Tadlock, editors, *Gays and Lesbians in the Democratic Process: Public Policy, Public Opinion, and Political Representation*

Robert Y. Shapiro, Martha Joynt Kumar, Lawrence R. Jacobs, Editors, *Presidential Power: Forging the Presidency for the Twenty-First Century*

Kerry L. Haynie, *African American Legislators in the American States*

Marissa Martino Golden, *What Motivates Bureaucrats? Politics and Administration During the Reagan Years*

Geoffrey Layman, *The Great Divide: Religious and Cultural Conflict in American Party Politics*

Sally S. Cohen, *Championing Child Care*

Peter L. Francia, John C. Green, Paul S. Herrnson, Lynda W. Powell, and Clyde Wilcox, *The Financiers of Congressional Elections: Inverstors, Ideologues, and Intimates*